The
Golden Century
of
Italian Opera
from Rossini to Puccini

The
Golden Century
of
Italian Opera
from Rossini to Puccini

William Weaver

Thames and Hudson

for John Fleming and Hugh Honour

'Mercè, diletti amici'

First published in the USA in 1980 by
Thames and Hudson Inc., 500 Fifth Avenue,
New York, New York 10110
First paperback edition 1988

© 1980 John Calmann and King Ltd

This book was designed and produced by
John Calmann and King Ltd, 71 Great Russell Street,
London WC1B 3BN

Library of Congress Catalog card number 80–81143

Printed in Hong Kong by Mandarin Offset

 *Contents*

ACKNOWLEDGEMENTS

This book was conceived, commissioned, and supervised through the final revision by the late John Calmann. My thanks, which can no longer be expressed to him in person, must be offered here, sadly, in print.

In the course of searching for documents and illustrations I have had the kind collaboration of numerous libraries, collections, and archives. My thanks therefore go also to the direction and staff of the Museo Teatrale alla Scala, the Raccolta Civica 'G. Bertarelli', the Archivio Ricordi, and the Archivio Fratelli Fabbri in Milan; the Istituto di Studi verdiani in Parma; the Biblioteca del Conservatorio di Santa Cecilia, the Biblioteca del Teatro 'Burcardo', and the Fondazione Primoli in Rome. I am also happy to express my gratitude to the John Simon Guggenheim Memorial Foundation for its support and to the Foundation's President Gordon N. Ray.

In addition to this assistance from institutions, I was also generously helped by many friends, beginning with John Fleming and Hugh Honour, to whom this book is rightfully dedicated since they prompted its commission and also put their wideranging library and their apparently endless store of knowledge at my disposal. I am happy to thank also, in Florence: Sir Harold Acton, Thekla and John Clark, James Holderbaum and Paolo Tosi; in Rome, Guido Agazzi, Francesco Crispolti, Kazuo Nakajima, Anna and Luigi Malerba, Walter Talevi and Jole Tognelli; in Milan, William Bowman, Adele Comin, Giancarlo Costa, Luigi Ferrari, Paolo Tosi; in Naples, Enrico Tellini; in Pescia, Rolando Anzilotti; in Turin, Enrico Gianeri; in Paris, Harold Barnes; in New York, John Ferrone, Gerald Fitzgerald and Elliott Stein; in London, John Black, David Britt, Elizabeth Forbes, and Madeleine van der Hecht.

My neighbours in Monte San Savino helped me in countless ways, and I am grateful to them: Licia and Pippo Greghi, Andrew Porter, Floriano Vecchi.

A brief note on the translation of titles: where an opera is very well known and it is clear what the title means (*La sonnambula*, for instance), I have not translated it. In the case of arias, they are generally referred to in Italian not by a title as such but by their first few words, which very often make little sense when translated into English. As they are usually well enough known by the Italian title I have also left them untranslated. Where the meaning of an opera title is not immediately clear it has been translated.

Introduction

IN 1819, in Venice, Lord Byron met, charmed, and seduced
Countess Teresa Guiccioli. He was introduced to her at a
Conversazione, but after that first encounter, they saw each
other frequently at the Teatro La Fenice. The terrible moment
came when Count Guiccioli told his infatuated wife that they
were leaving the city, whereupon the distraught Teresa rushed at
once to find Byron. She knew exactly where to go: the opera
house. He was there, and, in her own account, she 'almost
involuntarily followed him into his box and told him of her
troubles. This box was generally used by men only, and was
always the target of Venetian curiosity. One can imagine that this
was increased a hundredfold by the young lady's presence!'

Teresa does not mention which opera was being performed
(it was, appropriately, Rossini's *Otello*), and she surely heard not a
note of it. The rest of the audience, too, was probably less
interested in Rossini's music than in the real-life drama unfolding
in the box. No matter: a successful opera in those days was
repeated night after night, and night after night the small, devoted local audience would return to the theatre, which in the
Italy of that time functioned as a club, the principal gathering-
place for citizens of every rank.

Teresa left Venice, but the 'affair of the Box' continued to be
discussed. Some weeks later Byron followed her to the provincial city of Ravenna, where Guiccioli was a leading figure and was
responsible for the direction of the opera house. On arriving
there, the poet presented a letter of introduction to Count
Giuseppe Alborghetti, and the Count cordially invited the new-
comer to his box at the opera that evening. There, in conversation (talking during the music was the custom), Byron mentioned the Guicciolis. 'Alas,' his host said innocently, 'you will
not be able to see the young lady, as they say she is at death's
door.' Teresa's narrative, written long afterwards, continues: 'At
this abrupt news, Byron lost his head, and unable to control his
emotion, replied that if the lady should die, he hoped he would
not survive her.'

Another 'affair of the Box'. Anyway Teresa soon recovered,
and the liaison continued. Byron settled in Ravenna and, performing his social duty, made a handsome contribution to the

costs of the opera season. When finally the quarrel came with Count Guiccioli, it was as much about operatic matters as about adultery. Byron had wanted the Ravenna theatre to engage the Spanish soprano Maria Malibran, then at the beginning of her career, but already costly. The parsimonious Count refused, and battle was joined.

The opera house is prominent in every account of nineteenth-century Italian life. Travellers, arriving in a city, headed straight for the opera. Friends and lovers met there. As Effie Ruskin wrote to her in-laws from Milan, in 1849: 'We were at the Opera the other night. It was full of Austrian Officers with a sprinkling of their wives and daughters but no Italian Ladies.' Later, when the Ruskins were staying in Venice, they—and especially Effie—enjoyed the Fenice, where John, as his wife recounts, 'had been writing a Chapter on Chamfered edges all during the Opera.'

In another letter, Effie says: '. . . the third Military ball next week is not to take place as the Cavalchina is to be given in the Fenice. This Cavalchina is the old masked Ball of Venice which finishes the Carnival and they keep it up till the morning and then Lent begins. . . . The immense Theatre is boarded over and the boxes hung with mirrors and the masks enter the boxes & do anything they like. We may take a turn or two amongst them but it is not considered comme il faut for Ladies to mask or dance.'

Italy, even as late as 1849, was still, as the phrase went, a geographical expression. Verdi, in the 1830s, had needed a passport to travel from the Duchy of Parma to Austrian-occupied Milan. Rossini was a citizen of the Papal States; Donizetti, officially, was Austrian. But Italian unity was on the move, and the Italian opera house was also playing a new role. On 28 June 1862, in Palermo, when Garibaldi proclaimed his ideal of the unification of Italy with the cry 'O Roma o morte' (Rome or death), it was from box 10 of the second tier of the theatre.

At the very beginning of the nineteenth century, Italian opera was in a period of decline. Here, for example, is the list of composers whose works were performed at La Scala in the 1800–1801 season (and the list would be much the same in Italy's other opera houses): Zingarelli, Nicolini, Mayr, Gazzaniga, Portogallo, Orlandi, Pollini, Puccita, Nasolini, Mosca. Most of these are nonentities, whose names survive only in musical histories or theatrical chronicles. The most distinguished are Mayr, later the teacher of Donizetti, and Gazzaniga, whose *Don Giovanni Tenorio* had anticipated Mozart's more famous work. But, for the most part, the music of these men is forgotten.

Who else was there at that time? Piccinni died in 1800, in France. Cimarosa died on 11 January 1801. Rossini was a boy of eight, Donizetti a toddler, Bellini an infant. Paisiello, at sixty-one, had another fifteen years to live, but his active career was past. Paer and Cherubini were already established abroad, and Spontini was about to join them.

Then, a decade or so later, Rossini exploded on the scene, his unmistakable genius asserting itself immediately. At first he was criticized for being too 'German', for sacrificing voices to orchestral effect, but he still swept all before him, dazzling princes and populace. Just as he was retiring from the stage, there was the brief and brilliant meteor of Bellini and the generous outpouring of Donizetti. And, in the mid-1840s, as Donizetti sank into madness, Verdi was enjoying the first flush of success.

Verdi's life nearly spans the nineteenth century; and his powerful talent tended to extinguish rivals, however gifted. So Verdi is often seen as an isolated phenomenon, although the theatres in his day were just as hungry for novelty and audiences were just as curious about new musicians as they had always been.

As the century ended and, with it, the reign of Verdi, there was a furious war of succession. Puccini emerged as victor, but left the field strewn with victims. Then, as he grew older, many opera-lovers assumed that he, too, would have a musical heir. Several candidates were proposed, but none was quite able to seize the throne.

And so, when Puccini died, the golden century was over. Italian operas continued and continue to be written, and some of them have had success. But the figure of the international monarch of the lyric stage has vanished for good.

The story of the kings of Italian opera, from Rossini to Puccini, has been told many times. Good, in some cases definitive, biographies are available of all the major composers, and many of the minor ones. Scholars have analysed the operas; critical editions of scores are being prepared and issued.

And yet many aspects of the story remain to be investigated. We know about the composers' lives and about their operas, but too often these have been discussed in isolation, out of their context. The world in which those operas were written, heard, applauded or jeered, remains only partially known. And, in most studies, it is seen with modern eyes, not as it appeared to people at the time.

The brief essay that follows aims to suggest some of the avenues still to be explored. We know that the audience at the first night of *Il barbiere di Siviglia* received the opera with hostility, but we know less about who was in that audience. That Roman public in 1816 was, in any case, quite different from the Milanese audience of Verdi's first operas and from the solid burghers of Turin who hailed Puccini's *Manon Lescaut*.

The audience, important as it is, represents only a part of the operatic panorama. There were also the impresarios, the publishers, the newspapers and, in the latter half of the century, the critics. Of course, there were the singers. Their story, too, has often been told; but their relationship with the composer, which changed throughout the century, was of great significance.

The world of Italian opera in the past century (and the first part of this century) intersected other cultural worlds. Distinguished painters—Francesco Hayez at their head—designed or supervised the designing of many productions. If Italy's leading writers, Leopardi and Manzoni, did not write librettos, they were involved in opera all the same. Leopardi was an alert opera-goer; Manzoni allowed his novel *I promessi sposi* to be turned into an opera. At the end of the century, Giovanni Verga's naturalistic stories of Sicilian life led to the emergence of the *verismo* movement in opera, while the works of D'Annunzio served a number of post-*verismo* composers.

In Naples, at the end of 1943, while the war was raging not many miles to the north, the Teatro San Carlo was bravely reopened (all performances had to be matinées because of the blackout at night). In war-shattered Milan, almost the moment hostilities ceased, the city's first major effort was the repairing and reopening of La Scala. In 1820, Lady Morgan had written: 'After the Duomo, there is no shrine in Milan so attended, no edifice so prized, as the Theatre of the Scala.' More than a century and a half later, her observation still holds true, and it could just as easily be applied to other theatres in other Italian cities: the San Carlo in Naples, the Regio in Turin, the Fenice in Venice. This book is meant to be a record and, to some extent, an explanation of that singular devotion, which began in Italy and reached its peak in the nineteenth century, but which has long spread far beyond Italian borders and has persisted, happily, well into our own time.

William Weaver

Monte San Savino, January 1980

Chapter 1

ON 15 December 1815 Gioacchino Rossini signed a contract to write a new opera for the Nobile Teatro di Torre Argentina in Rome. The composer was only twenty-three years old, but he was already known throughout Italy and was on the threshold of his great international career. He had composed more than a dozen operas, including *Tancredi* and *L'italiana in Algeri*, phenomenal successes; and he was under a long-term contract to the Teatro San Carlo in Naples, where he was the darling of the public, of the theatre's impresario Domenico Barbaja, of Barbaja's mistress, the brilliant Spanish soprano Isabella Colbran (eventually to become Signora Rossini), and of Barbaja's employer, King Ferdinand I of the Two Sicilies.

Fortunately, Rossini's agreement with Naples allowed him ample leave to compose for other cities and to travel whenever it was necessary to supervise the staging of these new works. And so he was in Rome, in the last months of 1815, to attend to the production of his *Il turco in Italia* at the Teatro Valle, for which he was also to compose a new opera, *Torvaldo e Dorliska*, staged there on 26 December.

But what of the other party to this new contract? Duke Francesco Sforza Cesarini was forty-four, member of an old Roman family. Instead of devoting himself to the traditional pastimes of his class—shooting, racing, play-going—he had been bitten by the theatre bug, and since 1807 he had been running the Argentina, a family property, with singular lack of success. His losses during his first season had been 7,000 *scudi*; in 1808 he lost more than 10,000; and the deficit grew with each season.

The contract he offered Rossini might seem, today, unduly severe for such a prominent composer. But these were the normal terms of the period. First, Rossini had to deliver the opera within a month of signing. He was also bound to 'adapt it to the voices of the singers . . . and make all those changes which may be deemed necessary . . . for the singers' demands.' To make this task more difficult the Duke still had not, at the date of signature, managed to assemble his troupe.

Rossini was also required to be in Rome no later than the end of December. He had to supervise the preparation of his opera (stage directors, as such, did not yet exist), he had to be present at

1. (*Overleaf*) Contract for Rossini's *Il barbiere di Siviglia*. 15 December 1815. The contract between Rossini and Duke Francesco Sforza Cesarini, impresario of the Teatro Argentina in Rome, calls for the composer to deliver the opera within a month, to adapt it to the singers who would be engaged for the season, to be present and available in Rome from the end of December, and to conduct the first three performances. In the event Rossini was not given the second act of the libretto until 29 January. A week later the Duke died. His duties, however, were immediately assumed by a professional theatre manager, Nicola Ratti, who supervised the preparation and the première, on 20 February 1816. The contract also provided Roman lodgings for Rossini in Palazzo Pagliarini, Vicolo de' Leutari, a short walk from the theatre. The baritone Luigi Zamboni, the first Figaro, lived in the same building.

Nobil Teatro di Torre Argentina
A dì 26 Xbre 1815

Con la presente benchè privata scrittura da valere quanto publico, giurato istrumento convengono le infrascritte parti contraenti nel modo seguente cioè —

Il Sig.r Duca Sforza Cesarini Impresario del sud.o Teatro ferma, e stabilisce per la prossima futura Stagione di Carnevale dell'Anno 1816: il Sig.r Maestro Gioacchino Rossini, il quale promette, e si obliga di comporre e porre in scena il Secondo Dramma Buffo che si rappresenterà nel futuro Carnevale sud.o nell'indicato Teatro a forma del Libretto, che gli verrà dato dal sud.o Sig.r Impresario, o nuovo, o vecchio che sarà ai primi di Gennaro, quale dovrà dal med.o Sig.r Maestro Rossini porsi in Musica a seconda delle qualità, e convenienze de Sig.ri Cantanti, obligandosi ancora di fare occorrendo tutte quelle variazioni che saranno necessarie tanto per il buon esito della Musica, quanto per le circostanze, e convenienze de med.i Sig.ri Cantanti in avvisandolo del Sig.r pagarli, perchè così &, e non altrimenti &. —

Promette parimenti, e si obliga esso Sig.r Maestro Rossini di portarsi, e trovarsi in Roma per adempire al sud.o incarico non più tardi della fine del Mese di Xbre dell'Anno corrente, e di consegnare al Copista il primo Atto perfettamente compito nel dì 20 del Mese di Gennaro 1816, dico il 20. di Gennaro per poter essere pronti a fare le prove e concerti, e di andare in scena quella Sera che sarà destinata dal med.o Sig.r Impresario, non più tardi però del dì 5 Febraro circa di d.o Anno, e così il d. Sig.r Maestro dovrà similmente consegnare al Copista a tempo debito il Secondo Atto per aver tempo d'impararlo, concertarlo, e provarlo per essere in ordine per andare in scena nella Sera d.a di sopra, altrimenti il d.o Sig.r Maestro si sottoporrà a tutti i danni, perchè così &, e non altrimenti &. —

Sarà parimenti obligato il med.o Sig.r Maestro Rossini, conforme promette e si obliga di dirigere la sud.a sua Opera, e di assistere personalmente a tutte le prove e concerti tutte le volte, e quando sarà necessario s...

in Teatro che fuori a piacere del Sig.r Impresario, e parimente di assistere le prime tre sere consecutive che si daranno in Scena la sua Opera,
di dirigerla al Cembalo perché così pattò, e non altrimenti &.

In compenso poi di sue virtuose fatiche il Sig.r Impresario promette e si obliga di
pagare al Sig.r Maestro Rossini la Somma e quantità di Scudi Quattro cento Romani, subito che avrà terminate le tre sere di sua assistenza al
Cembalo, e non altrimenti &.

Si conviene ancora che in caso di interdizione, o sospenzione di Teatro,
per effetto di Principe o per qualunque altro infortunio debba osser-
varsi il solito che si pratica nei Teatri di Roma, e di altre Piazze Este-
re in simili casi perché così &, e non altrimenti &.

E per osservanza di tutte e singole cose contenute nel presente contratto il
Sig.r Duca Sforza Cesarini da una parte, ed il Sig.r Maestro Giovacchino Rossini dall'altro obligano loro stessi, beni ed eredi nella più ampla forma
della R. C. A., volendo essere tenuti in caso di qualunque inadempimen-
to all'emenda dei danni scambievolmente &, per i quali si obligano nella
più stretta e valide forme di qualunque Piazza Estera perché così pat-
to e non altrimenti &.

E per la piena osservanza la presente sarà firmata dal Sig.r Impresario,
ed altra simile dal Sig.r Maestro Giovacchino Rossini.

E più il Sig.r Impresario gli accorda l'Alloggio durante il p.te Contratto nel
med.o alloggio, che si passa al Sig.r Luigi Zamboni.

Gioacchino Rossini

ITALY
1814-1859

Scale of Miles
0   50   100

3. Teatro Argentina, Rome.
The original building of the Teatro
Argentina in Rome was constructed in 1732
by Duke Giuseppe Sforza-Cesarini, near the
house of the bishop Giovanni Burcardo,
'episcopus argentinus' (i.e. a native of
Strasbourg, the ancient Argentoratum,
hence the theatre's name). Noted for its
excellent acoustics, the Argentina served
the architect Gianantonio Selva as his
model for the Teatro La Fenice in Venice.
A new façade was applied in 1826 (and is
still extant). The interior has been altered
several times, and was drastically, and not
entirely happily, remodelled in the 1970s.
Besides Rossini's *Il barbiere di Siviglia*
(20 February 1816), the Argentina saw the
world premières of the same composer's
Adelaide di Borgogna (27 December 1817),
Donizetti's *Zoraide di Granata* (28 January
1822), Verdi's *I due Foscari* (3 November
1844) and his *La battaglia di Legnano* (27
January 1849). In 1845 Fanny Elssler made
her Roman debut at the Argentina, which
also welcomed many leading Italian actors.
After World War II, the theatre was used
for symphony concerts, but has now
become the home of the capital's Teatro
Stabile, or municipal repertory company.
The opera being performed here is *Stella*
by the Sicilian composer Salvatore
Auteri-Manzocchi (1845–1924).

2. (*Left*) Map of Italy showing the
individual states (1814–1859).

any rehearsals if the impresario felt he was needed, and he had to
attend the opera's first three performances, which he would
conduct, as was customary, from the cembalo. At the end of the
third performance, the Duke would hand Rossini his fee: 400
Roman *scudi* (the prima donna, when she was engaged, would
receive 500 *scudi* per performance). The Duke would also provide the composer's lodging.

The contract further specifies that Rossini was bound to write
his opera 'on whatever libretto, new or old, will be given him by
the afore-mentioned Duke, impresario'. As it turned out, Rossini, in this respect, did not fare badly. The impresario's first
choice as librettist was Jacopo Ferretti, the thirty-one-year-old
director of the government salt-and-tobacco monopoly. A gifted
amateur poet, Ferretti had already supplied texts for such popular composers of the day as Francesco Morlacchi, Niccolò Zingarelli, Valentino Fioravanti, and Giovanni Simone Mayr; the
following year, he would collaborate with Rossini on *La
Cenerentola*. But on this occasion the libretto that Ferretti produced failed to satisfy the Duke, who then turned to Ferretti's
exact contemporary, Cesare Sterbini, a man of equal gifts but of
less experience. Sterbini was also an employee of the Papal
government, and he had just worked with Rossini, having provided the libretto of the *dramma semiserio* in two acts *Torvaldo e
Dorliska*, presented at Rome's other active opera house, the

15

Teatro Valle, without success, only eleven days after Rossini and the Duke had signed their contract.

The contract between Sterbini and the Duke was dated 17 January 1816; the poet was required to deliver the first act of the text by 25 January and the second act four days later. Obviously, Rossini had been granted an extension, but he still managed to deliver the music of the opera's first act on the morning of 6 February. The delivery-date of the second act is uncertain, but it cannot have been much more than a week later.

The libretto Sterbini produced was *Il barbiere di Siviglia*, or rather, as it was first called, *Almaviva, ossia l'inutile precauzione*. The explanation for this change of title is simple: there already existed a well-known operatic version of the Beaumarchais comedy, produced in 1782, with libretto by Giuseppe Petrosellini and music by Giovanni Paisiello.

Actually, recasting an extant libretto—or, indeed, appropriating it, without changes, for a new opera—was accepted practice before and throughout the nineteenth century. A later example is Puccini's *Manon Lescaut*, composed less than a decade after Massenet's opera based on the same story. But Rossini was fearful by nature. Paisiello was still alive, his opera was popular, and the old composer had a number of supporters, who might react adversely to the new work.

Rossini took the—futile—precaution of writing to his illustrious predecessor. As he recounted later: 'I wrote a letter to Paisiello, declaring to him that I did not mean to compete with him, being aware of my inferiority, but wanted only to set a subject that delighted me, while avoiding as much as possible the specific situations in his libretto.' And, in fact, Ferretti's libretto is quite different from Petrosellini's.

At the same time, Rossini and Ferretti took yet another precaution, drafting a 'Notice to the Public', printed as a foreword to the libretto which would be sold in the foyer of the Argentina for the more interested members of the audience to follow during the performance. This preface said, among other things: 'The comedy of M. Beaumarchais entitled *Le Barbier de Séville ou La Précaution inutile* is presented in Rome, adapted as a comic opera with the title *Almaviva ossia l'inutile precauzione*, with the intention of fully convincing the public of the sentiments of respect and veneration which animate the Author of the Music of the present work towards the most celebrated Paisiello, who has already set this subject to music under its original title.

'Summoned to assume the same difficult assignment, il Signor Maestro Gioacchino Rossini, rather than suffer the accusation of desiring a foolhardy rivalry with the immortal author who preceded him, has expressly asked that *Il barbiere di Siviglia* be entirely versified anew and that numerous new situations be added. Some other differences between the plot of the present work and the aforementioned one given at the Comédie Française were caused by the necessity of introducing the

4. Jacopo Ferretti (1784–1852).
An Arcadian poet and bureaucrat in the Papal government in Rome, Ferretti was much admired as an improviser of verses. He began his career as a librettist inauspiciously: revising other writers' texts—without pay—for Duke Sforza Cesarini. His first signed text was *Baldovino* for Nicolò Zingarelli in 1811. He wrote *Matilde di Shabran* and then, in 1817, *La Cenerentola*. By the end of his career he had written almost seventy librettos for a number of composers, among them Donizetti whom he provided with *L'ajo nell'imbarazzo* (1824), *Il furioso all'isola di San Domingo* (1833), and other librettos.

5. (*Right*) Floor-plans of five theatres: (top row, l. to r.) Teatro Regio, Turin; Teatro Argentina, Rome; Teatro della Canobbiana, Milan; (lower row, l. to r.) Teatro alla Scala, Milan; Teatro San Carlo, Naples.
An early nineteenth-century engraving shows the relative size of five leading Italian opera houses. The Argentina is, like all Roman theatres, cramped, with little foyer space; while the San Carlo and La Scala enjoy more space, both in the hall and on stage. Piermarini, the architect of La Scala and the Canobbiana, is credited with inventing the horse-shoe auditorium, but as these plans indicate, at most he perfected an already existing architectural tradition.

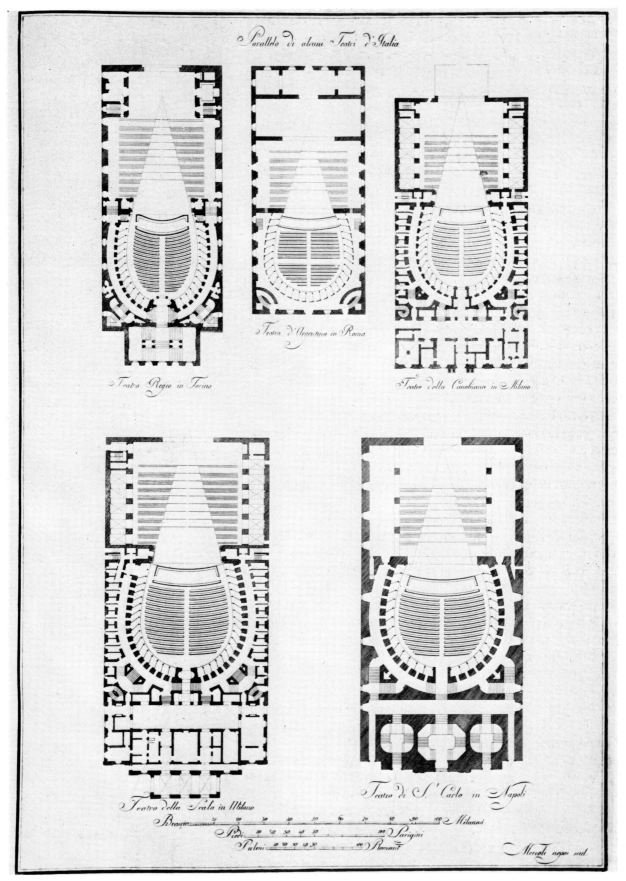

Parallelo di alcuni Teatri d'Italia

Teatro d'Argentina in Roma

Teatro Regio in Torino

Teatro della Canobiana in Milano

Teatro della Scala in Milano

Teatro di S.º Carlo in Napoli

Braccia — — — — — — — — Milanesi
Piedi — — — — — Parigini
Palmi — — — — — Romani

Mercoli napol. del.

Choruses, because they are demanded by modern usage and also because they are indispensable to the musical effect in a theatre of considerable size.'

Actually the size of the Argentina was not considerable. There were six rows of boxes, with thirty-one small boxes in each row. The stalls comprised forty rows of benches with backs.

Rome's largest theatre, the Teatro Apollo, was closed that season. The smaller Teatro Valle traditionally specialized in *opera buffa*, while the Argentina, in the past, had been the home of serious opera. But the Cardinal Secretary of State, responsible for theatrical matters in the city, had decided that the Argentina, for the 1816 season, should also present comic works. And, to the irritation of the public, the Duke Sforza Cesarini had eliminated the corps de ballet that year, for economic reasons.

The interiors of Roman theatres at this time were built entirely of wood and were decrepit and unsafe. The stairs, passages and boxes were cramped and dirty. The narrow benches in the stalls were even more uncomfortable, and the straw cushions which the spectator could rent for the evening were as hard as the wood.

In 1815 the papal authorities had commissioned two architects, named Stern and Camporese, to inspect the theatres. In their report they said: 'Complaining about the discomfort and the filth of our theatres would be simply a repetition of what the whole world has been saying, to our disgrace.'

The chorus at the Argentina totalled sixteen; the members of the orchestra numbered thirty-five. All were poorly paid amateurs. Some years later, in 1830, two young but competent foreign judges reported their opinion of such orchestras and such opera performances in Rome. One of these visitors was the twenty-one-year-old Felix Mendelssohn, who wrote home: 'The orchestras are worse than anyone could believe; musicians and a proper feeling for music are both wanting. The two or three violinists play just as they choose and join in when they please; the wind instruments are tuned either too high or too low; and they execute flourishes like those we are accustomed to hear in farmyards.

'I heard a solo on the flute, where the flute was more than a quarter of a tone too high; it set my teeth on edge, but no one remarked it, and when at the end a shake came, they applauded mechanically.'

Hector Berlioz, six years Mendelssohn's senior, was in Rome at the same time; his *Memoirs* paint an equally unflattering picture of the city's musical life: 'The choruses are rather below that of the Opéra-Comique in point of warmth, intonation, and ensemble; the orchestras are formidable and imposing in the manner of the Monégasque army, possessing every single quality which is normally considered a defect. At the Teatro Valle the 'cellos number precisely one, a goldsmith by trade, in which respect he is more fortunate than one of his colleagues, who earns his living

6. Geltrude Righetti Giorgi.
The contralto Geltrude (here called
Gertrude) Righetti (1793?–1862) was born
in Bologna, where she and Rossini became
friends when they were both children. She
made her debut in 1814 and was
immediately popular, both in her native city
and in Rome. But on her marriage to the
lawyer Luigi Giorgi, she retired from the
stage. That retirement was extremely brief,
because in September 1815 Duke Sforza
Cesarini, the Roman impresario, engaged
her, at Rossini's suggestion, for the part of
Rosina in *Il barbiere di Siviglia*. In 1817 she
created Rossini's *Cenerentola*, again in
Rome. Apparently her health was poor, and
she retired permanently from the stage in
1822. Louis Spohr (who heard her at the
Teatro della Pergola, Florence, in
November of 1816) described her voice as
'full, strong . . . with an extraordinary range
of two and one-half octaves'. But he added:
'Like most singers whom I have heard in
Italy, she indulges in too much
ornamentation, and, therefore, gets less out
of her sumptuous voice than is to be had. I
am told, moreover, that she contributes
nothing of her own, but rather accepts what
is drilled into her, with the result that her
ornaments which are precisely the same,
note for note, every night, soon become
tiresome' (trans. by Henry Pleasants). She
was considered a gifted actress.

by repairing cane-bottomed chairs. In Rome the word "symphony" is used, like the word "overture", to designate a kind of noise which theatre orchestras produce before the rise of the curtain, and to which no one pays any attention.'

These were typical of the forces who were to perform Rossini's opera. The composer was more fortunate in his principals. The Rosina was a young contralto, Geltrude Righetti Giorgi, whom Rossini had known since childhood. Though still young, she had retired from the stage a short time previously, on her marriage to Sig. Giorgi; her Roman appearance marked her return. Sterbini's description of Rosina in the libretto can be taken as an accurate portrait of Geltrude: 'Plump—clever—black hair—pink cheeks—eloquent eyes—hands that inspire love . . .'

The tenor was the Spaniard Manuel Garcia, forty years old, father of a seven-year-old daughter Maria, later to be internationally celebrated as la Malibran, and an eleven-year-old son Manuel II, who would make his debut, in 1825, as Figaro in this same *Barber*. Garcia had been singing in Italy for five years, and had just created the tenor lead in Rossini's *Elisabetta, regina d'Inghilterra* in Naples.

The highest-paid member of the company was the buffo Luigi Zamboni, the Figaro, who received 700 *scudi*. He was almost fifty years old, with a reputation as a superb interpreter. One of the minor members of the troupe, the bass Zenobio Vitarelli, had a less enviable reputation as a formidable bearer of the evil eye.

His reputation was no doubt reinforced by what happened in the course of the rehearsals. On 9 January, Duke Francesco wrote to the Cardinal Secretary of State: 'Your Excellency will understand what it means to put on a two-act composition in a week's time . . . Having to do things this way, rehearsals, scenery, decorations, and all is something I don't like. And the result will be to open . . . with the actors all out of breath. . . . Last night, after having worked hard all day long, I spent from one to five at night rehearsing the whole first act, with the direction of Rossini, and being in a theatre, with this cold, is like being on Mont Cénis; so Rossini, the prima donna, the tenor and everybody did nothing but shiver, and I came home so numb that it took me an hour to get warm.'

A week later the poor Duke suddenly died. His duties as impresario were promptly assumed by Nicola Ratti, secretary of the ducal house, who kept up the pressure on the artists, since the widowed Duchess was eager to recoup some of the money expended by her profligate husband.

Finally the opening night of *Almaviva* arrived: 20 February 1816. Several contemporary descriptions exist of that tumultuous first performance, but perhaps the most reliable, and certainly the most interesting, is the account written, in 1823, by Geltrude Righetti Giorgi herself. 'Garzia [sic], after tuning his

guitar on the stage, which aroused the laughter of the indiscreet, sang his arias with little spirit, and they were received with contempt. I was prepared for anything. Timidly, I climbed the ladder which was to take me to the balcony, to say these few words: "Segui, o caro, deh segui così." ["Continue, beloved, pray continue thus."] As the Romans had always overwhelmed me with applause in *L'italiana in Algeri*, they expected that I would reward them with a pleasant, amorous cavatina. When they heard only those few words, they exploded in whistles and brawling. After that, what had to happen, happened. Figaro's cavatina [Largo al factotum], though masterfully sung by Zamboni, and the beautiful duet between Figaro and Almaviva, also sung by Zamboni and Garzia, were not even heard.'

Rosina herself was applauded, after 'Una voce poco fa', and Rossini also had to stand up at the cembalo and take a bow. It looked as if the evening were saved. Not so. 'Booed on all sides, we came to the finale . . . Laughter, catcalls, and piercing whistles, and silence was established only to be broken by even louder demonstrations.'

The fiasco was, to some extent, pre-arranged. There was a pro-Paisiello faction in the theatre that night, and there were also some noisy supporters of the rival Teatro Valle, annoyed that the

7. Autograph of 'Largo al factotum' from Rossini's *Il barbiere di Siviglia*, 1816. Figaro's 'aria di sortita', or entrance aria, 'Largo al factotum', was sung masterfully by Luigi Zamboni, on the opening night, according to Geltrude Righetti Giorgi; but she adds that the aria was not even listened to, in the tempestuous atmosphere of that famous première. On the night of the second performance, when the changeable public hailed the opera with enthusiasm, Rossini had prudently remained at home. There he was wakened by the tenor Manuel Garcia, who, according to Rossini, said: 'Hurry, come on. Listen to those shouts.' The street was full of people, shouting—and quoting Figaro—'bravo, bravissimo Figaro!'

Argentina was invading their opera buffa territory. According to at least one report, a cat appeared on the stage. Don Basilio, making his entrance, stumbled over a nail. And Rossini also caused some hilarity when he took his place in the orchestra wearing a hazel-coloured suit with gold buttons, too tight for him.

But, no doubt, the audience was spoiling for a fight. Dickens, some years later, noted the 'uncommonly hard and cruel character' of the Italian theatre public, who seemed 'always to be lying in wait for an opportunity to hiss'. He added, however, in explanation: 'As there is nothing else of a public nature at which they are allowed to express the least disapprobation, perhaps they are resolved to make the most of this opportunity.'

Dickens was actually writing about Genoa, but the audiences in Rome in 1816 were not very different; and as far as the suppression of public opinion went, the situation was surely much worse. The city was small, firmly ruled by Pius VII, who was recently returned from exile and imprisonment, and his astute Secretary of State Cardinal Consalvi. The poet Giacomo Leopardi, visiting Rome at about this time, wrote: 'All the population of Rome is not enough to fill St Peter's Square . . . All the greatness of Rome serves only to multiply distances and the number of steps you have to climb to visit whomever you want. These immense buildings, and these streets interminable in consequence, are so many spaces thrown between human beings, instead of spaces that contain human beings.'

Though he was still a young man, the intensely intellectual Leopardi, arriving in the Papal capital, had hoped to find stimulating conversation. He was bitterly disappointed: . . . 'The frivolity of these animals surpasses the bounds of the credible. If I were to tell you all the ridiculous notions that serve as subjects of their conversations, and which are their favourites, a folio page would not suffice. This morning (just to give you an example) I heard a long and grave discussion of the fine voice of a Prelate who sang Mass the day before yesterday and of his dignified behaviour in performing this function. They asked him how he had managed to acquire these fine talents, and if at the beginning of the Mass he had felt any sort of nervousness, and such things. The Prelate replied that he had learned through long attendance at the Chapels, that this training had been very useful . . . that he was not at all nervous, and a thousand very witty things. I then learned that several Cardinals and other personages had congratulated him on the happy outcome of that sung Mass. Assume that all subjects of Roman talk are in this vein.'

Musically, the Romans were notoriously ignorant. 'The names of Weber and Beethoven are virtually unknown,' Berlioz wrote in 1830. And Mendelssohn, at the same time, discussing music with a learned priest of the Sistine Chapel, heard the older man remark that someone had mentioned to him 'a young man of great promise called Mozart'. Berlioz, reporting this encounter, commented: 'The smarter *dilettanti* know that he is dead. . . . I know of one who had got hold of a score of *Don Giovanni*. After studying it for some time at the piano he told me frankly, in confidence, that this 'old music' seemed to him to surpass M. Vaccai's *Zadig e Astartea*, which had lately been staged at the Apollo Theatre.'

This was the type of audience that judged—and condemned—Rossini's *Almaviva*. Having enjoyed itself hooting and laughing at the première, however, the fickle public changed its mind on the second night and decreed a triumph.

Rossini, distressed by the jeers of the opening night, had taken to his bed, with a convenient and undefined illness. After the second night's success, as Geltrude Righetti Giorgi tells it, 'we went, all of us, to the imaginary invalid, whose bed was surrounded by many distinguished Roman gentlemen, who had hastened to compliment him.'

If the opening night hostility had upset Rossini, it cannot have shocked or surprised him. By 1816, young as he still was, he had had a long and varied experience of the opera world, since he had virtually grown up in the theatre.

In 1792, the year of Rossini's birth (on 29 February), his father,

Giuseppe, was employed by the town of Pesaro as its trumpeter and crier; his mother, Anna Guidarini, a singer, had retired from the stage only temporarily. Later, as the senior Rossini's life was affected, sometimes dramatically, by the political uncertainties of those Napoleonic years, the family moved its residence frequently. Often Gioacchino was left with his maternal grandmother, while his parents performed—Giuseppe in the pit, Anna on stage—in brief provincial opera seasons in Jesi, Ferrara, and in more important cities like Bologna and Trieste.

Stendhal has described, ironically but believably, how these provincial seasons were organized: 'An impresario (he is often the richest nobleman of a small city; this role inspires respect and affords pleasures, but as a rule it is ruinous), a rich nobleman, as I was saying, assumes the management of the theatre of the city where he shines; he puts together a company, always made up of the *prima donna*, the *tenore*, the *basso cantante*, the *basso buffo*, a second woman and a third buffo.'

It should be added that, with the rise of the merchant class, this provincial impresario was not always a nobleman. Sometimes he could be a wealthy dealer in coal or in horse-flesh. And his negotiations with agents and with sopranos were carried on in the spirit of trade: the quality of the voice was sometimes secondary to the soprano's looks and morals (or rather, lack of them).

Stendhal continues: 'The *impresario* engages a maestro (composer), who writes a new opera for him, taking care to suit his arias to the voices of the people who are to sing them. The impresario buys the poem (libretto): this is an expense of from 60 to 80 francs. The author is some wretched abbé, parasite in some rich house of the town. The role of parasite, so comic, so well depicted by Terence, is still in its glory in Lombardy, where the smallest town has five or six houses with a thousand livres income. The impresario, who is the head of one of these houses, entrusts the management of all financial affairs to a steward, who is generally the great rogue who acts as his comptroller; and he, the impresario, becomes the lover of the prima donna: the great object of curiosity in the little city is to discover if he will offer her his arm in public.'

Finally, as Stendhal concludes, the company gives its first performance 'after a month of comic intrigues which are the news of the town. This *prima recita* is the greatest public event for the little city. . . . Eight to ten thousand people argue for three weeks about the beauties and defects of the opera with all the power of concentration that heaven has given them, and especially with all the power of their lungs. This first performance, when it is not interrupted by a scandal, is usually followed by twenty or thirty others, after which the company scatters.'

Soon Rossini was taking an active part in this world. His early musical education was haphazard, but by the time he was ten his parents discovered that he had a beautiful voice. And at twelve,

8. Stendhal (Henri Beyle). Painting attributed to Jean-Auguste-Dominique Ingres (1780–1867).
Stendhal (1783–1842) lived in Italy for several extended periods and wrote a number of books on Italian subjects, including *Promenades dans Rome; Rome, Naples, Florence* (ably translated by Richard Coe); and *Chroniques italiennes*, as well as idiosyncratic 'lives' of Metastasio and Rossini. Although these works were, for the most part, pot-boilers, on a level far below the author's great novels, they still contain—amid inaccuracies—much amusing and pertinent information about the habits and tastes of the time and furnish countless examples of Stendhal's wit and powers of observation. An inveterate opera-goer, Stendhal was devoted to La Scala, where today, appropriately, his bust is displayed in the foyer.

he made his operatic debut; with his clear treble, he replaced an indisposed basso buffo, during a makeshift season in Ravenna. The following year, still a boy soprano, he sang a small role in Paer's popular opera *Camilla*, in Bologna. There was a suggestion that he be kept a soprano forever, through an operation still customary at that time in Italy. But the danger was avoided. Before long Rossini was acting as accompanist for recitatives, composing odd bits of music as required, and—according to his own later accounts—enjoying at this tender age the charms of the mature prima donnas.

In Bologna he continued studying music seriously, and in 1807 he began studying counterpoint with the celebrated Padre Mattei. While still at the Conservatory (or Liceo musicale, as it then was), Rossini met the remarkable Mombelli family: the tenor Domenico and his children. Rossini afterwards described them: 'Mombelli was an excellent tenor; he had two daughters, one a soprano, the other a contralto; they got a bass to join them, and as a complete vocal quartet, with no outside help, they gave opera performances in Bologna, Milan, and other cities.'

In Bologna, they were giving a little opera by Marcos da Fonseca, known as Portogallo, after the country of his birth. A patroness of Rossini wanted an aria from it, but when Rossini asked Mombelli for a copy, the tenor refused. In those days, when there were no copyright laws and when operatic scores were rarely published, physical possession of a work amounted to ownership. The thirteen-year-old boy then attended a performance, wrote out a complete piano score from memory, and showed it to Mombelli. Impressed, the tenor asked Rossini to compose some music for him. Taking a libretto written by his (second) wife Vincenza, who was a niece of Boccherini and a sister of the choreographer Viganò, Mombelli passed the text to Rossini, a few pages at a time. Rossini set the words to music, a duet one day, an aria another, an ensemble the next, in no particular order. In the end, he had completed his first opera, *Demetrio e Polibio*. Naturally, since Mombelli paid for the numbers, the work now belonged entirely to him; he and his daughters did not perform it until 1812, by which time Rossini had already made his debut as an operatic composer with another work.

This debut also came about through an operatic friendship. In the course of their travels, Giuseppe and Anna Rossini had got to know another musical couple, the chorus-master and composer Giovanni Morandi and his wife, the singer Rosa Morolli. They had been engaged by the Marchese Cavalli in Venice for his Teatro Giustinian a San Moisé, which was giving a season of *farse*, one-act comic operas. At a certain point in the season, one of the composers engaged to write a new opera failed to deliver it, and the Morandis recommended the gifted but untried Rossini. The eighteen-year-old rushed to Venice, was handed the libretto of *La cambiale di matrimonio*, and set it in short order. It opened on 3 November 1810; and Rossini's debut was an auspicious success.

Other commissions—including two more from San Moisé— quickly followed. Demand for new works, in those days, was intense, and the discovery of a fertile young composer was a welcome event. Some of these early operas were well received; others, like *L'equivoco stravagante*, failed. But less than two years after his modest Venetian debut, Rossini was at La Scala in Milan, with the *melodramma giocoso La pietra del paragone*, which opened on 26 September 1812. It was given fifty-three times during that first season: Rossini had arrived.

The following year, in Venice, his serious opera *Tancredi* had an even greater success at the Teatro La Fenice. Its irresistibly

MARIA MARCOLINI

9. Maria (Marietta) Marcolini. Engraving by G. Maina, c. 1812.
The contralto Maria Marcolini (born c. 1780), also known as 'La Marcolina', sang in the première of an early Rossini opera, *L'equivoco stravagante* (1811), which closed—because of its 'scandalous' libretto, involving a trans-sexual disguise—after three performances. The following year she created the role of the Marchesa Clarice in *La pietra del paragone* at La Scala, on 26 September, with immense success; and in 1813 she was the first Isabella in *L'italiana in Algeri*. Rossini and La Marcolina were obviously musically well-attuned. She continued singing his operas—including the phenomenally popular *Tancredi*—until her retirement in 1820. Her gifts as an actress (especially in comedy) and her exceptional virtuosity made her an ideal interpreter of the Rossini of these pre-Naples years.

catchy aria 'Di tanti palpiti' was soon being sung, hummed, whistled throughout the city; and according to one early biographer, a judge, in sentencing a criminal, quoted the line 'ti rivedrò' ('I'll see you again'). A few weeks later, Rossini enjoyed another success, in a different Venetian theatre, with *L'italiana in Algeri*. According to rumour, the success also brought with it the favours of the prima donna, Marietta Marcolini, who, as Stendhal says: 'a charming *buffa* singer, then in the flower of her genius and youth, not wanting to be in arrears with Rossini, sacrificed Prince Lucien Bonaparte to him.'

Rossini's fame had not so much grown as exploded. But his next operas, written in the flush of his triumphs, failed to please. Rossini savoured the bitterness of fiascos at La Scala and even in Venice, where he was a favourite. Then, at some point in 1815, he apparently met the colourful and influential Domenico Barbaja, impresario of the Teatro San Carlo in Naples. And on 15 May of that year, Rossini wrote to a friend, the Venetian librettist Luigi Prividali: 'I leave the day after tomorrow for Naples.'

Chapter 2

IN the Museum of La Scala in Milan there is a portrait of Domenico Barbaja. The anonymous painter portrays the impresario in a curious pose, standing, his body bundled in a heavy coat, the trunk thrown back, the eyes looking slyly towards the viewer. In a framed space, to the subject's left, there are three tiny figures: Rossini, Bellini, and the soprano Giuditta Pasta. But what strikes the viewer is Barbaja's smile: wry, and self-satisfied. And by the time the portrait was painted, around 1825–30, he had every reason to be pleased with himself.

10. Domenico Barbaja, *c.* 1825–30.
This painting by an anonymous artist dates from the period when Domenico Barbaja (1778–1841) had assumed the management of La Scala, after his brilliantly successful years in charge of the Teatro San Carlo in Naples. He was also in charge of the other important Milanese opera house, the Teatro alla Canobbiana. In the background of the painting the figures of Rossini, Bellini, and Giuditta Pasta can be discerned: three artists in whose careers Barbaja played a decisive role. This is the only known surviving portrait of the great impresario.

Born of a poor family in Milan in 1778, Barbaja had begun his career as a scullion in a wine-shop. Then, as the novelist Giuseppe Rovani recounted in his historical novel *Cento anni*: 'driven by his genius, in the same year that Volta invented the pile, he discovered the lofty secret of mixing whipped cream with coffee and chocolate, hence the undying word *barbajata*, which raised him a monument more solid than granite.' In 1808 he was granted the gambling concession at La Scala, and in October 1809 he became impresario of the royal theatres of Naples, the San Carlo and the Fondo, later the Teatro dei Fiorentini.

Rovani's description, based on scrupulous research, continues: 'This man, then, except for his special knowledge concerning cocoa and mocha, was of a legendary ignorance; but he had a genius for making money, without paying attention to the means, with no ideas of honesty. . . . In his position as impresario therefore, he was an inexorable usurer of composers, singers, and dancers. He sniffed thus the odour of true merit, like a fox that, even from afar, raising its muzzle in the air, catches the scent of a pullet.'

In 1815, he was on the scent of Rossini, and engaged him to come to Naples. Though Barbaja made no secret of his ignorance, he was proud of his instinct and his acumen. He belonged to the new race of impresarios, quite different from noblemen like Duke Francesco Sforza Cesarini or Marchese Cavalli. For Barbaja, opera management was a lucrative source of income as well as prestige. He hired some of the best singers of the time: besides Pasta and Isabella Colbran, he also engaged Garcia, Nozzari and Donzelli. He brought new composers, like Rossini and, later, Donizetti, to Naples. But boldly, in a period where novelty counted most and older operas were rarely revived, he also presented outstanding works of an earlier generation, like Spontini's *La vestale* and Gluck's *Ifigenia in Aulide*.

The Teatro San Carlo that Rossini saw on his arrival in Naples in 1815 was not the theatre of the same name that stands today on the same site. The leading Neapolitan opera house at that time was an older theatre, erected in 1736, at the wish of Naples's first Bourbon king, Charles III, whose love of architecture gave the city the stylish aspect it still, to some extent, retains. The original San Carlo, built by the architect Medrano, was described in Charles's time by Samuel Sharp:
'The King's Theatre, upon the first view, is, perhaps, almost as remarkable an object as any man sees in his travels. The amazing extent of the stage, with the prodigious circumference of the boxes and the height of the ceiling, produce a marvellous effect on the mind. . . . Notwithstanding the amazing noisiness of the audience during the whole performance of the opera, the moment the dances [i.e. ballet] begin there is a universal dead silence. . . . Witty people, therefore, never fail to tell me, the Neapolitans go to *see* not to *hear* an opera. . . . It is customary for

gentlemen to run about from box to box between the acts, and even in the midst of the performance; but the ladies, after they are seated, never quit their box the whole evening. It is the fashion to make appointments for such and such nights. A lady receives visitors in her box one night, and they remain with her the whole opera; another night she returns the visit in the same manner. In the intervals between the acts, principally between the first and second, the proprietor of the box regales her company with iced fruits and sweetmeats. . . . The seats have elbows, which circumstance, I believe, is peculiar to this theatre. The pit here is very ample: it contains between five and six hundred seats, with arms resembling a large elbow chair. . . . The seat of each chair lifts up like the lid of a box, and has a lock to fasten it. There are in Naples gentlemen enough to hire by the year the first four rows next to the orchestra, who take the key of the chair home with them when the opera is finished, lifting up the seat and leaving it locked. By this contrivance they are always sure of the same place at whatever hour they please to go to the opera; nor do they disturb the audience, though it be in the middle of a scene, as the intervals between the rows are wide enough to admit a lusty man to walk to his chair, without obliging anybody to rise.'

The three lower ranges of boxes were also hired by the year; the other boxes could be bought by the performance. Unlike the boxes of the Roman theatres, the San Carlo's were spacious, accommodating twelve people standing, as well as the three ladies usually seated at the front.

Rossini could hardly have arrived in Naples at a more auspicious time. With the fall of Napoleon and of Murat, whom the Emperor had installed as King of Naples, the Bourbon king Ferdinand—son of the builder of the San Carlo—was about to return to the city, which Stendhal described as the 'only capital in Italy'. It is uncertain how long Rossini stayed in Naples on this first visit, but if he remained over a month, he was probably in the audience of the San Carlo on the night of 19 June, when the king returned to his box, enthusiastically welcomed.

All reports agree that the theatre had never been so brilliantly lighted, nor had there been, as one observer wrote, 'more perfect and more seemly joy. The King was moved to tears; and when his bust appeared on the stage amid the banners of all the Allied Powers, the theatre resounded with applause and continued cheering for half an hour. The King was seen to wipe his eyes, and acknowledge the transports of the public with fervent thanks.'

The contract that Rossini signed at this time with Barbaja, to become effective in the autumn of 1815, placed the composer in charge of the two Naples opera houses, required him to write two operas a year, and provided him with an annual stipend, which has been variously described. Rossini, in later life, told his

friend Hiller that it amounted to 8,000 francs; Stendhal, never very reliable in such matters, says 12,000. In any case, it was a comfortable sum, and the contract also allowed Rossini to compose and produce new operas elsewhere.

While Rossini was in Rome, completing *Il barbiere di Siviglia* for the Argentina, a disastrous fire destroyed the San Carlo, on the night of 12 February 1816. The blaze broke out after a ballet rehearsal, and was caused by sparks from a lamp that had been left burning on the stage. Naturally, the Neapolitans blamed it all on the Jacobins. King Ferdinand came to inspect the smouldering ruins and expressed the wish to see the same ballet on his next birthday, 12 January 1817. Barbaja, with the help of the architect Antonio Niccolini, managed to have a new theatre built in less than a year, thus cementing his position in the royal household.

Rossini had, however, presented his first Neapolitan opera, in fulfilment of his contract, at the old San Carlo, a few months before its destruction, on 4 October 1815. It was *Elisabetta, regina d'Inghilterra*, a vehicle for Isabella Colbran, who was particularly admired in noble, tragic roles. In fact, *Elisabetta* is characterized as a 'dramma': in other words, a sad story with a happy ending (Elizabeth pardons Leicester). After the fire, Rossini's next Neapolitan operas were given either at the Fondo

11, 12. The Teatro San Carlo, Naples: (*left*) during rebuilding in 1816, and (*right*) after the rebuilding was completed.
The original Real Teatro di San Carlo was built in 1737 by order of Charles III, the first Bourbon king of Naples. Construction of the house was part of his larger plan to enrich and beautify his new capital, a plan continued under his successors. When the first San Carlo burned down in 1816, Charles had long since left the city, to become king of Spain; but his son, Ferdinand I of the Two Sicilies, was equally concerned about the city's magnificence. He commanded the prompt rebuilding of the opera house, and—thanks to the alacrity of the impresario Domenico Barbaja and of the architect Antonio Niccolini—the renewed San Carlo opened on 12 January 1817. It has survived ever since, escaping serious damage even in World War II, and remains one of the glories of Naples.

or the tiny, but charming Fiorentini, which Stendhal described as 'fresh and pretty'.

Then, on 12 January 1817, the king's birthday, came the gala re-opening of the San Carlo, whose rebuilding had cost 200,000 ducats. Stendhal was in Rome at the time, but this did not prevent him from giving an elaborate description of the occasion in one of his books. Obviously, these pages were based on first-hand reports from others and on his own acquaintance with the theatre, made some time later.

'Standing once more in the theatre, I found again that sense of awe and ecstasy. If you search to the farthest frontiers of Europe, you will find nothing to rival it—what am I saying? Nothing to give so much as the vaguest notion of its significance. This mighty edifice, rebuilt in the space of three hundred days, is nothing less than a *coup d'état*: it binds the people in fealty and homage to their sovereign far more effectively than any *Constitution*. . . . From prince to waiter, all Naples is drunk with joy.' The reference to a Constitution is unfortunate; it was the demand for a constitution that was to inspire the Carbonari revolution three years later.

The Teatro San Carlo one sees today is not very different from the theatre of Rossini, Stendhal, and Ferdinand I. The auditorium is still 'a symphony in silver and gold'. The gold ornaments still decorate the front of the boxes and the proscenium. And, as Stendhal went on to say: 'There is a marvellous chandelier, all glittering with light, mirrored and refracted on all sides, as it falls upon the gold and silver of the reliefs—an effect which would be entirely lost if the ornamentation were two-dimensional. I can conceive of nothing more majestic or more magnificent than the sumptuous royal box, which is set over the central doorway, borne aloft by two huge golden palm-trees, each of natural size; the hangings are wrought out of leaves of metal, the faintest red in colour.'

And Stendhal also praised the painted ceiling, 'a faultless mirror of that taste in art prescribed by the French school'; this ceiling—on the subject 'Apollo presenting to Minerva the world's most famous poets from Homer to Alfieri'—is the work of Giuseppe Cammarano, whose son Salvatore was also employed at the San Carlo as a set-painter until he turned to poetry and became the librettist, years later, of *Lucia*, *Il trovatore*, and other beloved operas.

The theatre's reopening was, of course, marked by a gala cantata; and, again according to Stendhal, the happy event nearly ended in disaster, because at a certain point in the performance the audience began to notice a cloud of dark smoke filling the hall. Murmurs ran from box to box. The Duchess of C*** leaned towards the writer and 'whispered in accents of splendid terror: *"Ah! Santissima Madonna!* The theatre is on fire!"'

And she assumed it was the Jacobins again. 'They tried once and failed; now they want to try another time.' While pondering the best escape route from a narrow third-tier box, Stendhal noticed that the 'smoke' had a peculiar smell. It was not smoke at all, but condensation. The freshly-built house was still thoroughly damp and was drying out, thanks to the heat of the crowd and the illumination.

Like other observers, Stendhal complained of the talking; but conversation in the boxes, during the performance, was the rule also at La Scala, in the Roman theatres, and at Italian opera houses generally. The auditorium also was brightly lighted from beginning to end. Indeed, the new San Carlo, for some of the ladies, was over-illuminated. They felt themselves on display all evening, and those who had been to Milan recalled, with nostalgia, the convenient curtains on La Scala's boxes, which could screen them from curious eyes.

Rossini's life in Naples was undoubtedly pleasant. No one knows exactly when his love affair with la Colbran began, but apparently she succeeded in transferring her affections from Barbaja to the composer without causing any trouble. The city, too, was particularly enjoyable. A handsome capital, it had the usual complement of embassies, with routs, receptions, gaiety. It also attracted, because of its incomparable situation, a number of travellers; and it had a large permanent foreign colony, with a dominant English element.

The Bourbons were absolute monarchs, but still there was in

13. Teatro alla Scala, Milan, painting by Angelo Inganni (1807–80).
This is La Scala much as it appeared to Rossini, Bellini, Donizetti, Verdi, and Puccini, and—as far as the exterior of the building is concerned—much as it appears today. Giovanni Ricordi's music shop and printing establishment was, in its early years, just to the left of the main entrance of the theatre.

14. Teatro alla Scala, Milan: interior, c. 1830.
The interior of the house is here much as Donizetti and Bellini must have seen it, as they supervised the staging of their early operas there. This is also the view that the young Verdi must have had, later in the 1830s, when he attended the theatre as an obscure student.

Naples an atmosphere of intellectual enquiry, philosophical debate, and serious study. Neapolitan intellectuals—then as now—were often eccentric; yet they were cosmopolitan, original, and hospitable. A typical example was the Marchese Francesco Berio di Salsa, now remembered only as the librettist of Rossini's *Otello* and *Riccardo e Zoraide*. The poor Marchese has been roundly excoriated especially for the *Otello* text, because it bears little resemblance to Shakespeare. Actually, Shakespeare was virtually unknown to the Italians at the time, and the aristocratic writer almost certainly based his libretto on the more fashionable and more popular version of the Othello story by the French actor-poet Jean-François Ducis, whose neo-classical adaptations of Shakespearean plots were widely performed in Italy. The erudite Marchese, who was supposed to know much of Homer, Sophocles, Terence, Corneille, and Alfieri by heart, probably was also familiar with Shakespeare's own sources.

Lady Morgan described the *Conversazione* at the Palazzo Berio as 'a congregation of elegant and refined spirits, where everybody converses and converses well; and best (if not most) the master of the house'. Berio was an omnivorous reader, and visitors would see the latest English novels and poetry on the tables in his living room. Lady Morgan once found him writing, *all'improvviso*, a beautiful ode to Lord Byron, after having read for the first time '*that* canto of *Childe Harold*, so read and so admired by all in Italy'.

At a typical gathering in the Marchese's drawing room there might be the sculptor Canova, the poet and *improvvisatore* Gabriele Rossetti (father of the more famous poets Dante Gabriel and Christina), the philosopher and historian Melchiorre Delfico (who later fled Naples for political reasons and found refuge in the Republic of San Marino), and the Duke of Ventignano. The Duke, like the Marchese Berio, was an amateur poet and sometime librettist. He furnished Rossini with the text of *Maometto II* (later revised, in French, as *Le Siège de Corinth*).

Lady Morgan lists other leading lights of Naples, also regular visitors to the Palazzo Berio, and concludes: 'While *Duchessas* and *Principessas*, with titles as romantic as that which induced Horace Walpole to write his delightful romance of "Otranto", filled up the ranks of literature and talent—Rossini presided at the pianoforte, accompanying alternately, himself, Rossetti in his improvvisi, or the Colbran, the prima donna of the San Carlo, in some of her favourite airs from his own *Mosé*. Rossini at the pianoforte is almost as fine an actor as he is a composer. All this was very delightful, and very rare!—'

The liaison with la Colbran, and her pre-eminent position at the San Carlo, had a determinant effect on Rossini's music at this time. For the major theatre or for the Teatro del Fondo (during the reconstruction of the San Carlo), Rossini wrote only opera seria, tailored for the gifts of his prima donna. He saved his comic talents for the smaller Teatro dei Fiorentini or for his productions in other cities. On state occasions—a happy recovery of the king's health, a royal betrothal—he turned out appropriate allegorical cantatas, often re-using old music of his own, or persuading some friendly fellow-composer to lend a hand and ghost-write some of the piece.

Not all his works were hailed with enthusiasm. His fantastic opera *Armida*, which contains, unusually for him, several love duets (supposedly inspired by Isabella), was sumptuously staged, but aroused a certain hostility. The score was considered too 'German'—an adjective applied in those days to anything that departed from the simplest, tried-and-true formulas. Even *Mosè*, staged during Lent (hence the Biblical subject), got a cold welcome at its première. It was revived in later seasons, however, and with a happier outcome. For its second production, Rossini added the famous Prayer ('Dal tuo stellato soglio'). And Stendhal relates an entertaining, if unlikely result of this beautiful number. 'Cotugno, the leading physician of Naples [he was physician to the royal family], said to me after the wild success of *Mosè*: "Among the other praises one can give your hero [Rossini], add also the title of murderer. I can cite for you more than forty attacks of nervous brain-fever, or violent convulsions, in young women too gripped by music; and the only cause is the prayer of the Hebrews in the third act, with its superb change of key."'

After Stendhal's and other writers' descriptions of the showy, talkative Neapolitan audience, Dr Cotugno's complaint suggests that not all the San Carlo opera-goers were insensitive.

Early in 1821, Rossini was back in Rome. Giovanni Torlonia, Duke of Bracciano, possessor of a wealth already considered legendary, had bought the Teatro Apollo and was determined to make it the city's leading theatre. He had the house completely restored and added 'sumptuous reception rooms, and assigned others for gambling, for the exhibition of objects of art, for billiards, for wardrobes, adorned with rich hangings and excellent furniture'. The Duke also added an elegant café, in two large rooms, and a trattoria, whose model kitchens were visited and observed with admiration by the Romans.

Rossini was commissioned to write *Matilde Shabran*, later known as *Matilde di Shabran*, and he was to be paid 1,000 *scudi*, more than twice what he had been given for the *Barber*. His poet was Jacopo Ferretti, who had written an earlier Roman success for him, *La Cenerentola*.

But Rossini was in no hurry to get to work. It was Carnival time, the season when sleepy, provincial, hidebound Rome came suddenly and briefly to life.

Among Rossini's Roman friends was the painter and writer Massimo d'Azeglio, later an outstanding Italian statesman. In his autobiography he wrote of that carefree time: 'Paganini and Rossini were in Rome: la [Caterina] Lipparini was singing at Tor di Nona [Apollo], and in the evening I often went out with them

15. (*Overleaf*) Isabella Colbran. Painting by Heinrich Schmidt (1740–1821).
This portrait was painted in 1817, when Colbran and Rossini were already lovers but not yet married. Celebrated for her interpretations of classical heroines, la Colbran is seen here as Sappho in Giovanni Simone Mayr's *Saffo* (1794), his first opera, also known under the title of *I riti di Apollo Leucadio*. In 1817, the year of this portrait, the soprano also created the role of Desdemona in Rossini's *Otello* and the title role of his *Armida*.

16. (*Page 37*) Gioacchino Rossini as a young man. Painting by Vincenzo Camuccini.
Camuccini (1771–1844) was a leading artist in Rome in the early years of the nineteenth century. He met Goethe and was a friend of the English *dilettanti* who visited the city. In 1806 he was appointed Principal of the Accademia di San Luca; he was Inspector General of Paintings under Pius VII, who created him a Baron in1830; and he arranged the Vatican Gallery for Gregory XVI. He painted chiefly historical, classical scenes, but he also executed a few portraits. This one probably dates from around 1815, the time of *Il barbiere di Siviglia*.

and with other fellow-lunatics my age. Carnival was approaching and one evening we said: Let's do something in fancy dress.'

The three young men decided to dress up as blind beggars and to sing for alms. They put together some lines of doggerel, and Rossini set them to music. He made his friends rehearse diligently for their debut on the Thursday before Lent. 'Our costumes, it was decided, would be very elegant underneath, and covered with poor patched tatters. In other words, an apparent and tidy wretchedness. Rossini and Paganini were then to be the orchestra, strumming two guitars; and they thought to dress up as women. Rossini, with great taste, amplified his already abundant figure with handfuls of straw, and it was something inhuman! And Paganini, thin as a rail and with that face of his that seemed the neck of a violin, looked even more skinny and gnarled.'

The trio, in d'Azeglio's account, had an enviable success, singing and begging along the Corso, and later at a private party.

On the Corso, they probably also witnessed another traditional Roman Carnival event: the riderless horse-race. Some years later, William Wetmore Story described it: 'Boom! goes the cannon. It is the signal that the races are about to begin. The carriages at once turn into the by-streets, the crowd flocks closer together, and there is a suspension of hostilities between parties who have been pelting each other all day with flowers. . . . Sud-

17. Teatro Apollo, Rome: interior, 1882. The Roman Teatro Tor di Nona, on the banks of the Tiber, opened in 1671, but was demolished in 1697 by Pope Innocent XII. In 1773 it was rebuilt, only to burn down in 1787. After several more versions, it was given the name of Teatro Apollo in 1795. In 1820, when the house became the property of Prince Giovanni Torlonia, it entered its glorious, final phase. In the following year Rossini staged the world première of his *Matilde di Shabran*, conducted by Paganini. In 1839, the colourful Vincenzo ('Cencio') Jacovacci (1811–81) became the Apollo's impresario and remained in that position until his death. He was responsible for introducing Verdi's *Il trovatore* (19 January 1853) and his *Un ballo in maschera* (17 February 1859). In 1882, after Jacovacci's death, his successor Federico Tati sponsored the posthumous première of Donizetti's *Le Duc d'Albe* (given in Italian as *Il duca d'Alba*), the occasion of this illustration. The cast included Abigaille Bruschi-Chiatti, Leone Giraldoni (title role) and Julián Gayarré. In 1889 the theatre was demolished for good, to make room for the embankments along the Tiber, which ended the floods that had long plagued that quarter of Rome (in 1853, on the opening night of *Il trovatore* the audience had been obliged to wade to the theatre entrance).

denly there is a movement, and down come the papal dragoons, their swords clattering and their horses galloping, while the crowd opens before them. . . . Arrived at the Venetian Palace, they wheel about, and again come clattering down the Corso. . . . Around the starting-place in the Piazza del Popolo is built an open square of wooden *palchi*, where the magistrates of the city and their invited guests are seated. A rope is drawn across, and in the open space beyond the horses which are to run come plunging and rearing. They are covered with spangles and crackling tinsel, and balls armed with sharp points that swing loosely over their backs. Starting, rearing, kicking, and with difficulty held back by their grooms, they press against the rope and strive madly to escape. The signal is given, the rope is loosed, and away they go. . . . Sometimes, frightened by the din, and irritated by the goads, they start aside into the crowd and leave wounded and killed behind them. There is almost no Carnival race without its victims.'

Rossini's japes with his friends and his enjoyment of Carnival delayed the composition of the opera, which finally opened on 24 February 1821, only ten days before the season had to end. At the last minute, pressed by the understandably angry Duke Torlonia, Rossini had called in the younger composer, Giovanni

18. Horse-race on the Corso, Rome, 1817. Painting by Théodore Géricault. In 1816, the year Rossini's *Il barbiere di Siviglia* had its première at the Teatro Argentina in Rome, the young painter Théodore Géricault (1791–1824) visited the city. Both composer and painter were thus in the Papal capital at Carnival time, when a main attraction was the famous 'corsa dei barbari', the race of riderless horses from Piazza del Popolo to Piazza Venezia. Géricault, who had a passion for horses, painted several aspects of the race and its preparation. Other visitors to Rome that same season were the Piedmontese painter-writer (and future statesman) Massimo d'Azeglio and Nicolò Paganini.

Pacini, to lend a hand. The first night was stormy, despite the presence of Paganini as conductor (filling in for an indisposed colleague). The Duke tried to withhold the second half of Rossini's fee, due after the third night; and Rossini had to appeal to the Cardinal Governor of Rome.

The Cardinal made the Duke pay up, and Rossini went back to Naples some time in March. His last opera for the San Carlo was *Zelmira*, on a libretto by Andrea Leone Tottola, who belonged to the unhappy category of the 'theatre poet'. Given the job by Barbaja, Tottola turned out dozens of librettos, year after year (his first text was written in 1802 and he continued work until his premature death in 1831). He was the opposite of the noble dilettantes, like the Marchese Berio and the Duke of Ventignano. For Rossini he also wrote *Mosé, La donna del lago, Ermione* and others.

Colbran, of course, sang the title role of *Zelmira*, when it opened on 16 February 1822. As a result of the short-lived Carbonari revolution in the summer of 1820, the kingdom of Naples was occupied by Austrian troops. Barbaja had temporarily lost his position at the San Carlo as a result of the uprising and the subsequent turmoil; and though he would soon regain his Neapolitan post, he signed—a few weeks before Rossini's première—a contract which made him impresario of the Kärntnertortheater, the court theatre of Vienna. As he set off to assume his duties in the Austrian capital, he took his leading soprano and his star composer along with him.

On 5 January 1822, a Neapolitan paper wrote: 'Rossini, the ornament of Italy, is about to leave our country.' The article added that, after a visit to Vienna, London, and Paris, Rossini would then return to Naples. He did not. On 7 March 1822, Rossini left the city for good.

19. (*Page 40*) *Lo scappellotto*. Engraved drawing by Matania for a special number of *L'illustrazione italiana*, 1901.
On 6 January 1816 the Emperor Francis I of Austria, visiting Milan, which was then under Austrian rule, attended a gala performance at La Scala of a cantata, *Il ritorno di Astrea*, text by Vincenzo Monti, music by Joseph Weigl, with the popular Marietta Marcolini among the singers. In the stalls one young man, defying a police order, failed to remove his hat. Because of the crush, the police were unable to reach him, so the exasperated military governor of Milan, General Sarau, leaned from the box (where he was seated near the Emperor) and knocked the young patriot's hat off.

20. (*Previous page, above*) Bergamo in the early nineteenth century.
Italy's greatest composers of the nineteenth century came from outlying, provincial cities, or small towns: Rossini from Pesaro, Bellini from Catania, Verdi from Busseto (or, more specifically, the hamlet of Roncole), Puccini from Lucca. Donizetti was born in Bergamo in 1797, in a dark, dank basement (now open to the public and still oppressively gloomy). Fortunately, the city had a flourishing musical tradition. Donizetti and his teacher Mayr are both buried in the church of Santa Maria Maggiore.

21. (*Previous page, below*) View of Posilippo from Naples.
The cape of Posilippo, in the first decades of the nineteenth century, was a suburb of Naples (now it has been practically incorporated into the city), where people with means had villas, gardens, and follies. Among the owners of such villas was the impresario Domenico Barbaja—he died at Posilippo in 1841—who frequently invited there his favourite singers and composers. Rossini was one such guest, and so was Donizetti who later wrote an album of salon songs entitled *Nuits d'été à Pausilippe*.

22. (*Right*) Simone Mayr and friends. Painting by Luigi Deleidi, *c.* 1840.
Mayr, Donizetti's teacher, was notoriously fond of wine, and this painting seems to make an affectionate reference to this little weakness of his. In the garden of a Bergamo tavern, the host, Michele Bettinelli, is seated at the table, left, guarding some bottles. The central group consists of Donizetti, his life-long friend Antonio Dolci (another, less eminent pupil of Mayr), and Mayr himself. The figure at right is a self-portrait of Luigi Deleidi, a local artist nicknamed 'Il nebbia' (Fog).

$\mathcal{F}$ Chapter 3 $\mathcal{F}$

ON 28 February 1822 the *Giornale del Regno delle Due Sicilie*, published in Naples, announced the programme of the approaching summer season at the Teatro Nuovo, a small and popular theatre which specialized in opera buffa and in dialect works. That year it was to present operas by Pasquale Sogner, Valentino Fioravanti, and Giuseppe Mosca; and, the announcement added, there would also be 'a production of Signor Gaetano Donizetti, a young pupil of one of the most valued Maestros of the century, Mayer [sic], much of whose glory could be called ours, since he modelled his style on that of

23. *La gazza ladra* by Gioacchino Rossini, set design.
Rossini's opera semiseria was first produced at La Scala on 31 May 1817, with a cast that included the soprano Teresa Giorgi-Belloc and the bass Filippo Galli. The sets were designed by Alessandro Sanquirico (1777–1849), the great romantic designer, who was active at La Scala until his retirement in 1832. He was interested in every aspect of stage production, and—as his career coincided with the installation of gas lighting at La Scala—he was responsible for many innovations in the illumination of sets and action. This set represents the Court-Room (Act II, scene ix), 'in a large villa near Paris'.

24. (*Right, above*) *La regina di Saba*, set design.
Turin, in the last decades of the nineteenth century, enjoyed a particularly lively musical life. Its newly-established Conservatory flourished, a series of 'concerti popolari' introduced the great symphonic literature to wide audiences, and the Teatro Regio presented seasons of special interest, as did the city's other, smaller opera houses. The Regio followed a policy of alternating new Italian works (among them Puccini's *Manon Lescaut* in 1893 and his *La Bohème* in 1896) with foreign works new to Italy. The Italian

première of Carl Goldmark's first and most successful opera, *Die Königin von Saba* (Vienna, 1875) took place at the Regio on 1 March 1879, and was a triumph. The opera was given in Italian translation, as were all foreign operas in Italy at this time. The illustration shows the final scene of Act IV.

25. (*Right, below*) *La sonnambula*, final scene. Lithograph by P. Oggioni.
This naive contemporary illustration of the last scene of *La sonnambula* probably does not depict the opera's first production (at the Teatro Carcano, Milan, on 6 March 1831), which starred Giuditta Pasta and Giovanni Rubini. Here, in fact, the Count seems to be dressed as an army—or police —officer; and young Elvino, the tenor whom he is restraining, looks more like a crazed vagabond than the rich landowner he is meant to be. The picture is more likely an artist's fantasy, though it may well have been inspired by one of the popular opera's numerous, makeshift provincial productions.

26. Gaetano Donizetti. Watercolour by B. Martini, 1815.
This awkward, but engaging portrait shows Donizetti at the time of his studies under the legendary Padre Mattei in Bologna. There Donizetti wrote his first opera, the one-act *Pigmalione* (op. post.) and a number of other works. His period of study ended in November 1817.

the great luminaries of the musical art who developed in our midst. From what we hear, it seems that this pupil of Mayer is not unworthy of such a teacher. A sample of his work presented on the stage of the Teatro Argentina in Rome was welcomed with the most flattering applause.'

Donizetti's teacher had been Johann Simon Mayr, born in Bavaria but of Italian background. He re-Italianized himself, changing his given names to Giovanni Simone, and making his debut as an opera composer in Venice in 1796. In 1802 he settled in Bergamo, as *maestro di cappella* in the church of Santa Maria Maggiore; and in 1805 when the Istituto musicale was founded in the city, he became its director. He continued, however, to write operas, which were performed with success all over Italy. After studying with him, Donizetti had left his native Bergamo to continue his studies at the even more famous school of Padre Mattei in Bologna. But to the opera-wise Neapolitans, the name of Mayr, whom they had often applauded in the city, meant more than that of the illustrious pedagogue of Bologna.

Donizetti had arrived in Naples only a few days before the appearance of the article in the *Giornale*. Rossini left the city about a fortnight later. The two composers must surely have spent some time together; they would have had a number of common acquaintances (Rossini, after all, had studied with Padre Mattei also), but it was only later that they became friends.

Donizetti was just five years younger than Rossini; in terms of career, however, in that spring of 1822, the two artists were practically a generation apart. Donizetti, like his older colleague, had shown musical talent at an early age, and had made his operatic debut—in Venice, like Rossini—when he was only twenty. But in the four years since then his career had progressed relatively slowly. Rossini, after his debut at eighteen, had become famous in the space of two years. Donizetti had to struggle more. His first works, mostly little farces, had made scant impression. His only substantial success so far, in January of that same 1822, had been the work referred to by the *Giornale*, an opera semiseria entitled *Zoraide di Granata*, given in Rome. Its success had been sufficient to procure the composer's exemption from military service.

It was Lent when Donizetti arrived in Naples, so instead of operas, the San Carlo was presenting oratorios on Biblical themes. In preparation at the time was a work of Mayr's, *Atalia*. Donizetti had come to the city early with the intention of helping in the rehearsal of the piece, which had been written three years earlier.

He wrote to his teacher in despair, especially about the leading female singer, Flora Fabbri, who was to appear 'after two years in which she hasn't been singing. And that's not all; she has a very cloudy contralto voice, so Sig. Rossini has had to revise the whole part. At rehearsals he complained Jesuitically about the singers, that they weren't performing the music properly. Then, at the orchestra rehearsals, there he was chatting with the prima donnas instead of conducting.' Donizetti then went on to enumerate the cuts that were being made—all, of course, without the composer's consent, in keeping with the relaxed customs of the time.

Meanwhile Donizetti was busy writing his opera for the Teatro Nuovo: *La zingara*, with a libretto by the overworked Tottola. The première took place on 12 May 1822, and two days later the composer wrote about it to a friend in Rome, Signora Anna Carnevali. For comic effect, Donizetti wrote in the third person:

'So the fortunate Donizetti opened on Sunday with *La zingara*, and the audience was certainly not miserly with compliments. They were abundant, I might almost say; the more so because in Naples people don't applaud much.

'. . . This evening His Majesty comes to us for the first time.

'The papers yesterday confirmed the opinion of my talent expressed by the Romans.'

27. *Norma* by Vincenzo Bellini: the Temple of Irminsul. Set by Alessandro Sanquirico. The première of Bellini's *Norma* took place on 26 December 1831, the opening night also of the Carnival season. The cast included Giuditta Pasta in the title role, with Giulia Grisi—a young girl of twenty—as Adalgisa. Though the opera was jeered at this first performance, the second night was a success, and *Norma* was performed a record thirty-four times that season.

Among the admirers of *La zingara* was the twenty-year-old Vincenzo Bellini, who had come to Naples from his native Sicily for the purpose of studying at the prestigious Conservatory. An older student and budding composer, Carlo Conti, arranged for Bellini to meet Donizetti. And a third student, Bellini's friend and future biographer Francesco Florimo, later wrote: 'The day that this introduction took place was a day of rejoicing for Bellini. On coming back from the visit, he said to me, still all excited: "Besides the great talent that this Lombard has, he is also quite a handsome man, and his physiognomy, noble, sweet and impressive at the same time, inspired liking and respect."'

One may legitimately doubt that Bellini expressed himself in precisely these terms, but it is possible that his first feelings towards Donizetti were friendly. Later, when Bellini had begun his rise to fame, and the careers of the two men were running parallel, the younger man's attitude towards Donizetti underwent a transformation. Bellini's obsessive jealousy and envy, openly expressed in any number of his letters (and in his actions), are the least attractive aspect of his character. But in these first Neapolitan days, when Donizetti himself was only on the lowest rung of the ladder, the two men were on good terms.

28. Vincenzo Bellini. Painting attributed to Giuseppe Cammarano, *c.* 1826.
This unfinished portrait, painted not long before Bellini left Naples in April of 1827, is attributed to Giuseppe Cammarano (1776–1850). The painter was a member of an exceptional family of writers, artists and actors. Giuseppe's father, Giancola, was the great Pulcinella of his day. Giuseppe's son Salvatore was the librettist of Donizetti's *Lucia di Lammermoor*, Verdi's *Il trovatore*, and many other operas. Salvatore's brothers were painters, as was his son Michele, who achieved more than local fame. This picture may be a copy of Giuseppe Cammarano's original, but in any case, the portrayal—less flattering than most portraits of Bellini—is considered by experts a convincing likeness.

29. Felice Romani. Engraving after the bust by Pompeo Marchesi.

Felice Romani (1788–1865) was the most famous and most sought-after librettist of his time. He was also one of the most prolific: he produced more than a hundred texts, some of which were set several times by different composers. His first libretto, *La rosa bianca e la rosa rossa* (1813), was written for Donizetti's teacher Simone Mayr, for whom Romani also wrote the more famous *Medea in Corinto* (also 1813). He supplied texts for Rossini (among them *Il turco in Italia*, 1814), Donizetti (*Anna Bolena*, 1830; *L'elisir d'amore*, 1832, and several others); Mercadante (*Amleto*, 1822); and Meyerbeer (*L'esule di Granata*, 1822), as well as for a number of minor composers. But his greatest achievements were with Bellini, whom Romani sponsored in Milan and for whom he wrote *Il pirata* (1827), *La straniera* (1829), *Zaira* (1829), *I Capuleti ed i Montecchi* (1830), *La sonnambula* (1831), *Norma* (1831), and *Beatrice di Tenda* (1833): in other words, all of Bellini's mature operas except *I puritani* (1835). Romani was also an influential journalist and editor, and published verses and essays. As a critic, he was staunchly classical, anti-romantic (though, for operatic reasons, he reluctantly adapted plays by such arch-romantics as Victor Hugo). Marchesi (1783–1858) probably made the bust around 1840.

Donizetti's easy-going nature was suited to the temperament of Naples; he liked the city, and in a short time it was to become his home, in so far as an itinerant composer of the early nineteenth century could have a home. Meanwhile, however, other cities and other experiences awaited him. In October of that year, 1822, he tried his wings for the first time at La Scala. The opera—semiseria—was entitled *Chiara e Serafina*; and on this occasion Donizetti was privileged to have, for the first time, a libretto by Felice Romani, the outstanding theatrical poet of the time and an important figure in Milanese cultural life.

But even the lustre of the name of Romani—whom we will come to know better presently—could not decree a success. The Milanese audience was suspicious of Donizetti's nascent fame, acquired in the rival cities of Rome and Naples. The opera failed. Donizetti eventually went south again, and after an opera seria (*Alfredo il grande*) at the San Carlo on 2 July 1823, and an opera buffa (*Il fortunato inganno*) at the Nuovo on 3 September, he finally enjoyed another resounding success, with an opera buffa, *L'ajo nell' imbarazzo* (The Tutor Embarrassed), at the Teatro Valle in Rome on 4 February 1824. The libretto was by Rossini's Roman librettist Jacopo Ferretti, who had taken the plot from a popular comedy by the Roman writer Giovanni Giraud. The opera was one of the first of Donizetti's works to circulate widely and rapidly among other Italian theatres, and it soon went abroad: to Vienna in 1827, to Dresden the following year, and then to Rio, Lisbon, Nice, Berlin, and Constantinople.

Success did not solve Donizetti's financial problems. He was still paid modestly for his work (and, as was the custom, sold the property of his scores outright), so he had to keep working in order to support himself. At about this time therefore he agreed to serve as musical director of the Teatro Carolino in Palermo.

The Sicilian capital was not fortunate in its theatres. The Carolino—named after Queen Maria Carolina—was the best of them. It had opened in 1809, in the presence of Maria Carolina and King Ferdinand, then in exile from Naples. It was a small house with a cramped stage, and no public rooms (aristocratic members of the audience, however, could repair to an exclusive club in the Palazzo Santa Lucia next door). The house was not really replaced as Palermo's leading opera theatre until the inauguration of the Teatro Massimo in 1897. The Carolino still stands, and is now called the Teatro Bellini.

When he was in Palermo, Donizetti also had to teach at the Conservatorio del Buon Pastore, and he probably took up these duties shortly after his arrival. Some time later, he wrote to Mayr: 'Would you like to know how this musical boarding-school is progressing? Ah, mercy! Horrors! Ragged boys, dreadful voices, no teachers of *bel canto*; in other words, a synagogue, a perfect synagogue [since it is highly unlikely that Donizetti had ever set foot in a synagogue, he probably meant something like 'a bedlam']. Among the instruments there are some promising students, but their teachers are dogs like me. I won't go into the concerts. In any case, because of my way of doing things, I refuse to crawl to anybody. It isn't worth the effort here anyway. They look on theatre people as wretches, and so nobody pays any attention to us, as we pay none to them. I had understood from the very outset that the profession of poor opera composer is very unhappy, and only necessity keeps me at it. But I assure you, dear Maestro, that I suffer very much from these animals whom we need for the performance of our efforts.'

Donizetti's *L'ajo nell'imbarazzo* and Mayr's little farce *Gli originali* had been the successes of the summer season, but the composer was embittered to see that, while his income was minimal, there were ballerinas who received 2,500 ducats for a two-month stint. The orchestra of the Carolino was of decent size, however unskilled. Its forty-three players included thirteen violins, two violas, three cellos, five double-basses, one piccolo, two flutes, two oboes, two clarinets, two bassoons, three horns, two trumpets, two trombones, one bass serpent, and three-desk percussion. The chorus consisted of eight women and eleven men.

After the success of *L'ajo nell'imbarazzo*, Donizetti mounted his *Alahor di Granata*, which was favourably received. But, all

in all, his Sicilian stay was a disaster. The Carolino did terrible business, and the composer—like the singers—was paid irregularly. With great relief, he set sail for Naples on 14 February 1826.

From there, on 30 May, he wrote again to Mayr: 'This evening at the S. Carlo they will perform *Bianca e Gernando* (not Fernando, because that's a sin).' This opera, by Bellini on a libretto by Domenico Gilardoni, had originally been called *Bianca e Fernando* (and later, it returned to this title), but because the king of Naples was named Ferdinando, the royal censors thought it prudent to change the operatic character's name to the unlikely 'Gernando'.

Donizetti then went on: '. . . by our Bellini, his first production, beautiful, beautiful, beautiful, and especially considering this is the first time he's written an opera [actually, the second: Bellini's student piece *Adelson e Salvini* had been performed in the conservatory's little theatre the previous year]. It is all too beautiful, as I will realize when my own opera is given in two weeks' time.'

Donizetti's new opera was a one-act work, *Elvida*, written for a royal gala. At the same time he was rehearsing the *Ajo nell'imbarazzo* (re-christened *Don Gregorio*) for the Nuovo. As might have been expected, the latter had a success; *Elvida*—with

a cast that included Henriette Méric-Lalande, Giovanni Rubini, and Luigi Lablache, all first-rate artists—was received only fairly well. All the same, the composer's position in Naples was gradually being consolidated. He wrote to his father: 'You are looking for money? Alas! Honour, yes, that I could give you, but pecunia . . . here at the Teatro Nuovo, to whom I sold the score, I received for the rehearsals and everything 40 ducats, at the San Carlo for *Elvida* 200 . . . in any case I'll try to help you as best I can. Success is difficult to achieve; then we'll see . . .'

From Naples, Donizetti went back to Rome, partly because he was writing an opera for the Teatro Valle, but even more because he was courting the pretty young Virginia Vasselli, sister of his close friend Antonio (Totò), a successful lawyer. But he returned to Naples for more operas at the Nuovo and the San Carlo, and in the spring of 1828 he was in Genoa, where his *Alina, regina di Golconda* was given at the newly-inaugurated Teatro Carlo Felice.

On 1 June 1828 Donizetti married the nineteen-year-old Virginia in the bride's parish church, Santa Maria in Via, near the Piazza Colonna. The marriage was brief (Virginia died nine years later), but happy, despite the bride's poor health. The Donizettis, shortly after the wedding, went to Naples and settled in Vico Nardones, within walking distance of the San Carlo.

Donizetti was now under contract to Barbaja (again in command in Naples), who required him to compose twelve new operas for the Neapolitan theatres and also to conduct at the Teatro Nuovo. For this work Donizetti was paid two hundred ducats per month, plus an extra fifty *scudi* for his conducting at the Nuovo. Obviously, the financial security guaranteed by this contract had enabled him to marry.

The contract also allowed him to travel and produce operas in other cities. In 1830 he returned to Milan, where he was engaged to write the opera that would open the season at the Teatro Carcano, a small house which presented both opera and spoken theatre (it was more distinguished in the latter department).

The Carcano, however, had just been taken over by a new and ambitious management that had engaged not only Donizetti but also the rising star, Bellini, and the gifted soprano Giuditta Pasta.

Donizetti's new opera was to be *Anna Bolena*, and again the librettist was Felice Romani (who had also promised to supply a text for Bellini, to whom he was now bound by deep friendship).

32. Teatro Carcano, Milan. Festa di società, Carnival, 1852–3.
Built by the nobleman Giuseppe Carcano, the theatre bearing his name opened on 3 September 1803. After a successful period as an opera house, the Carcano specialized in drama, and some of the leading actors of the nineteenth century appeared there, among them Luigi Vestri, Achille Majeroni, Alemanno Morelli, Gustavo Modena, Adelaide Ristori, Ernesto Rossi, and Eleonora Duse. There were also seasons of opera, usually brief, throughout the nineteenth century. Of these the most illustrious was in 1830–31, when on 26 December 1830, Donizetti's *Anna Bolena* was performed for the first time, and on 6 March 1831, Bellini's *La sonnambula* received its première. In 1913 the old interior was demolished and rebuilt in art nouveau style. Eventually the house became a cinema.

The writer was a man of fifty-two, with a long and illustrious career behind him, and with many fertile years ahead of him. A graceful poet, an acute (if conservative) critic, he was also a respected classical scholar. He began his activity as a librettist with texts for Mayr, *La rosa bianca e la rosa rossa* and *Medea in Corinto*, and went on to write several librettos for Rossini, including the irresistible *Il turco in Italia*. He was not a theatre drudge, like Tottola or Gilardoni, though he was at times employed on a fixed basis by La Scala, nor was he an aristocratic dilettante like the Marchese Berio. Carrying on the noble tradition of Metastasio and Apostolo Zeno, Romani was a man with serious ideas about the operatic theatre, even if he sometimes had to bow to popular taste and adapt works by romantics like Byron and Hugo, whom he detested. He was, in sum, a professional writer. Born into a well-to-do family, he had been forced, by financial reverses, to earn his living (and support his younger brothers) at an early age.

Following the custom of the time, Romani almost never invented a story: his sources were earlier librettos, dramas (the French repertory was particularly suitable), even ballets (his libretto of *La sonnambula* was derived from a scenario written by Scribe for a ballet-pantomime by Hérold in 1827). For the Apulian composer Saverio Mercadante, he wrote an *Amleto*, but like the Marchese Berio's *Otello*, it was based less on Shakespeare than on the neo-classical Ducis, of whom Romani approved. With equal facility, Romani produced comedy, tragedy, and semiseria. And when he was not writing librettos (he could turn out as many as four in eight months), he was contributing to journals, and was in great demand as a provider of words for ceremonial cantatas and occasional pieces.

Late in life, Romani married the young Emilia Branca, daughter of a well-known Milanese music-lover and host. Long after her husband's death, Signora Romani wrote a biography of him. In it, she describes Donizetti as he was at this time; and, incidentally, she gives a picture of the bourgeois Milanese society of the period:

'Though he did not possess a beautiful bass voice, Donizetti sang quite charmingly, and in a humorous and amusing fashion, the buffo repertory, and especially little Neapolitan airs and songs, both traditional ones and others he composed himself, as well as songs written in other dialects, while he accompanied himself brilliantly at the piano. He played very well. He was a handsome man; tall, a slender figure, he had a broad brow crowned with curly black hair, and regular features. He was more casual than elegant; he had a very good-natured appearance, and a straightforward, open, slapdash manner, *butta là*, as the Milanese would say. . . . He was likeable beyond all description, and the fair sex went mad for him. At gatherings he never had to be begged to sit down at the piano and accompany singers, whether amateurs or professional artists, enlivening the timid with his jokes, encouraging the awkward, praising the experienced.'

Donizetti was a regular visitor to the soirées in the Branca home, where Emilia would have seen him when she was a little girl. There he would have met not only Romani but other poets like Andrea Maffei (later Verdi's good friend) and Giulio Carcano (translator of Shakespeare). The leading composers of the day were also *habitués* of the house: Mercadante, Lauro Rossi, and others. It was the custom for the poets to improvise verses, the composers to set them to music on the spot, and the singers to perform them, with the ink still wet. 'Donizetti and Romani, almost always united,' Emilia Branca Romani writes, 'created the most beautiful and delightful little things, sometimes merry, sometimes pathetic, for solo voice or for several voices. . . . Oh! those beautiful and delicious evenings! Romani and Donizetti kept them more alive than any, because the two were the life of everything.'

This was the atmosphere in which *Anna Bolena* was completed. Romani delivered the finished libretto on 10 November 1830. A month later, Donizetti had completed the score and rehearsals began. The première took place on 26 December, the feast of Santo Stefano and the traditional date for the opening of the Carnival opera season. *Anna Bolena* was a success—the greatest Donizetti had enjoyed up to that time—both with the audience and with the press.

Among its admirers was the patriot Giuseppe Mazzini. Himself an amateur musician, Mazzini had ideas about the future of Italian music, as he had ideas about the future of Italy herself. There was little abstract discussion of opera at that time, little theorizing. Opera was more merchandise than art. But Mazzini, dreaming of an Italian nation, also dreamed of a national, epic music, a new path for opera. And, as he looked around, Donizetti seemed the composer most suited to lead the way.

'To be sure,' he wrote in 1836, 'many of those aspects of innovation which have been cited as necessary to the development and future regeneration of music prove to have been applied often, whether through the instinct of genius or deliberately, it does not matter, in the operas of Donizetti. . . . The individuality of the characters, so barbarously neglected by the servile imitators of Rossini . . . , is achieved in many of his operas with rare vigour. . . . Who has not heard in the musical expression of Henry VIII the stern language, at once tyrannical and artful, that history assigns him? . . . *Anna Bolena* is the sort of opera that approaches the musical epic.'

This was the opera that brought Donizetti real national fame, and also some international attention. In 1831, Pasta repeated her interpretation of the title role in London (with Rubini and Lablache); the following year the opera was heard in Vienna, Budapest, Madrid, Graz, Brünn, and Malta. In 1839 it reached New Orleans, and in 1843, New York.

33. Donizetti, note to Felice Romani, 1833.
For the Carnival season at the Teatro della Pergola in Florence in 1833–4, the impresario Alessandro Lanari commissioned Donizetti to write a new opera. The libretto was to be by the famous Felice Romani, who had already provided the composer with texts in the past (including *L'elisir d'amore* and *Anna Bolena*). Overworked as usual, Romani sent the verses bit by bit. At one point, Donizetti—who was also pressed by many commitments—simply turned Romani's letter over and, on the back, wrote these hasty instructions for the opera, *Rosmonda d'Inghilterra*: 'Omit Arturo altogether,' he says, 'make Rosmonda's part bigger and give her an aria not interrupted by anyone. End the opera with the tenor's aria. Have the first act trio with Ros., Clifford, and Arturo become a duet. Don't neglect Ros, in the finale or, at least, in the stretta.—The introduction shorter if possible.—And whatever my friend Romani wants to do with it or cut out of it.' Though the note has no date, it probably belongs to the last months of 1833, when Donizetti was in Milan preparing his *Lucrezia Borgia* (another Romani text), which opened the Scala season on 26 December and was immensely successful. On 27 February 1834, *Rosmonda d'Inghilterra* opened at La Pergola with Fanny Tacchinardi-Persiani, future creator of Lucia, in the title role. Gilbert-Louis Duprez was also in the cast. Despite Donizetti's instructions, Romani did *not* omit Arturo, and the part (a *travesti* role) was sung by Giuseppina Merola, with whom Donizetti was reported to have had a brief affair. The opera was a success.

56

Levar del tutto Arturo.

Ingrandir Rosmonda, e dargli Cavatina non interrotta da alcuno.

Finir L'opera coll'Aria del Tenore.

Divenir Duetto il Terzetto dell'atto 1.° fra Rosi Clifford, e Arturo.

Non trascurasi Rosi nel finale, o almeno nella stretta. —

L'Introduzione più corta se è possibile. —

E tutto ciò che piace all'Amico Romani da farci o da levarci. —

Donizetti

The bold management of the Teatro Carcano scored a double victory in that 1830–31 season. On 6 March 1831, some ten weeks after the première of *Anna Bolena*, Vincenzo Bellini presented his *La sonnambula*. Originally, Bellini had thought to compose an *Ernani*, requiring Felice Romani to prepare a text from Victor Hugo's drama of 1829. But the plan was abandoned (surely to Romani's relief), as Bellini wrote to a friend on 3 January 1831: 'You know I am no longer composing *Ernani*, because the story would have had to undergo some modifications for the police. Therefore Romani, rather than be compromised, has given it up, and now he is writing *La sonnambula*.'

Bellini's reference to the police, casual as it sounds, indicates a growing, pressing problem for composers and librettists. Official censorship plays a major, and deplorable, role in the history of nineteenth-century opera. In Naples, there were the censors of the Bourbon rulers, bigoted and (rightfully) fearful of revolutionary ideas. They were to ban Donizetti's *Poliuto* and reject Verdi's *Un ballo in maschera*. The Papal authorities in Rome, and in other cities of the Papal States, regularly made a hash of librettos. Thus in Rossini's *L'italiana in Algeri*, the heroine was not allowed to sing '*Pensa alla patria*' but was made instead to

34. Donizetti's *Anna Bolena* at Her Majesty's Theatre.
Donizetti's first really great success, *Anna Bolena*, after its première at the Teatro Carcano in Milan (26 December 1830), quickly made the rounds of other theatres; and on 8 July 1831, it reached the stage of Her Majesty's, in London. In his *Recollections* the critic Henry Chorley wrote: '*Anna Bolena*, brought hither under the protection of Madame Pasta's royal robes, was permitted rather than admitted, though in this historical English opera might be discerned something of Donizetti's own; and though three of the characters—those of the Queen (Pasta), Percy (Rubini), and Henry the Eighth (Lablache), were played and sung to perfection.'

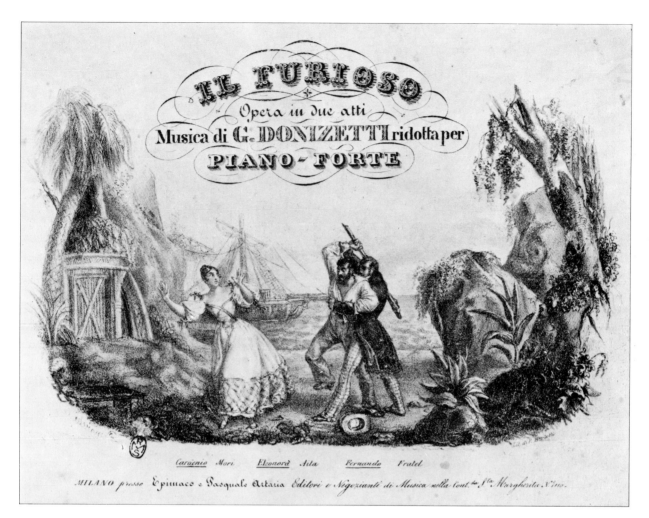

IL FURIOSO

Opera in due atti

Musica di G. DONIZETTI ridotta per

PIANO-FORTE

Caraenio Mori Eleonora Aila Fernando Fratel

MILANO presso Epimaco e Pasquale Artaria Editori e Negozianti di Musica nella cont.da S.ta Margherita N.o 1118.

35. Donizetti's *Il furioso all'isola di San Domingo*, 1833. Frontispiece of piano score. Donizetti's opera about a man driven mad ('furioso') by his wife's adultery, set on an exotic Caribbean island, was first performed at the Teatro Valle in Rome on 2 January 1833. Its cast was headed by the young baritone Giorgio Ronconi (later to create the title role in Verdi's *Nabucco* and to become a favourite Verdi interpreter) and by the tenor Lorenzo Salvi (creator of Riccardo in Verdi's *Oberto*). The work belongs to the 'opera semiseria' genre, in which sad, even tragic events are concluded by a happy ending: a genre not popular with more modern audiences. In Rome, at its première, *Il furioso* was greeted with enthusiasm and given a number of times that season and the seasons following. By the end of the century, however, it had virtually disappeared from the repertory and was forgotten until recent years, when it has been revived with success.

cry, nonsensically, '*Pensa alla sposa*'. And as late as 1863 the authorities decided that the title of Verdi's *La forza del destino* might sound deterministic, and so the opera was called *Don Alvaro*.

In Milan, the Austrians, in their long occupation of the city, set the tone of operatic life. Stendhal, writing of another period, said that La Scala was 'gay without being boisterous, and ruthlessly stripped of *gravity*'. That gaiety was not to last much longer. In the 1830s, perhaps, La Scala was still the 'salon' that the French writer had described; but as political unrest mounted, the theatre was to turn into an arena.

For Bellini, in 1830–31, the Carcano was also an arena, where another round in his one-sided battle with Donizetti was fought (one-sided because the unenvying, generous-minded Donizetti remained completely unaware of the conflict). From the time of their meeting in Naples, some years before, almost to the moment of Bellini's death, the paths of the two musicians crossed and re-crossed. The story of Italian opera, in this brief period, is the story of these two men.

Chapter 4

WHEN Bellini and Donizetti first met in Naples, in
1822 at the time of the latter's *La zingara*, Bellini, still
at the conservatory, was unknown. But, in 1825, his
student work *Adelson e Salvini* attracted attention, and the following year—as Donizetti had predicted—his *Bianca e Gernando* was
successful at the Teatro San Carlo, where Barbaja was again in
full charge.

The shrewd impresario had recently joined a partnership with
some Milanese businessmen, who operated La Scala and the

36. (*Left*) Teatro della Canobbiana, Festa da ballo, 1825.
The Canobbiana was a kind of smaller Scala, designed by the same architect, Giuseppe Piermarini, and inaugurated on 21 August 1779, a year after the opening of the larger house. The audience was predominantly middle-class, as opposed to the more aristocratic public of La Scala. In 1894, the Canobbiana, after a long period of decline, was transformed by the publisher Edoardo Sonzogno into the Teatro Lirico. This was destroyed by fire in 1938, then rebuilt in its present form.

37. Saverio Mercadante. Lithograph by Melchiorre Delfico.
Delfico (1825–95), the Neapolitan caricaturist, was a great friend of Verdi, whom he drew many times. In this rare lithograph, dating from about 1860, he portrays the older composer Mercadante (1795–1870), whose career began in 1819 and continued for almost half a century. Verdi had great respect for Mercadante, as did Rossini and Bellini. His operas, skilfully, even elegantly written, enjoyed considerable popularity in their own time; and Mercadante wrote for the leading Italian houses and for the Théâtre Italien in Paris. Despite recent attempts to revive his works, they have not returned to the repertory. Born in Altamura, Puglie, Mercadante spent most of his life in Naples, where he died. In 1862 he went blind, and though he continued to compose, his career was essentially over. In his later years he was the director of the Naples Conservatory.

Teatro della Canobbiana; and he encouraged Bellini to believe that for the 1827–28 season he would be engaged to compose the *opera d'obbligo* for the major Milanese theatre. This 'obligatory opera' was the new work which, by regulation, impresarios had to provide for their subscribers each season. For Bellini, such a contract meant an immense leap forward.

He left Naples in April of 1827, armed with several important letters of introduction. One was from Barbaja to his partner Villa. Another was from Bellini's teacher at the conservatory, the old composer Niccolò Zingarelli, introducing his pupil to Felice Romani. In Milan, Bellini already had one important acquaintance: the slightly older composer Saverio Mercadante, who had also studied with Zingarelli and was well-known to the Milanese audience.

It was Mercadante who helped Bellini find lodgings with Francesco Pollini and his wife, both musicians and also friends of Zingarelli. The couple became Bellini's surrogate parents; some of his most interesting and affectionate surviving letters are addressed to them.

The introduction to Romani was equally happy. The librettist also took the handsome young Sicilian under his wing. And Romani's influence, along with the help of Mercadante, persuaded Barbaja's Milanese associates to commission an opera from Bellini. To help matters, Romani offered to write the libretto without fee. His offer was not accepted, but it was further proof of Bellini's merit.

As Romani wrote, after the composer's death, recalling the first days of their friendship: 'I alone could comprehend that poetic spirit, that impassioned heart, that mind eager to soar beyond the sphere in which it had been confined both by the rules of schooling and the servility of imitation, and it was then that I wrote for Bellini *Il pirata*, a subject that seemed to me suited to strike the most responsive chord in his heart.'

Bellini was not such a novice as Romani suggests, nor did he lack self-assurance, even in dealing with the older and far more experienced librettist. In the course of working on *Il pirata*, he wrote to his friend Florimo: 'Romani yesterday gave me the rest of the duet which—especially the cabaletta—is unspeakably cold, and has nothing to do with the sublime first act. I asked him to change it, but he proved recalcitrant, and I don't know whether he will produce a new text for me this morning, or whether I must redouble my pleas, because this one I will absolutely not set, since it is dreadfully bad.'

Bellini and Romani evidently ironed out their differences, for the opera was completed in time, and the première of *Il pirata* took place at La Scala on 27 October 1827. Bellini, as was customary, did not just write the music; he also prepared the singers, all of them familiar to him from Naples. The soprano was Henriette Méric-Lalande, then twenty-nine; she had made her Scala debut the previous August. The baritone Antonio Tamburini was twenty-seven and had been singing for nine years (his debut at La Scala had taken place in 1822). The oldest of the trio was the tenor Giovanni Rubini, who was thirty-three and well-known in Milan, particularly as an interpreter of Rossini.

It was, however, this most experienced artist who made Bellini work hardest. Bellini's was a new kind of music, which required a passionate expressiveness at odds with Rubini's ingrained, more aloof style. After accusing the tenor of being cold, without feelings, Bellini finally managed to achieve his ends. Subsequently Rubini became a specially valuable interpreter of Bellini's operas, as did Tamburini.

Shortly after the opening, Bellini wrote an ecstatic letter to his beloved uncle Vincenzo Ferlito in Catania. The letter, with its characteristic, shaky syntax and garrulity, is worth quoting at length, not least because it represents a first-hand account of an opening at La Scala: 'Rejoice, together with my parents and relatives: your nephew has been fortunate in having such a success with his Opera that he cannot express it, and neither you nor all my family nor I myself could have dreamed of such an outcome.—Saturday, 27th of the current month, it was staged. After the dress rehearsal there had already been a rumour that it contained good music, and so the hour strikes when I am called to the piano, I appear, and the public receives me with great applause. The overture begins, which pleased them very, very much. The Introduction consists of a single chorus, which was somewhat badly sung, but as it takes place in the midst of a storm, the public didn't notice, but there was very scant applause at the end. Rubini's entrance aria: such a furore that it cannot be expressed, and I had to stand up a good ten times to thank the public. The prima donna's cavatina: also applauded. Afterwards a chorus of Pirates with Echo, which was very appealing because of the novelty of having rendered the echo so well, and at the end, going off stage, the voices keep singing with another orchestra, which is arranged behind the scenes, nothing but wind instruments. All this makes such an effect, and I receive so much applause that, because of my profound emotion, I was seized by convulsive weeping, and I could barely control it after five minutes. Then come the scena and duet for Rubini and Lalande, and at the end the audience, all shouting like madmen, made such a racket it seemed an inferno. . . .

'The curtain falls, and imagine the applause; and then calling me onto the stage. I presented myself, and I received the general approval of such a cultivated audience, which then called me out together with all the singers.

'The second act begins with a women's chorus, which I harmonized well, but since it was not well performed, because the women are few and off pitch, it passed coldly. . . . Finally Rubini's scena and La Lalande's created such enthusiasm . . . the Italian language has no terms to describe the tumultuous spirit that seized the public. . . . Yesterday evening, at the second performance, the applause increased, and as on the first evening, I was called out on the stage three times.'

On Monday 5 November an important article appeared in the *Gazzetta privileggiata di Milano*, which read, in part: 'Situations and effects: this is what poet and composer must aim at in order to delight profoundly and be moving. Overlooking many previous operas which, thanks simply to these requisites, were hailed in the major theatres, we will cite the *Pompei* of Pacini. . . .'

This mention of a rival composer was not calculated to please Bellini, but he could not help but enjoy what followed: 'Bellini . . . had the fortune to be trained in a school where the true principles of the beautiful are maintained. . . . Having seen how so many composers, young and old, allow themselves today to be swept away by the Rossinian torrent, he seems to have studied deliberately how to elude the flood. And without clashing head-on against the prevailing taste, he has managed to restore song to the path of lovely simplicity, animating it with those harmonic combinations in accompaniment which serve to underline it but not overwhelm it. . . .

'The music of *Il pirata* has the characteristics which are necessary to be effectively dramatic: simplicity, sweetness, vigour, passion.'

This remarkably perceptive reporter then goes on to describe the public's reaction, and his account tallies with Bellini's. But not all the theatrical journalists of the time were so gifted with insight or so scrupulously honest. Daily papers, in the modern sense, were practically non-existent; and the space allotted to music was scant. There was no such thing as a music critic. Some specialized papers covered theatrical events; the most important, at the time, was *I Teatri*, published in Bologna, with correspondents in all the major cities. Some of these correspondents were corrupt; and at best they were mere chroniclers of events.

Bellini often imagined—and sometimes rightly—that his fellow-composers were intriguing against him. In a letter to his friend Florimo, written at about this time, he discusses a characteristic plot: 'Il Sig.r Pacini is not content with devising intrigues down there [Naples]; he manoeuvres here as well. He has already arranged for a letter to reach la Ungher [Caroline Unger, Viennese soprano then at La Scala], which may or may not have been written by Vinter [Berardo Winter, tenor], in which he describes the furore aroused by *Margherita* [*Margherita, regina d'Inghilterra*, opera by Pacini then being given at the San Carlo, with Winter]. And la Ungher has sent this letter to the theatrical reporter to have it printed in the paper *I Teatri*. And I am told that this journalist, who formerly was no flatterer of Pacini, as you see in his papers when he speaks of *Pompei*, is now all for Pacini; and this change is the effect of some little sum sent him by Pacini, because for this journalist money is a strong argument in making him change his opinion. So you can surmise what a trap this is, and perhaps they were able to speak to this journalist

39. La Scala, floor plan of second rank of boxes. Engraving by Giuseppe Piermarini, late eighteenth century.
This floor plan shows the rich life that revolved around the performances. Number one is the 'box of the Prince' with a withdrawing-room behind it (2). Number 6, at extreme left, led to the apartment of the Prince. In the lower left corner of the plan there are (9) private rooms for suppers, a kitchen (10) to the right, and a larder (11). There was also a pastry-shop (7).

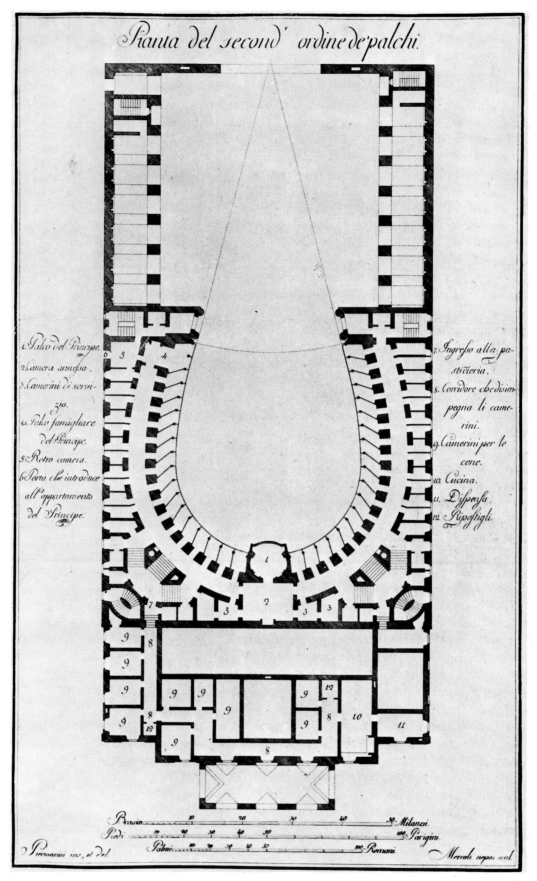

1 Palco del Principe.

2 Camera annessa.

3 Camerini di servizio.

4 Palco famigliare del Principe.

5 Retro camera.

6 Porta che introduce all'appartamento del Principe.

7 Ingresso alla pasticceria.

8 Corridore che disimpegna li camerini.

9 Camerini per le cene.

10 Cucina.

11 Dispensa.

12 Ripostigli.

Piermarini inv. et del.

Mercoli nepos sculp.

about me. But until I write more music, so that he can speak of it, who knows what will happen? Anyway, true merit does not need support and plots.'

Actually *I Teatri* had written favourably about the Scala production of *Il pirata*, but when the same opera was given, under Barbaja's auspices, in Vienna, the paper reported a fiasco. In a later number, it had to publish a correction since by that time the Viennese triumph of Bellini's opera had become common knowledge in Italian operatic circles.

In his novel *Gli artisti da teatro*, the one-time singer and later librettist Antonio Ghislanzoni, amid characters of pure fantasy, introduces others clearly based on his own experience of the theatre. Among these figures is the scurrilous, venal Moltrasio (based on the Florentine journalist Enrico Montazio), who sells his pen for cash or the prima donna's favours. The author first describes him in these terms: 'The new character . . . is named Lodovico Moltrasio, editor of the paper *La rivista toscana*, terrifying to artists, impresarios and theatre managements for his satirical articles. Endowed with a very mediocre talent and an arrogance proof against anything, he was able to gain among his fellow-citizens the reputation of being the best among critics, though all knew his sordid venality and the other base passions that almost always governed him as he dictated his injurious polemics. . . . He sold his praises at so much a line, extorting the money with cowardly threats, terrorizing and bullying. No artist would dare appear on the stage . . . if first he hadn't given Moltrasio one of those meaningful handshakes that leave a metallic imprint.'

Adverse reports in newspapers could not arrest Bellini's career now. By the time the Scala season closed, on 2 December 1827, *Il pirata* had had fifteen performances. Shortly after the beginning of the new year, Bellini received a visit and, with it, the offer of a contract for the following Carnival season in Genoa. He wrote to Florimo a few days later, reporting the event and adding: 'but since the company is not yet complete, I didn't want to commit myself as yet; and my answer was that they should finish signing up the artists. Then, if the artists suited me, I would immediately accept the offer.'

For a composer barely twenty-six years old, still fresh from his Scala debut, this was high-handed behaviour. Again Bellini was showing his confidence in his own talents. His letter also underlines another practice of the time: new operas were written, indeed tailored, for individual singers. Bellini had written *Il pirata* with Méric-Lalande, Rubini, and Tamburini in mind (even if he then had to bend them to his will); and so he would write his new work for whatever singers he found. In his refusal to sign the contract at once, he was actually being more prudent than most of his colleagues, who often found themselves forced to compose for artists past their prime or with personal defects, quirks, or demands.

66

40. Giovanni David.
Giovanni David (1790–1864) was a tenor, like his father Giacomo (1750–1830), the great interpreter of Cimarosa and Paisiello. After studying with his father, Giovanni made his debut in 1808, in Siena. By 1814 he was at La Scala, singing Don Ottavio in *Don Giovanni* (Filippo Galli was the Don) and taking part in the premières of two new operas, Rossini's *Il turco in Italia* and Mayr's *Le due duchesse*. In 1816 he was engaged by Barbaja for the San Carlo, and there his long association with Rossini really began. In Naples David sang in a whole series of Rossini's operas, between 1816 and 1822, including the premières of *Otello, La donna del lago, Ermione, Zelmira*. His repertory also included many Rossini roles that had been created by others. He accompanied Rossini to Vienna in 1822 and contributed to the composer's fanatical reception there. In 1828 he sang in the production of Bellini's *Bianca e Fernando* which inaugurated the Teatro Carlo Felice in Genoa. By 1831, when he was again in Rome, his voice was declining, and the poet Gioacchino Belli made unkind references to David in some sonnets. But the tenor continued singing until he lost his voice completely in 1840, when he opened a singing school (according to Donizetti it was not very good). Then, in 1844, he moved to St Petersburg, as stage director of its Italian Opera. He died there twenty years later.

The bearer of the Genoa offer was Bartolomeo Merelli, an important figure in Italian operatic life, where he was to remain active for several more decades. He was born in Bergamo, in 1793, and had been a companion of Donizetti's in Mayr's music school. He was forced to leave his native city, after being involved in a theft; so he moved to Milan, got a job as errand-boy in a theatrical agency, became an agent himself, and was soon organizer of theatrical seasons and impresario of various theatres. For Genoa, in fact, he was putting together the inaugural season of the brand-new Teatro Carlo Felice. Bellini's opera would actually open the splendid house, which seated 2,500, in the presence of King Carlo Felice himself. Donizetti was also invited to compose a new opera for the season (it was to be *Alina, regina di Golconda*), as was the older composer Francesco Morlacchi, who, in homage to the city, wrote *Il Colombo*, about Genoa's most famous son, Christopher Columbus. For the rest, the season included Rossini's *Barber*, his *Otello*, and *L'assedio di Corinto* (the Italian translation of his French refashioning of *Maometto II*). Felice Romani provided the librettos of the new operas and was in Genoa to help the composers stage them. Only Rossini, busy in Paris staging his new *Le Comte Ory*, was absent.

It was not until early February of 1828 that Bellini signed the contract with Merelli: his opera was scheduled to open the season on 7 April. There was not, therefore, enough time for him to procure a new libretto and write a wholly new work. With the agreement of the Genoese authorities, he decided to present a much-revised and extended version of his *Bianca e Gernando* (now *Fernando* again). The Genoa company, now signed up, included the soprano Adelaide Tosi and the tenor Giovanni David, for whom this opera had originally been composed (they had not sung it in Naples because the première was postponed).

Bellini was not keen on the libretto, by Gilardoni, and he was determined that Felice Romani should revise it. Romani, as usual, was busy. At the beginning of that year he was in Venice, where he wrote *I saraceni in Sicilia* for Morlacchi, and then he presumably went on to Trieste, where he supplied the text for *Il divorzio persiano* of Generali. And, of course, he had the other two Genoa librettos to write. He reached Milan only in mid-March, then he and Bellini travelled together to Genoa.

Once there, the composer immediately began having troubles with his prima donna, who had her own ideas about the deference due to a star singer from a young musician. On 5 April Bellini wrote to Florimo: 'She had looked over her two numbers at the piano and was not pleased with the first section of the cavatina. I wrote another one for her. She rehearsed the cavatina with the orchestra, and having sung it like a dog, hence achieving no effect with it, she wanted a different one. At the same time she rejected the stretta, which she said had no coloratura and was music written for children, and if I didn't change it, she said she would insert one of her "trunk" numbers.'

These *pezzi di baule* were an institution among singers in the early nineteenth century, when a composer's written score was anything but sacred. A prominent singer, on taking over a part already performed elsewhere with another artist, would examine the score carefully to see if it afforded the proper opportunities to show off. If it did not, the singer would ask the composer to make the necessary changes. If the composer was not present (and he was likely not to be, since composers rarely bothered about their works after the first production), then the singer would request—and pay—some other composer to write new music for the opera (that season in Genoa, Donizetti obligingly contributed a new—and very beautiful—number to Rossini's *L'assedio di Corinto*). And, if this solution was not feasible, the singer had another possibility: he or she could insert some aria, more or less in the right mood, from some other work, an aria, of course, that allowed the interpreter to shine. Every leading artist of the day travelled with a sheaf of these arias, and brought them out of the trunk as required.

On this occasion, Bellini managed to avoid this drastic solution. His letter continues: 'I replied that I would not change one note: not out of pique, but because I wanted *my* music to be performed, with the tempi established by me, and not at her whim; and I wanted the shadings also to be rendered as I had imagined them. She fought for two days, but seeing my stubbornness and how, because of our familiarity, I insulted her and treated her as a capricious woman, after I had served her with such care . . . she finally sang the numbers as I had given them to her. My dear Florimo, they were so effective that she came and asked my forgiveness . . . and that cabaletta, which she said I had written for children, brought the house down. Now we are the closest of friends, as if nothing had happened.'

41. Teatro La Fenice, Venice, on fire, 1836. From a drawing by Pividor. Destruction by fire was a common fate of theatres in the eighteenth and nineteenth centuries, when much of the structure was of wood, when illumination was by candles or by gas jets, and when fire-fighting was still a haphazard affair. The Teatro La Fenice was forty-four years old when it caught fire on the night of 12 December 1836. The flames spared only the outer walls, the foyer, and the Sale Apollinee, the handsome, neo-classical rooms on the upper floor, where the audience can tarry during intervals. The 1836–7 season opened, as planned, on 26 December, in temporary quarters at the Teatro Goldoni, while the house was being rebuilt. The Fenice—a true phoenix—rose rapidly from its ashes and reopened on 26 December 1837.

Bellini continued to be difficult and demanding, even with Barbaja, the impresario who had launched him. As that spring season came to an end, the theatres were already thinking of the next Carnival. And Bellini, swept up on the wave of success, was awaiting offers, which did not fail to come. One was from Barbaja, for La Scala. On 16 June, Bellini wrote to Florimo: 'I am writing you only a few lines, since I have little to tell you, though that little is juicy. This morning I signed a contract with Barbaja for an opera at Carnival in this Teatro della [sic] Scala. . . . The price, after many howls from him, has been fixed at one thousand ducats; this seems to me not a bad deal, and I believe you will find it good, because in my last contract for two operas I received five hundred ducats, and for the first, one hundred and fifty. I seem to have made a little leap forward. Is that right?'

In the same letter Bellini tells of an offer from the small but wealthy Tuscan city of Lucca, inviting him to produce *Il pirata*. To supervise this revival, he asked for all his travelling expenses, room and board (which he would pocket, since he was invited to stay with friends), and three hundred and forty ducats. In the event, Bellini did not go; he stayed in Milan, where he was in the midst of a passionate love affair with a married lady, Signora Giuditta Turina, and where he was also writing his next opera, *La straniera*, for Barbaja and La Scala.

69

Bellini's astute management of his career, even at this early stage, allowed him to support himself for months at a time between operas, unlike most of his colleagues, who had to scurry from theatre to theatre, composing at top speed. Bellini as a rule was able to write with a certain leisure, and also spent an unusual amount of time going over the libretto with his poet (who, for these years, was always Romani).

One measure of Bellini's solid, if sudden celebrity was the steadily increasing fees he could demand—and get—for his operas. After *La straniera* (14 February 1829, again a resounding success), he was invited to write another inaugural work, to open the first season at the lovely Teatro Ducale (now the Teatro Regio) in Parma, built under the supervision of Parma's grand duchess, Napoleon's music-loving widow Marie-Louise (or Maria Luigia, as she was known by that time). Bellini's opera was *Zaira*, for which he received 5,000 francs (or 1,135 ducats) and Romani received 700 francs. Though *Zaira* was a disastrous failure, Bellini was immediately signed to write for the Teatro La Fenice in Venice; in haste, Romani put together a Romeo-and-Juliet opera, *I Capuleti e i Montecchi*: the fee was 325 gold Napoleons (equivalent to 8,000 lire). For his next opera, *La sonnambula*, for another Milanese theatre, the Carcano, as Bellini

42. Teatro La Fenice, interior, 1837. Rebuilt after the fire that destroyed it in 1836, the renewed Fenice is the theatre that still stands today, very little changed. It was rebuilt according to the original plans by the architect Gianantonio Selva (1751–1819).

43. (*Right*) Giulia Grisi as Norma. Giulia, or Giulietta, Grisi (1811–69) made her Scala debut, after successful appearances in Bologna and Florence, on 20 September 1831, in the première of *L'Ullà di Bassora* by Feliciano Strepponi, father of the future Signora Verdi. The following season, barely twenty, Grisi created the role of Adalgisa in *Norma*. Though Adalgisa is now usually sung by a mezzo-soprano, it was originally the province of sopranos like Grisi, who frequently sang the opera's title role in later life. She is seen here as Norma, in Act One of the opera.

I. R. TEATRO ALLA SCALA.

In questa sera di Giovedì 15 Maggio 1834 si produrrà l'Opera

NORMA

Poesia del sig. FELICE ROMANI

Musica del Maestro sig. VINCENZO BELLINI.

PERSONAGGI

NORMA	Signore	MALIBRAN MARIA.
ADALGISA . . .	„	GARCIA RUEZ.
CLOTILDE . . .	„	RUGGERI TERESA.
POLLIONE . . .	Signori	REINA DOMENICO.
OROVESO . . .	„	MARINI IGNAZIO.
FLAVIO	„	VASCHETTI GIUSEPPE.

Dopo il primo atto

NUOVO PASSO A SETTE

fra il sig. *Priora*, e le signore *Rabel, Bonalumi, Braschi Amalia, Ancement, Romagnoli* e *Frassi Adelaide*.

Prezzo del Biglietto { Al Teatro lir. 6 } austriache.
{ Al Loggione lir. 3 }

I Palchi di quinta Fila si affittano al Camerino dell'I. R. Teatro suddetto.

Daranno accesso alle File chiuse due ingressi a dritta e sinistra nell'atrio del suddetto Teatro. — Ciascun concorrente conserva il Biglietto a garanzia del posto.

Lo Spettacolo incomincerà alle ore otto e mezzo.

Milano il 15 Maggio 1834.   Tipografia Pirola.

44. Announcement of revival of Bellini's *Norma* at La Scala, 15 May 1834.

In the spring of 1834, less than three seasons after its dramatic première at La Scala, Bellini's *Norma* was revived for three performances, sung by Maria Malibran (1808–36), making her debut there (although already famous from her appearances in Paris and London and elsewhere). She also sang in Rossini's *Otello*. The cast of this latter opera included the young Michael Balfe (1808–70) in the role of Iago: a puzzlement, since this is a tenor role and the future composer of *The Bohemian Girl* is usually described as a baritone. In the autumn season of 1834, Malibran returned to Paris to La Scala for more performances, received—as were the first—with delirious excitement by the audience, who compared her to Pasta, and to Pasta's disadvantage. Piqued, Pasta rushed back to La Scala for the next season to reclaim her crown, singing Norma, the role she had created and that Malibran had 'usurped' for her Scala debut. Pasta regained the fickle public's heart.

wrote to his uncle Ferlito in April of 1830: 'I asked a fee of 12,000 *svanziche*, that is to say 2,400 ducats, and half the rights of the score. With success, this means the opera will bring me 3,000 ducats in all.'

For his next contract, Bellini wrote to Ferlito a short time afterwards, 'for two operas, one to be written in the autumn of 1831 and one in Carnival of 1832, the impresario has already offered me 4,000 ducats [per opera]; but I insist on more, that is another 600 ducats.'

Bellini's next opera was *Norma*, which opened the Carnival season at La Scala on 26 December 1831. On its opening night, it was a calamitous failure, marked by loud jeering from the audience. Bellini blamed part of the fiasco on the intrigues of Pacini and his rich mistress Countess Giulia Samoyloff, and he may have been right, for at the second performance *Norma* was a success. The opera was given thirty-four times in that season.

But the shock of that terrible opening may have weakened the composer's poor health. Having written two operas in 1831, he slowed his already leisurely pace: his next opera was not presented until 26 December 1833, in Venice. This was *Beatrice di Tenda*, another and more lasting failure. Against Bellini's practice (and against his will), the opera had been written in haste, because of Romani's delay in delivering the libretto (he was 'promised' to half-a-dozen other composers that same season). After the catastrophic opening night, poet and composer blamed each other for the work's poor showing. There were angry letters exchanged in the local papers, and—for some time, at least—Bellini and Romani were enemies.

45. (*Below, left and right*) Scenes from Act II of *Norma* with Giuditta Pasta in the title role.

Bellini paid a visit to his native Sicily, where he had not been for years. There his self-confidence was restored by a royal welcome and the demonstrative admiration of his compatriots, for whom he was—and still is—a source of local pride. Then, when he was invited, at a considerable fee, to go to London and oversee the production of several of his operas there, he accepted readily. It was time for him to leave Italy, and his decision was reinforced by a crisis in his relationship with Giuditta Turina. Although he was unaware of it, he was not just making a journey to London: actually, he was moving to Paris, where his career, and his life, were soon to end.

46. Birthplace of Vincenzo Bellini, Catania. The room where Bellini was born, on the night of 2–3 November 1801, was in a dark apartment in the Palazzo dei Gravina Cruylas, in the centre of Catania. The building still stands, and the Bellini apartment is now a fascinating museum with invaluable memorabilia of the composer. Here the older Bellini gave Vincenzo his first music lessons, and here the precocious youth composed his first works. In 1816, the Bellini family moved to cheaper (but larger) lodgings; Vincenzo, however, did not accompany the others. He went to live with his grandfather, also a musician, until—thanks to a grant from the Catania city fathers—the young man was able to go to Naples for further study, in June of 1819.

Chapter 5

SOME time in November of 1823, almost a decade before Bellini left Milan on his first journey outside Italy, Gioacchino Rossini arrived in Paris. He was accompanied by Isabella Colbran, whom he had married, in Bologna, on 16 March of the previous year. They were bound for London, where

47. Caricature of Rossini in Paris.
This was published in 1819 when *Il Barbiere di Siviglia* was first heard at the Théâtre Italien. He is supporting Manuel Garcia (Almaviva), Joséphine Fodor (Rosina) and Felice Pellegrini (Figaro). Fodor was also the first London Rosina, at the King's Theatre.

both of them had professional engagements; but their stay in Paris was not just a restful break in their trip. Rossini could hardly travel anywhere in Europe, by now, without causing a stir.

Twelve of his operas had already been performed at Paris's popular Italian-language opera house, the Théâtre Italien (or des Italiens). Some of them, true, had been given in bastardized versions, but even these made their contribution to the composer's renown. His Parisian admirers were legion, and he attended banquets and receptions, frequenting the most important salons, including that of the Duchesse de Berry, for whom he sang some of his arias, accompanying himself at the piano. The band of the Garde Nationale played a serenade under his windows; and on 16 November, there was what one paper described as a 'colossal picnic' with more than one hundred and fifty guests. Among them was the actress Mlle Mars, reigning star of the Comédie and, a few years later, the first Doña Sol in Hugo's *Hernani*; with her there was an equally illustrious colleague,

49. (*Above*) Manuel Garcia sr.
After studying in his native Spain, where he made his debut, Manuel Garcia sr. (1775–1832) travelled all over the world, including the United States and Mexico. He was also an occasional composer. As a tenor, he specialized in the operas of Mozart and Rossini, for whom he created Almaviva in *Il barbiere di Siviglia*. He also sang Rossini's *Otello*. He was much admired as a teacher; his pupils included his remarkable children: Manuel jr., Maria Malibran, and the contralto Pauline Viardot.

48. (*Left*) *Judith and Holofernes*. Painting by Horace Vernet.
Born in Paris, son and grandson of popular painters, Horace Vernet (1789–1863) served from 1829 to 1835 as director of the French Academy in Rome, in the Villa Medici, where his charges included the refractory Berlioz. On commissions, first from Louis Philippe, then from Napoleon III, Vernet painted vast battle panoramas, still to be seen in the galleries of Versailles. The interest in this Biblical scene lies in the identity of the model for the Judith. She was Olympe Pélissier, Vernet's mistress, later to become the second wife of Rossini and a leading Parisian hostess. Vernet exhibited this painting in Rome in 1831, but it was in all likelihood executed earlier. The model for Holofernes was the composer Federico Ricci (1809–77), a friend of Vernet, who also painted a formal portrait of him.

50. Manuel Garcia jr., 1854.
Teacher of Johanna Wagner, Jenny Lind,
Charles Santley, and countless others, the
second Manuel Garcia (1805–1906) was
born in Catalonia. He studied in Naples
under Zingarelli, then in Rome, then in
Paris (harmony, under Fétis). He made his
debut in New York, but disliked singing in
public, so returned to Paris in 1829 and
embarked on a teaching career which was to
last about seventy years. As a biographer
and friend, John Mewburn Levien, wrote:
'Being of a scientific turn of mind he now
also determined to study the voice
physiologically, and attended the military
hospital where La Rey, one of Napoleon's
surgeons, assisted him in his
laryngo-anatomical investigations.' These
investigations led to the invention of the
laryngoscope, an instrument whereby,
thanks to mirrors, the human larynx could
be examined and studied. This portrait was
made at about the time Garcia presented
his invention to the public.

Talma, supreme interpreter of Corneille, Racine, and Voltaire.
A host of composers also attended: Auber, Boieldieu, Hérold,
Panseron; and singers like Giuditta Pasta, Laure Cinti (better
known, a few years later, as Cinti-Damoreau, an important
Rossini interpreter in France), and Manuel Garcia, the tenor
who had created the role of Almaviva, seven years earlier, at
the Argentina in Rome. Another guest was the painter Horace
Vernet. Was his mistress, Olympe Pélissier, with him on this
occasion? We do not know. It would have been an amusing
coincidence, for she was to become, in the not too distant future,
Rossini's mistress and, after Isabella's death, the second Signora
Rossini.

Under Louis XVIII—who received Rossini on the composer's
return from London—Paris was a glittering, stimulating city, and
it was to become even more so during the next decades. Rossini
obviously felt at home there, so when the king and his Director
of Fine Arts urged the composer to take over the direction of the
Italien, Rossini was tempted to accept. If at first he demurred,
it may have been because he was reluctant to offend the
sensibilities of the current director, also an Italian composer,
Ferdinando Paer. Finally, Rossini agreed to act, in effect, as
co-director with Paer, who did indeed take offence, although he
was persuaded to work in harness with his younger, more famous
compatriot.

Louis XVIII died on 16 September 1824, shortly after his
meeting with Rossini, but his brother and successor, Charles X,
respected their agreement. Rossini was also granted (at his own
impelling suggestion) an annual stipend, independent of his
composing and directorial duties. After a trip to Bologna to
arrange his affairs there, he returned to Paris in the autumn of
1824, to settle in the French capital for an indefinite time.

The Théâtre Italien has a long, chequered, fascinating history,
still to be adequately written. Italian opera first became popular
in France in the mid-eighteenth century, when Pergolesi's in-
nocuous little intermezzo *La serva padrona* sparked the notorious *guerre des bouffons*, between partisans of Italian music and
partisans of French music, and inspired Rousseau's *Lettre sur la
musique française* as well as pamphlets by Diderot and others.
Similar polemics rocked Paris later in the century, when Piccinni's supporters and Gluck's disputed the relative merits of
the two composers. And, in the late 1820s, when Rossini arrived,
two Italians were in eminent positions in Paris: Paer at the Italien
and, at the Conservatory, Luigi Cherubini, who had been its
director since 1821 and was to hold the position until his death
in 1842.

Rossini had admirers, many of them; but the admiration was
not universal. A large sector of the press was against him, more
for chauvinistic than for musical reasons. And, no doubt, some of
the French composers who attended the gala 'picnic' swallowed
the praises sung to Rossini with a generous helping of bile. Those

PANTHÉON MUSICAL.

Paris: Bureau central de Musique: 29, Place de la Bourse.

French composers were all minor figures, no match for the overpowering genius of Rossini, whom they accused, naturally, of ruining music. The greatest French musician of the first half of the nineteenth century, Hector Berlioz, was only in his twenties, still a few years away from the composition of his youthful masterpieces (the *Symphonie fantastique* dates from 1830–31), and many decades away from due recognition.

So the last years of the 1820s, in Paris as in Italy, were undisputably Rossini's. First he staged his operas in the original at the Théâtre Italien: *La Cenerentola* was a success there on 6 October 1825 (with Rubini making a splendid Paris debut), then *La donna del lago* and *Otello* (both with Rubini), and on 6 December, *Semiramide*, a novelty for Paris, first with Fodor-Mainvielle (who lost her voice during the opening night performance), then with Giuditta Pasta. Pasta and Rubini both appeared in *Zelmira* on 14 March 1826. For a while the only non-Rossini opera in the repertory of the Italien was Meyerbeer's *Il crociato in Egitto*, a work sponsored by Rossini, whose friendship for the German-turned-Italian and soon-to-turn-French composer was profound and lasting.

There was a sizeable Italian colony in Paris at the time, but the majority of the audience at the Italien was, naturally, French. Characteristically, the theatre is mentioned in *Le rouge et le noir*. Stendhal's hero Julien Sorel could not have failed to attend the Italien, imitating his aristocratic friends. But there would also be

51. Panthéon Musical. Caricature after a drawing by C.-J. Travies, 1843.
This multiple caricature gives a good idea of the musical scene in Paris in 1843. Verdi has not yet arrived (*Nabucco*, his first work to reach the city, was given at the Théâtre Italien in December 1844). Rossini, extreme right, resting on his laurels, is seen as a river god from whose flow of music lesser composers draw. Meyerbeer, extreme left, dressed as his own Robert le Diable, is known to be working on both *L'Africaine* and *Le Prophète*, which he is keeping in a cage. Berlioz, leaning from a coach, is writing his travel impressions for the *Journal des Débats*, and Donizetti—dominating the assembly in the centre—is under full steam, flinging music right and left. The panorama also includes Adolphe Adam, Ambroise Thomas, and such now-forgotten composers as Labarre, Clapisson, Crisar, Montfort, and Rossini's friend Prince Carafa, whose body is shaped like a wine carafe.

52. Filippo Galli as Assur in Rossini's *Semiramide*.
Son of a well-to-do Papal official, Galli (1783–1853) began his musical career as a child prodigy. He made his professional debut in 1801 in Naples, as a tenor; but some years later, reputedly as the result of a grave illness, he became a bass. In 1812 he appeared in the first performance of Rossini's *L'inganno felice* and formed a warm friendship with the composer. Galli took part also in the premières of Rossini's *La pietra del paragone* (1812), and—as a brilliant Mustafà—in *L'italiana in Algeri* (1813), as well as in *Il turco in Italia* (1814), another 'Turkish' role. He also created roles in *Torvaldo e Dorliska* (1815), *Maometto II* (1820), and *Semiramide* (1823). In 1830 he was the first Enrico in Donizetti's *Anna Bolena*. He retired in 1840 and moved to Paris, where he taught singing and died in poverty.

53. (*Right*) Giacomo Meyerbeer. Engraving by A. Lorentz, 1850s.
After an early career in Italy, the German-born Giacomo Meyerbeer (originally Jakob Liebmann Beer, 1791–1864) settled in Paris in the 1820s and with *Robert le Diable* (1831) achieved a phenomenal success, which made him world-famous. This opera was followed by *Les Huguenots* (1836) and *Le Prophète* (1849). With advancing age, Meyerbeer worked more and more slowly, and the intervals between his operas grew longer. This caricature, published in *Le Charivari* in Paris, refers to these silences; the original caption said that the composer's 'torrent of harmony' flows too slowly.

a number of artists in the audience. These, after all, were the years of Henry Murger and Arsène Houssaye. One of the first entries in Delacroix's *Journal* refers to an evening at the Italien, where the young artist seemed impressed most by the female members of the audience. The entry ends: 'Today I thought with great satisfaction about the lady at the Italien.'

Rossini's contract with Charles X also required him to compose for the Opéra, in French. His first work there was *Le Siège de Corinth*, an extensive revision of an earlier Neapolitan work, *Maometto II*. Its première took place on 19 October 1826, and—as a contemporary report went—'not only was every number saluted by a triple salvo of applause, but also after the performance the entire audience wanted to enjoy Rossini's presence. For almost half an hour, the Maestro was called persistently onto the stage; finally the call-boys appeared, to announce that he had left the theatre.'

This first French opera of Rossini's also marked the beginning of his relationship with the publisher Troupenas, who paid six thousand francs for *Le Siège de Corinth*.

After the triumph of *Moïse et Pharaon* in 1827 (a reworking of the Neapolitan *Mosé in Egitto*) and the adequately successful *Le Comte Ory* in 1828, Rossini's *Guillaume Tell* opened at the Opéra on Monday 3 August 1829. It was to be Rossini's last work for the stage, though this fact was, of course, not known at the time. Even Rossini himself may not have been entirely aware of it, but at thirty-seven, he was tired. He seemed to be in good health (though he was not) and, as his massive new opera amply demonstrated, he was not running out of ideas. But theatrical life apparently had lost its charms for him. Two years earlier, his father had said, in a letter to a friend: 'Gioachino [sic] has given me his word that he wants to retire from everything in 1830, come home, and enjoy acting the gentleman, being allowed to write what he wishes.'

Though Rossini stopped writing operas—not with a firmly-announced decision, not with a sharp break, but rather with a gradual detachment—he did not entirely abandon the opera house. Later, in 1830, when he and Isabella were practically separated and she had settled in her villa outside Bologna, he actually lived in a small, top-floor apartment in the Théâtre Italien building, the Salle Favart.

55. (*Right*) Giuditta Pasta. Painting by Gioacchino Serangeli (1768–1852). This painting was probably executed in 1818, the date of a Fine Arts Exhibition at the Brera Academy in Milan, where the painter exhibited a work entitled 'Portrait of a woman singing', apparently this same work. In 1818 Pasta was briefly in Milan, after a two-year absence in Paris and London. Pasta (1798–1865) was on the threshold of her career: she first won real fame in Paris in 1821, after which she sang often in London, St Petersburg, and in Italian houses. She continued singing until 1850, although her voice had begun to lose its beauty and power as early as 1837. She sang in the first performance of Rossini's *Il viaggio a Reims* (1825), created the title roles in Bellini's *La sonnambula* and *Norma* in 1831 and in *Beatrice di Tenda* (1833). She was also the first Anna Bolena in Donizetti's opera (1830).

54. Gilbert-Louis Duprez, as Arnold in Rossini's *Guillaume Tell*, 1837. The tenor role of Arnold in Rossini's *Guillaume Tell* was created (at the Paris Opéra in 1829) by Adolphe Nourrit (1802–39); but at the work's Italian première, in Lucca two years later, the part was sung by Gilbert-Louis Duprez (1806–96). After his debut in France in 1825, as Almaviva in *Il barbiere di Siviglia*, Duprez came to Italy, where at first he was confined to minor roles or comic opera. But the year 1831 represented a turning-point: in Turin he sang his first big, serious part, Gualtiero in Bellini's *Il pirata*, and then the impresario Alessandro Lanari signed him for the Lucca season, where his rightful position in the front rank of tenors was confirmed. He returned to his native country only in 1837, and on 17 April of that year he made a sensational debut at the Opéra, as Arnold. In 1851 he retired. He published an interesting volume of memoirs (*Souvenirs d'un chanteur*, 1880).

PANTHEON CHARIVARIQUE

Compositeurs.   Le Charivari (Journal)

Rare en second genie au renom populaire,
Entre tous Rossini brille au rang le plus haut.
La critique aujourd'hui ne lui sait qu'un défaut:
C'est celui de ne plus rien faire.

56. Rossini in Paris, c. 1830. Caricature by Benjamin.

Although Rossini was popular in Paris, where he lived for most of the latter part of his life, he also encountered some hostility. This is reflected in this caricature from *Le Charivari*, which shows the composer with a sack of money under one arm and a sheet of paper with 'easy music' written on it, protruding from his left pocket. In the background, the Opéra seems to be collapsing, perhaps a reference to the notion that Rossini's music meant the downfall of traditional opera. The verses beneath the caricature are more flattering; they conclude: 'Critics nowadays find in him only one fault: that of writing nothing more.' Rossini's operatic silence, after *Guillaume Tell* in 1829, was very quickly a popular subject of speculation.

By that time the July Revolution of 1830 had taken place. The reactionary and unpopular Charles X, who the year before had signed a new and even more advantageous contract with Rossini, had been swept away. Louis-Philippe, the new Citizen King, was a cultivated man, but not a great music-lover. Rossini now had to sue the French government for his annuity of 6,000 francs: the suit dragged on for five years, but in the end Rossini won it.

Rossini, young as he still was, acted—until his death in 1868—as a kind of musical doyen in Paris, especially towards the Italian artists who were drawn to the city. The seasons at the Italien were certainly brilliant; Théophile Gautier, a few years later, called it the 'théâtre *fashionable* par excellence'. One visitor, in Rossini's time, was the young Frederick Chopin, who on 8/9 November wrote to a friend: 'I . . . am happy at what I have found in this city: the finest musicians and the finest Opera in the world. I have met Rossini, Cherubini, Paer, etc. etc.'

Chopin warned his friend, who was travelling in Germany, what to expect in the French capital: 'One finds here at the same time the greatest luxury and the greatest filth, the greatest virtue and the greatest vice; at every step there are posters concerned with ven. . . diseases—noise, racket, confusion, and more mud that you can conceive. . . . One day, for thirty sous, you eat the most abundant meal in a restaurant illuminated by gas and covered with mirrors and gilt; the next day you might lunch in another where they serve you a portion of bird, making you pay three times as much.'

Inevitably Chopin went to the Italien. On 12 December he gave another friend a report on his opera-going: 'I have never heard the *Barbiere* as I did last week with Lablache, Rubini, and la Malibran (Garcia). I have never heard *Otello* as with Rubini, Lablache, and Mme. Raimbeaux. . . . You cannot imagine what Lablache is. Pasta, they say, has declined, but I never heard anything more sublime. La Malibran subjugates with her marvellous voice. She dazzles like nobody else! Wonder of wonders! Rubini, excellent tenor, sings full voice, never with the head voice. His roulades last at times two hours . . . His mezza-voce is incomparable. I also heard la Schröder-Devrient, who doesn't arouse the same furore here as in Germany. She played the role of Desdemona and Madame Malibran that of Otello [which Rossini had written for a tenor]. La Malibran petite and the German enormous! It seemed as if the German was going to smother Otello. It was expensive to attend this performance. Twenty-four francs for all seats to see la Malibran completely black and in a role for which she is not renowned. Soon they will give *Il pirata* and *La sonnambula*.'

57. Maria Malibran in the last act of Rossini's *Otello*. Painting by Henri Decaisne. Malibran, daughter of Manuel Garcia (she sang under the name of her feckless first husband) made her Covent Garden debut on 4 June 1830, in a mixed programme which included the last act of Rossini's *Otello*, with the tenor Domenico Donzelli (creator of Pollione in *Norma*) in the title role. In 1833 Malibran reappeared in the great London house, again in a heterogeneous bill. She sang once more an excerpt from *Otello*, this time with Wilhelmina Schröder-Devrient as the Moor. Their duet had been preceded by Beethoven's *Fidelio* and was followed by the first act of Weber's *Euryanthe*. The role of Desdemona was a favourite of Malibran's, especially in the early years of her short career; she sang it in America and later at the Théâtre Italien (15 April 1828), where Alfred de Musset was among her most articulate admirers.

58. (*Left*) Giovanni Battista Rubini.
Watercolour, 1835.
Rubini (1794–1854) first sang, at the age of
eighteen, in the chorus of the Teatro
Ricciardi of Bergamo, the city nearest his
native village. He made his official debut
in 1814, in Pavia, then went on to Brescia,
Venice, and Naples, in 1815. He had been
brought to this last city by the impresario
Barbaja, who renewed Rubini's contract
again and again for a period of fourteen
seasons (until 1829), during which the tenor
sang forty-four roles. Meanwhile, through
his friend, the bass Lablache, he made his
Paris debut at the Théâtre Italien, in
Rossini's *Cenerentola* in 1825, with immense
success. In 1835, he created the role of
Arturo in Bellini's *I puritani* (he had
already created the leads in the same
composer's *Il pirata* and *La sonnambula*),
thus becoming the tenor member of the
famous '*Puritani* quartet', with Giulia Grisi,
Antonio Tamburini, and Luigi Lablache. He
was also a widely admired interpreter of
Rossini, Donizetti, and other composers of
the period. He retired in 1845 (though in
1847 he sang in Russia, where he had been
a favourite for some years). He is portrayed
here in his *Puritani* costume.

59. (*Above*) Teatro San Carlo, Naples,
interior. Painting by Cetteo di Stefano,
1835.
The opera being performed in this picture
is *Lara*, libretto by Giovanni Emanuele
Bidera, a house poet of the Neapolitan
theatre, music by the French composer
Henri De Ruoloz (1808–87). This was his
first opera. After his second, *La vendetta*,
given in Paris, he abandoned music and
devoted himself completely to industrial
chemistry. A more permanent offering in
the 1835 season at the San Carlo was
Donizetti's *Lucia di Lammermoor*, mounted a
few weeks before the De Ruoloz work. The
soprano Fanny Tacchinardi-Persiani starred
in both operas.

F. Galli   N. Molinari   G. Pasta   L. Henry   G. B. Rubini
G. Donizetti   G. Frezzolini   F. Romani   V. Bellini

Omaggio
AL MERITO
in occasione delle rappresentazioni date
nel Carnovale dell'anno 1830-31
nel Teatro Carcano
in Milano

Milano presso Epimaco e Pasquale Artaria, Negozianti di Musica, Stampe e Carte Geografiche Cont:S:Margherita N.mo.

60. Giuditta Pasta and other artists, 1830.
For the season of 1830–31, the
management of the Teatro Carcano in
Milan was assumed by the aristocratic
opera-lover Duke Litta along with two
wealthy merchants, Marietti and Soresi, all
bent on outshining La Scala itself.
Anticipation ran high. The composer
Mercadante wrote from Madrid to his
friend Francesco Florimo in Naples: 'I
would pay ready money to witness the
theatrical competition this next carnival
season in Milan.' La Scala's season did not
look promising: the programme consisted
mostly of revivals, with new operas by such
undistinguished composers as Feliciano
Strepponi and Carlo Coccia, and the
somewhat more illustrious Luigi Ricci.
Their stars were the Grisi sisters, Giuditta
and the quasi-debutante Giulia. For the
Carcano the new managers had signed up a
fine company, headed by the
thirty-two-year-old Giuditta Pasta, at the
peak of her career and fame. She is
portrayed here, in a 'homage' of the period,
with other Carcano artists, among them the
tenor Rubini, the bass Galli, and the buffo
Frezzolini (father of the future Verdian
soprano Erminia). Also seen is the
librettist Felice Romani, who provided the
texts for the new operas by Donizetti and
Bellini, respectively *Anna Bolena* (première,
26 December 1830) and *La sonnambula*
(6 March 1831). The composers are at
either end of the bottom row in this group.

As a matter of fact, there had been some performances of *La sonnambula* at the Italien the previous month; *Il pirata* was given there early in 1832, and *La straniera* later that same year. These productions were Bellini's introduction to the Paris audience. Soon the composer was to present himself in person.

In the spring of 1833, travelling from Milan to London, in the company of the soprano Pasta and her husband, Bellini stopped off in Paris en route; the visit was brief, but at least long enough to allow him to open negotiations with the Opéra. In London his operas had brilliant success and he was lionized by society. After a few months the composer returned to Paris. He was to remain there until his death, two years later.

Tall, blond, romantically handsome, Bellini quickly and easily gained entrée into Parisian salons. The most important of these was not so much French as it was Italian, or international: this was the drawing-room of the Milanese Principessa Cristina Trivulzio Belgioioso, a beautiful and intelligent exile. Separated from her husband and at first deprived of her patrimony, the Principessa had lived for a time in near-poverty in Paris. Then, through the intervention of the Austrian ambassador, she had managed to regain some of her wealth and her possessions. Now, at 28 Rue Montparnasse, she received the leading figures of Paris: Victor Hugo, Musset, George Sand, Dumas (not yet *père*), Heine, Michelet, Thiers, Thierry, Liszt, and Chopin. An ardent patriot, she was particularly welcoming to Italian political refugees, who would become more and more numerous as the fervent years of the Risorgimento approached.

Intimate friends were received at her house after noon, by invitation, and the talk continued until dinner-time, six o'clock. After dinner, the salon became an open house. Since Bellini had already met the Principessa in Milan, he probably received a special summons to Rue Montparnasse.

Heinrich Heine, like many members of the salon, was in Paris for political reasons; and he was without means. The Principessa had persuaded her friend Thiers, then Minister of the Interior, to grant the German refugee poet a pension. The difficult, often acid Heine was not liked by the Principessa's more easy-going guests; he took his revenge in sharp, arresting pen-portraits. In his *Reisebilder* there is an extended description of Bellini.

Years later, a lady asked Heine what the composer had been like. He answered: 'Well, he certainly was not ugly. But, mind you, to some questions we men are like you ladies: we cannot say yes. He was tall, slender, moved with grace, I would almost say coyly, and always elegant to the point of affectation. His face was regular, rosy, with rather long, curly hair of a pale, almost golden blond. A high and noble brow, straight nose, pale blue eyes, well-proportioned mouth, round chin. His features, however, had a certain imprecise quality, without pronounced characteristics: a face of milk that sometimes assumed a sweet-sour expression of melancholy which, in Bellini, made up for lack of wit.

But it was a superficial melancholy that glistened without poetry in the eyes and trembled without passion on the lips.' And Heine concludes with the much-quoted summation of Bellini: 'a sigh in dancing-pumps'.

Heine also made fun of Bellini's bad French. When the composer arrived in Paris, in 1833, he hardly spoke French at all, and for that matter even his Italian had a strong Sicilian accent, which must have sounded exotic enough in the drawing-rooms of Milan or in the foyer of La Scala. But for his purposes Bellini did not need a perfect command of French. He was in Paris on business, to consolidate his international fame, to win success with a new work in the city that was then the intellectual capital of Europe.

Before the end of the year Bellini had signed a contract with the Théâtre Italien for an opera seria. Because of his rupture, in Venice, with his usual librettist Felice Romani, he had to look for a new poet. Here the Principessa Belgioioso came to his aid. It was probably at her house that Bellini met a very distinguished refugee: Count Carlo Pepoli of Bologna. More or less the composer's age (his birth-date is given variously as 1797 and 1801), Pepoli had begun writing poetry as a boy and in 1825 had befriended Leopardi, who addressed to him a celebrated verse epistle. During the revolution in central Italy, in 1831, Pepoli had belonged to the provisional government and had signed a declaration abolishing the temporal power of the Papacy. He fought against the Austrians, was captured, imprisoned, then exiled. In Paris, obviously, time hung heavy on his hands (a few years later he moved on to London, where he taught Italian history and music-history at University College), so he was more than willing to provide Bellini with a text for his opera.

'I want to see how Count Pepoli will write this libretto for Paris,' Bellini wrote to Florimo in March 1834: 'I hope he will succeed, because he writes fine verses and has a facility.' In the same letter, however, Bellini went on to say: 'You will already know that they are advising Donizetti to move to Paris and to accept—at a price which I will find out—a contract Rossini might offer him to write an opera also for the Théâtre Italien. He [Donizetti] has already done everything in his power, and I believe he will receive the commission, and I don't know at what fee.' So his new opera was not the only thing on Bellini's mind.

By early spring of 1834, one of Bellini's problems—the choice of an opera subject—seemed to have been solved. He wrote to his uncle on 11 April: 'I have already chosen the argument for my new opera for Paris: it takes place in the time of Cronvello after he had Carlo I of England decapitated.' The composer then goes on to tell the story of *I puritani*, and lists the cast, already established, of course: 'Giulia Grisi will be the girl; Rubini the bridegroom; Tamburini a rival with sublime sentiments; and Lablache a relative of the girl, her only support in her great misfortune . . . I am enthusiastic with the subject, I find it truly inspiring, and Tuesday, at the latest, I'll begin to write the music.'

61. (*Previous page*) Il carroccio (La battaglia di Legnano). Painting by Massimo d'Azeglio.
The subject of the battle of Legnano, in which, on 29 May 1176, the Lombard League defeated Barbarossa, was particularly popular with Italian artists in the Risorgimento years, even before Verdi composed his opera, *La battaglia di Legnano* (1849). This oil by Massimo d'Azeglio (1798–1866) dates from the 1830s and is one of several that the artist devoted to the subject. A writer as well as a painter, d'Azeglio also left an unfinished novel, *La lega lombarda*, dealing with the same events. An even more famous painting of the battle by Amos Cassioli, executed in 1860, is in the Palazzo Pitti, Florence.

62. Vincenzo Bellini and Carlo Pepoli, draft outline of the scenario of *I puritani*, Acts II and III, 1834.
Count Carlo Pepoli, the librettist of Bellini's last opera, had been imprisoned, for patriotic reasons, in the early 1830s and, during his confinement, he contracted an eye affliction which made it often impossible for him to read or write. Thus, in 1834, when he was working with Bellini on the outline of *I puritani*, Bellini did some of the actual writing, at Pepoli's dictation. This draft of Acts II and III of the opera is in Bellini's hand (which Pepoli then authenticated in an autograph note of his own in 1840, when he was teaching Italian literature at University College). The draft varies considerably from the final text; thus Arturo, the hero, is here called Clifford, and Elvira, the heroine, is called Eloisa. A third hand, in the lower left margin, authenticates Pepoli's authentication of the document.

atto. 2d.

Coro di famigliari = deplorano le sorti di Eloisa al comparire della Zia l'attorniano e con interesse ne domandano le notizie — Ella rec.vo e più attristarsi un'aria di molte parole, che esprimeranno tutti i dettagli delle sorti folle di sua Nipote, e ciò che questa crede di vedere nello stato più abbattuto del suo male (*)

Arrivo di Malgravé, dopo l'aria, Rec.vo alla Zia romanza da dentro cantata da Eloisa, dopo la quale viene in scena e largo rec.vo oppure subito attacherà un terzetto come si trova nelle piece e come abbiamo convenuto a voce .——— Resta sola Eloisa, e piede — Grande ritornello avanti che attacchi il suo rec.vo Lo Zio ritorna seguito di Villanelle e prepara tutti provvisi di fiori e d'ispromenti per cercare di distrarla: qui ella venuto s'allegra (sempre fuor di sé) e succede un duetto con suo Zio, questi il vedendola più fuori di sé piange, — mentre quella vuol forzarlo alla danza, chiamandolo suo cavaliere ec: ec: Finisce il duetto, e dessa si ritira con le pastorelle frapponendo tra la folla anche lo Zio, che si vede sciogliersi fra tutti e torna in scena per innomprere nel suo dolore, più allora compresso ec: ec: Colpo di fucile, comparsa di Clifford in lontano — Rec.vo alla Zia, e dopo gran rec.vo e duetto con Eloisa come nella piece pel quale si giunge al finale.

Fine dell'atto 2d.

(1)

Lo Zio ordina al coro in scena e loro di avvisare le villanelle del paese per venire a recar fiori ec: ec: e ritorno a spasso Eloisa ec.

Questo scritto è di carattere di Bellini; l'annotazione è del Conte Pepoli, la Postuma è di Pietro Romani Pagliara

Questo soggetto dev'essere principali. del 2. Atto dei [...]

Siciliani (ho come la prima idea) per la distribuzione delle scene ec ch'io dettava al mio caro Bellini, quando l'infermità de' miei poveri occhi m'impediva assolutamente lo scrivere.

Questo primo ed informe bozzetto, ch'io immaginava e dettava, fu il solo, ma grande pregio di essere scritto dalla mano del dolcissimo Maestro Siciliano, e tenuta di memoria alla gentil Dama la quale principalmente lusingata del quanto fui scritto, e del quale io fui donato, [...]

91

63. Milan, Piazza del duomo, 1835.
The Milan cathedral was the city's religious
centre, as La Scala was its social centre. In
the young Verdi's time, the archbishop was
an Austrian prelate, whose authority
allowed him to censor operas as he saw fit.
The façade of the cathedral, begun in 1616,
was uncompleted for over two centuries.

64. *Semiramide* by Gioacchino Rossini:
interior of the sanctuary. Set design by
Alessandro Sanquirico, 1824.
After its première at the Teatro La Fenice
in Venice on 3 February 1823, Rossini's last
Italian opera, *Semiramide*, was quickly given
elsewhere. The following year, it was
presented at the San Carlo in Naples and at
La Scala. There the cast included Teresa
Giorgi-Belloc and Filippo Galli, and the
designer was Sanquirico, at the height of his
career. This is the set for Act II, scene iv.

The story was based on a three-act historical play by Jacques-Arsène Ancelot and Joseph-Xavier-Boniface Saintine entitled *Têtes Rondes et cavaliers*, which Bellini may very well have seen, since it opened at the Théâtre National du Vaudeville in Paris on 25 September 1833, after he had settled in the city. At various times, his opera was also called, misleadingly, *I puritani di Scozia*, to capitalize on the continental mania for Walter Scott and for Scotland, which had also inspired the libretto of *La donna del lago* and was to inspire Donizetti's *Lucia di Lammermoor*, given in Naples in the autumn of 1835.

Perhaps in order to compose in more peaceful surroundings, Bellini soon moved from the centre of Paris—where he was living in a strange tower near the Italien, and thus near Rossini —to Puteaux, outside the city. There he lodged with some new friends, apparently English, named Levys (or Lewis or Levis). When he was established there, he received confirmation of the news that Donizetti was also to write an opera for the coming season at the Italien: their paths crossed again. 'I had a fever for three days,' Bellini wrote to his uncle, 'as I realized the plot actually being prepared against me.'

The plot reminded him of others; he recapitulated his situation in the same letter: '. . . the Théâtre Italien made me offers which it suited me to accept, first because the fee was larger than what I had previously received in Italy, though not by much; then because the company was so magnificent; and finally in order to stay in Paris at the expense of others. But at that time Rossini was my most fierce enemy, only for professional reasons, etc. etc. . . . Rossini decided to have Donizetti commissioned also, because in that way, set up against me, he would suffocate me, exterminate me, with the support of Rossini's colossal influence.'

Deliberately, Bellini set out to win Rossini's heart, and his first move was to conquer the susceptible Olympe Pélissier, disliked by other friends of Rossini's. More a nurse than a mistress, Olympe clearly wielded power over the older composer, who may have been but was probably not Bellini's enemy. In any case, Bellini's tactics proved successful. Rossini actually looked at the score-in-progress of *I puritani*, made suggestions, and generally helped Bellini. In a later report to his uncle, Bellini said: 'Having won the friendship of Rossini, I said to myself: let Donizetti come now!'

Donizetti did come: he arrived in Paris early in the new year, 1835, in time to attend the dazzling première of *I puritani* on 24 January, with Grisi, Rubini, Tamburini, and Lablache (later to be known, since they often sang together, as 'the *Puritani* quartet'). A short time afterwards Donizetti wrote to Felice Romani: 'Bellini's success has been very good, despite a mediocre libretto. It still continues, though we have reached the fifth performance, and it will go on like this to the end of the season. I am telling you about it, because I know that you and he have made up. Today I begin my own rehearsals, and I hope to

65. Bellini's *I puritani*. First edition of vocal score. Frontispiece, 1836.
After Bellini's death, on 23 September 1835, at the age of thirty-three, the musical world went into mourning, as the engraving on this frontispiece of his last opera indicates. The publication is dedicated to Maria Malibran, who was to die only a short time later. Donizetti—whose *Lucia* had opened triumphantly at the San Carlo on 26 September—wrote a Requiem Mass for Bellini, a *Lamento per la morte di V. Bellini*, and a *Sinfonia* on Bellini melodies. The brevity of Bellini's brilliant career made him a perfect subject for romantic idealization.

give the first performance at the end of the month. I don't deserve anything like the success of *I puritani*, but I do want to please.'

Donizetti's opera was to be *Marino Faliero*, derived from Byron via a play by Casimir Delavigne (seen in Paris in 1820). Romani had turned down an invitation from Paris to write the libretto, so the composer had to be content with Giovanni Emanuele Bidera, a Sicilian actor-writer, then official poet of the Teatro San Carlo. But, not satisfied with Bidera's work, Donizetti found another political exile writer in Paris, Agostino Ruffini, and asked him to revise the text. Ruffini accepted, and became friends with Donizetti. In fact, the composer was friendly with the Ruffini family, which included another refugee brother, Giovanni, later the librettist of *Don Pasquale*.

The same quartet of singers who had created *I puritani* also starred in *Marino Faliero*, which opened at the Italien on 4 March 1835. It was a success. Donizetti was not a man to delude himself about the reception of his operas, so he can be taken at his word, when he wrote some ten days or so after the première to his old friend Antonio Dolci in Bergamo: 'I want to send you also a few words about the second and third evenings, which were very

66. Gaetano Donizetti.
This little-known portrait of Donizetti as a young man has been, somewhat improbably, attributed to Gerolamo Induno (1827–90), an important Milanese painter of the Risorgimento. It could possibly be the work of his older brother Domenico (1815–78); but it was in all likelihood painted by an artist in Bologna, where the work is still preserved, and where Donizetti studied under the celebrated Padre Mattei between 1815 and 1817.

brilliant. Rubini sang as I have never heard him, and for this reason had to repeat the cavatina and the aria every evening . . . Bellini's success with *I puritani* made me considerably nervous, but, since our genres are opposite, we thus both obtained a fine success and satisfied the public.'

Bellini, as usual, was less generous. In the already-quoted letter to his uncle Ferlito, he said: 'Well then, at the dress rehearsal they gave him immense applause, so much so that I, in a box with Rossini, laughed with him at this furore, as the opera at all the rehearsals had been sentenced to a short, a very short life, because it is the worst Donizetti has composed so far, and his operas now have reached the number of forty-eight. At the first performance the auditorium, that is the stalls, was full of claque, etc. etc., but since the Théâtre Italien is full, very full of subscribers, the claque were unable to impose on anyone, and *Marin Faliero* had a mediocre effect. . . . The newspapers, influenced by his behaviour, as he goes and acts the clown in all the houses of Paris and especially with the journalists, have tried to praise him.'

The letter is very long, almost delirious when Bellini is describing the Rossini-Donizetti 'plot', and then suddenly cool-headed when the composer discusses money, or says: 'It is still my plan to take a wife, if I find one with a dowry of at least 200,000 francs, of good character, well brought up, and not ugly.'

Bellini never had time to take a wife, or to write another opera. Some weeks after the end of the season, during which *I puritani* had been played seventeen times (*Marino Faliero*, opening much later, apparently had only five performances), Bellini went back to his rural lodgings in Puteaux. He stayed there through the summer, depressed and idle; negotiations with the Opéra went haltingly, in part because of his financial demands. His occasional letters are almost incoherent, with more plots and plans ('Oh! if Rossini were to leave Paris for good, that would also be the fortune of my Italian operas, as perhaps the impresarios would come to me for advice about the management of the Théâtre [Italien].')

In early September a rumour began to spread through Paris cultural circles that Bellini, invisible at Puteaux, was seriously and mysteriously ill. A young attaché from the embassy of the Kingdom of the Two Sicilies went out to investigate, but the gardener, at the gate of the villa, forbade him entrance. Two other attempts met with the same result. On 14 September the attaché returned with his uncle, the composer Carafa, who passed himself off as a physician and was allowed into the house, where he found Bellini alone, ill, in bed. The Levys were absent.

Principessa Belgioioso sent an Italian physician, Luigi Montallegri, out to Puteaux. On 20 September, he reported the composer's condition as 'alarming'; the following day he gave a more optimistic report. Then, on 23 September, the young attaché, Baron Augusto d'Aquino, noted in his diary:

'Having to go and spend the day at my sister-in-law's in Rueil, I leave early on horseback. At Pont de Courbevoie, I stop in Puteaux. The gardener is still inflexible. During the day, an appalling storm breaks out, and at about ten past five, completely drenched by the driving rain, I knock at the house of Mr Lewis. No answer . . . I push the gate, and it gives. After having tied up my horse, I enter the house, which seems completely abandoned. I find Bellini on the bed, apparently asleep . . . but his hand is ice-cold. I cannot believe the hideous truth. . . . The gardener reappears and tells me that Signor Bellini breathed his last at 5 o'clock, and that M. and Mme Lewis had gone to Paris, so he had had to go out to call someone and procure candles.'

The Lewises, or Levyses, were accused of poisoning Bellini; dramatic tales promptly circulated through Paris. More considered, modern opinion is that Bellini died of a flare-up of a chronic amebiasis, which his hosts—and his attendant doctor—mistook for cholera (then raging in southern France). If cholera had been discovered, he would necessarily have been taken to a public hospital, and so they forbade access to him. For the same reason they also kept clear of their own house.

Rossini arranged the solemn funeral ceremony, at which Rubini, Tamburini, Lablache, and the tenor Ivanoff (replacing la Grisi in the quartet, since the presence of a female singer would have been out of the question in a church at the time) sang an arrangement of 'Credeasi misera', the finale of *I puritani*. The body was buried in Père Lachaise (and moved from there to Catania in 1876). In Milan, Donizetti, unaware of Bellini's secret and obsessive dislike of him, conducted a commemorative ceremony and composed a Requiem. His *Lucia di Lammermoor* had had its triumphant première, at the San Carlo, on 26 September, three days after Bellini's death.

But Donizetti's career, too, was approaching its end, although the composer was only thirty-seven. The effects of syphilis, contracted many years before, were beginning to be felt. He had composed the tenor's death scene, 'Tu che a Dio spiegasti l'ali', in the last act of his most famous opera, during a blinding headache, a symptomatic warning.

Like Bellini's, Donizetti's career ended in Paris. He returned there on 21 October 1838, and took a flat at 4 rue Louvois. Adolphe Adam, composer of *Giselle*, lived in the same building, and in his *Derniers souvenirs*, left a description of the Italian composer as he was at this time:

'Donizetti was a big man, with a frank, open countenance; and his physiognomy was the index of his excellent character. You could not be with him and not love him, because he constantly afforded opportunities for you to appreciate one or another of his fine qualities. We lived in the same house. . . . We often visited each other; he worked without a piano, he wrote incessantly, and you could not believe he was composing, if the absence of any sort of rough draft had not made you certain. I

67. Self-portrait of Donizetti. Drawing, 1841.
By 1841 Donizetti was more or less established in Paris, where he lived in the Hotel Manchester, rue Grammont, though he still held the official post of Court Composer in Vienna. The previous year he had presented *La Fille du régiment* at the Opéra-Comique, *Les Martyrs* and *La Favorite* at the Opéra. In 1841 he was back in Italian opera houses: his *Adelia* was given on 11 February at the Apollo in Rome (with Giuseppina Strepponi and Lorenzo Salvi heading the cast) and—at the end of the year—his *Maria Padilla* opened La Scala's season on 26 December (with Sophie Loewe, Giorgio Ronconi, and Domenico Donzelli). Between these two premières he returned to France, where—in a spell of idleness, without a commission to fill—he composed the little French farce *Rita* (not performed until 1860, years after Donizetti's death). This self-caricature dates from that year, and was presumably done in Paris, since Donizetti wrote, in French, 'mon portrait fait par moi même' [sic] in the left margin.

Mon portrait fait par moi même

Donizetti
1851

noticed with surprise a little scraper, made of white horn, set carefully next to his paper, and I was astonished to see that instrument, which he cannot have used much. This scraper, he told me, was given me by my father, when he forgave me and agreed to my becoming a musician. It has never left me, and though I use it little, I like to have it near me as I compose; it seems to me that it carries my father's blessing. This was said so simply and with such sincerity, that I immediately understood what a great heart Donizetti had.'

Donizetti, while he lived in the rue Louvois, was at work on several projects at once: a light piece for the Opéra-Comique, which turned out to be the highly successful *La Fille du régiment*; and, for the Opéra, the noble, serious *Les Martyrs*, an extensive revision of a work written originally for Naples, *Poliuto*, not performed there because the censors considered the story—of Christian martyrs—unsuitable for the stage (librettists had to hew to a fine line: on one side the immoral, and on the other side the sacred). The Paris version of this work—though Berlioz described it as 'a credo in four acts'—was well-received. Soon Donizetti was invited to compose more operas for the Paris theatres.

He also had commissions from Italian theatres, but before leaving Paris temporarily, he presented at the Opéra *La Favorite*, one of his most complex works, on 2 December 1840. The sumptuous production featured ballets choreographed by Jules Perrot and interpreted by his wife Carlotta Grisi (cousin of the soprano Giulia), making her Paris debut. The following year Carlotta Grisi created the title role of *Giselle*.

Understandably, *La Favorite* was a success, not least because the cast was headed by the sensational, capricious Rosine Stoltz and the star tenor Gilbert-Louis Duprez. Eleven days after the première, Donizetti left for Italy. His next opera, *Adelia*, was given in Rome, at the Apollo, and is significant only because its leading singer was the twenty-five-year-old soprano Giuseppina Strepponi, later to become Signora Verdi. He next composed a work for La Scala: *Maria Padilla*.

Finally, at the end of March 1842, Donizetti was in Vienna, where the impresario Merelli had signed him up for a new opera at the Kärntnertortheater. His *Linda di Chamounix*, which opened on 19 May, had a stellar cast, but the names are new. These names—like Strepponi's—are those of the next operatic generation, the Verdi generation. They are Eugenia Tadolini (creator of Verdi's *Alzira*), the tenor Napoleone Moriani (known as the 'tenore della bella morte', for his splendid rendering of the death of Edgardo in *Lucia*; he was a valued interpreter of Verdi's *Ernani* and his *Attila*), and the baritone Felice Varesi (for whom Verdi wrote the roles of Macbeth, Rigoletto, and Germont *père*).

Donizetti's stay in Vienna was crowned, in late June, by his appointment as court composer, Maestro di Cappella e di Camera e Compositore di Corte, with an annual stipend of 12,000 Austrian lire. For him the position meant financial security as well as prestige; and as he happily pointed out in several letters to friends, this was the title that had been given to Mozart (in Mozart's case it had been a fairly empty honour). The post also allowed Donizetti generous leave, so he could write elsewhere. And he promptly did. He composed only one more opera for Vienna: *Maria di Rohan*, in 1843. His most significant, final works were for Paris (*Don Pasquale* for the Italien, 3 January 1843; *Dom Sébastien* for the Opéra, 11 November 1843) and for Naples (*Caterina Cornaro* for the San Carlo, 12 January 1844).

Donizetti did not go to Naples to supervise the production of *Caterina Cornaro*. His health was now deteriorating visibly. During the rehearsals of *Dom Sébastien*, there was a terrible quarrel with Rosine Stoltz (whose capacity for quarrelling was, by common consent, immense). The soprano, creator of *La Favorite* and also the mistress of Pillet, the director of the Opéra, refused to remain on stage while the baritone Paolo Barroilhet sang his solo barcarole. Exasperated, as the argument dragged on, Donizetti threw down his score, railed at the soprano, and walked out, as an early biographer of Donizetti said: 'furious, inflamed. His head was spinning. His legs were unsteady. If his *fidus Achates*, [Michele] Accursi, had not supported him, almost carrying him to the carriage, he would have fallen.' And another biographer, Léon Escudier, writing about the same incident, said: 'From that day on, Donizetti's brain was afflicted. From that day dated the fatal illness that gradually undermined his faculties and finally killed him.'

The audience reacted favourably to *Dom Sébastien*, although the critics were mostly hostile. Donizetti should have been able to console himself: the next night, his *Maria di Rohan* had its Parisian première, in its original language, at the Italien, and it was a reassuring success.

But his early biographers Alborghetti and Galli wrote: 'When *Dom Sébastien* was given for the first time . . . the Maestro bore on all his person the obvious traces of a profound change, both physical and spiritual. In the short span of a few months he seemed to have declined from the fullness of manhood into extreme old age: bent, his hair white, his eyes lustreless and hollow, his movements limp and languid. He moved his body with difficulty. Impatient, irascible, gruff, his character had changed as much as his facial expression. He provoked around him a curious reaction of envious rancour and base malice because what was simply the inadvertent expression of his sick brain was thought to be a deliberate new haughtiness.'

Somehow Donizetti kept on. From Paris he went to Vienna, then to Italy, managing to keep up his usual stream of witty, sometimes obscene letters, though they now occasionally lapsed into a deep and uncharacteristic melancholy.

The story of Donizetti's very last years makes painful, almost

unbearable reading. In the autumn of 1845, alarmed by reports of the composer's condition and by the fact that he had stopped answering his friends' letters, Antonio Vasselli, Donizetti's brother-in-law, his beloved Totò, wrote to the composer's brother Giuseppe, himself a composer, in Turkey. Giuseppe sent his son Andrea, a boy in his twenties, from Constantinople to Paris. There, aghast at the state in which he found his uncle, Andrea called in three specialists in nervous disorders.

Their elaborate report read, in part: '. . . in mid-1845, the signs of disease at work in his brain became more numerous and unmistakeable each day. M. Donizetti was no longer able to compose and produce as in the past; his ideas seemed less numerous than before; he easily succumbed to the heaviness of a frequent somnolence. His walk appeared heavy, his body tended to stoop, his whole physique took on an unhealthy aspect, a host of nuances [betrayed] a weakening of the faculties of comprehension and imagination. . . .

'Not only are his memory and other intellectual faculties marked by a lack of capacity and understanding, but further, false and unreasonable notions have intruded into the patient's reasoning, so that he imagines that he is being robbed, that he is being deprived of sums of money not really his. . . .

68. Donizetti with his nephew Andrea. Daguerreotype, 1847.
This daguerreotype of Donizetti in his last illness was made at no. 6 avenue Châteaubriand, the Paris house to which the composer was taken on 23 June 1847, after his nephew Andrea (who had come from Constantinople) had secured his release from the mental hospital at Ivry. After difficult negotiations with the authorities, Andrea managed to obtain permission to take Donizetti back to Bergamo, and there the patient was housed in the palace of Baroness Rota-Basoni. On the back of the picture is written: 'To the most kind Signora Rosa Basoni, Andrea Donizetti offers this sad souvenir as a testimony of his esteem. Paris, 3 August 1847.' Some years later Andrea himself went mad and died in the asylum at Aversa, near Naples, on 11 February 1864.

69. (Right) Letter from Donizetti to his brother Giuseppe. Late May, 1846.
From the asylum at Ivry, Donizetti – as the final stages of syphilis affected his mind and body more and more gravely – scrawled a few, desperate letters, his last. This one, to his brother Giuseppe in Constantinople, is almost undecipherable. It begins: 'Rejoice I am better. I hope that I will leave for Bergamo.' The music apparently cannot be identified. The date is 20 or 21 (or 26?) May.

Caro Giuseppe
20. Maggio — 26. Maggio.
Sto allegro io sono meglio

'His character has become either irritable or taciturn; the excitement of his genital organs no longer allows M. Donizetti to resist the impulse of his desires, and he increasingly compromises his health by giving rein to partly unhealthy desires.'

The report, dated 28 January 1846, recommended in conclusion that Donizetti be confined in an institution for treatment. A few days later his carriage took him from his apartment in the Hôtel Manchester to Dr Mitvié's clinic at Ivry. Donizetti, whose mind was clouded but not completely gone, had been told he was travelling to Vienna, where his duties as court composer summoned him. In Ivry, he was told that the carriage had broken down, and the asylum was passed off as a hotel. When he became

70. Table presented to Donizetti in Naples, 1837.
This olive-wood table, with movable lid, was presented to Donizetti by some Neapolitan friends. The portrait is flanked by a handwritten biography of the composer, then two panels of generic operatic scenes. The three outer bands contain the titles of his operas up to 1837, thus allowing us to date the table. It may have been given to Donizetti on the occasion of his moving – on 2 May 1837 – into a handsome, large apartment at no. 14 vico Nardones. There, on 30 July, Donizetti's beloved wife Virginia died, following the death of their new-born infant son. The next year Donizetti left Naples.

aware that he was staying in this 'hotel' for an unlikely length of time, his questions were parried with another elaborate lie: there had been a theft, his manservant was suspected, and the composer would not be able to pursue his journey while the investigation was in progress.

The choice of lie was unfortunate for a sick man who already had delusions about robberies. Somehow Donizetti began to think *he* was the suspect and the asylum was a prison. His last letters, in an almost illegible scrawl, are incoherent assertions of his innocence and heart-rending pleas for release. A typical one, in his broken French, was written to Countess Appony, wife of the Austrian ambassador in Paris: 'Madame come to Ivry . . . in an hour! . . . I too have been arrested—My manservant has stolen again?—my nephew's grief gives me courage! The young man is innocent: Have him released . . . oh! God! what sorrow—Tell H. Ex.—Count Appony that he loves me, I have been arrested in my carriage . . . I weep and am weak! . . . But I, I have three rooms: come, come, the good Lord will save us.

'I never did it . . . A matinée! Tomorrow if it is possible? Oh, I am dying . . . dying . . .

'They arrested my nephew, and it was the Servant! . . .

'Oh, how I weep, I am innocent! Would I steal my own possessions?—*They are mine . . .*'

And it is signed *Le pauvre Donizetti.*

As Donizetti became progressively paralysed, it was clear that the asylum was not necessary; he could be cared for just as well somewhere else. His family wanted him taken back to Bergamo, but for reasons never explained, the French police opposed his leaving the country. Finally the Austrian government intervened. Bergamo was then in Austrian territory, so Donizetti was an Austrian subject as well as an official of the Court.

By slow stages, the composer was taken back to his native city and received by a noble (in every sense) family there, the Baroness Rota-Basoni and her daughter, who kept him in their home, as an honoured guest, until he died. Old friends visited him; Rubini came and sang some of Donizetti's music to him, but there were no signs of understanding or recognition. In February 1848, Donizetti had a fever, then other symptoms developed. He was treated with leeches, mustard-plasters, vesicants. At five-thirty a.m. on April 8, he died.

But it was the year 1848. Carlo Alberto, king of Sardinia, had just invaded Lombardy. In Paris, Louis-Philippe had been overthrown, and there had been rioting in the streets of Vienna. As another early biographer, Annibale Gabrielli, wrote: 'Thus the death of Gaetano Donizetti passed almost unnoticed outside the circle of his most affectionate fellow-townsmen.'

 Chapter 6

IF the Paris of Rossini, Bellini, and Donizetti was a glittering capital, centre of an international society, with brilliant writers, exciting theatre and significant artists, the Milan of the young Giuseppe Verdi was almost the exact opposite: a small, provincial city, ruled by the Austrians, dirty, cramped, narrow in every sense.

Still, Milan was Italy's musical capital; it had La Scala, it was closer to Vienna and Paris than Naples was; and the Austrian authorities, whatever their faults, were opera-lovers. To the eighteen-year-old Giuseppe Verdi, who arrived there in the summer of 1832, the city must have seemed a metropolis.

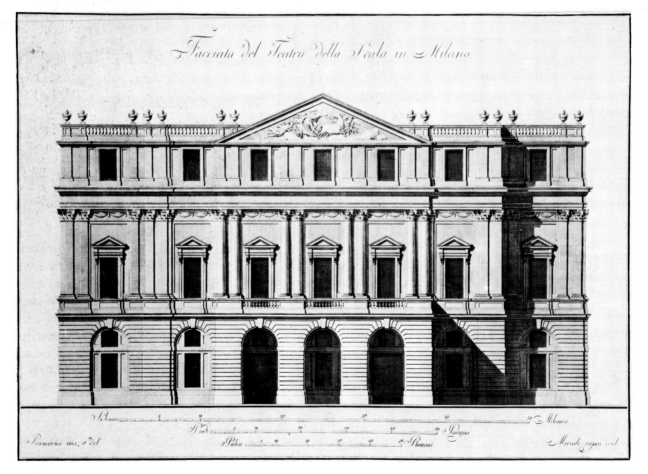

72. Verdi as a young man, *c.* 1836. Drawing by Stefano Barezzi.

Since this drawing was originally one of a pair (the other was of Margherita Barezzi), it is possible that they were made in 1836, at the time of Verdi's first marriage. The artist was Margherita's uncle, a successful painter and later a distinguished restorer. This drawing, formerly in the Stefanini collection in Busseto, now hangs in the newly-refurbished 'salone Barezzi', the drawing-room of the Barezzi house, where the young Verdi gave Margherita piano lessons and conducted the Filarmonici, the local amateur orchestra of which Antonio Barezzi, the composer's patron and father-in-law, was an active member.

71. (*Left*) La Scala, façade. Drawing by Giuseppe Piermarini.

During the night of 25 February 1776, the Teatro Ducale in Milan burned down. The theatre's box-owners immediately decided to rebuild it, but there was some question whether or not to use the same site. One of the advocates of a new location was the architect Giuseppe Piermarini (1734–1808); a political progressive, he probably wanted to shift the opera house away from the restricting ambiance of the court and move it closer to the general public. In the end the authorities decided to build two theatres: the larger one was to become La Scala, and the smaller, the Teatro della Canobbiana. Piermarini was the architect of both. He worked on La Scala for two years. The façade gave him particular trouble, and five different versions of its survive in his drawings. This is the version finally approved. The portico—a new element in theatre design—was demanded by the box-owners, whose instructions insisted on 'a covered entrance for carriages'. The same clients wanted the classical pediment, which Piermarini accepted reluctantly, as he had accepted the portico.

Besides Roncole, his native hamlet, and neighbouring villages like it, Verdi had seen only the market town of Busseto, where he had lived and studied, and had perhaps visited Parma, a handsome, elegant capital, but tiny and, compared to Milan, backward and unstimulating.

Antonio Ghislanzoni, years later, wrote a humorous, sketchy *History of Milan* between 1836 and 1848. Some of his observations illustrate the atmosphere in which Verdi found himself. 'Nobody mentioned politics—The streets were illuminated by oil lamps, and the glow of the flames quite blinded the passerby. —The Milanese boasted of their cleanliness, and the pavements, all the same, were crossed by trickles that did not smell of musk. The cathedral, admired by foreigners, served as urinal for the more civilized, who, to the greater offence of the edifice, were numerous.—The city woke around eleven; the true *lions* did not appear in public until one o'clock. . . . The fashion of moustache and full beard encountered stubborn and furious opponents. Many fathers became angry with their sons or nephews for a slight hirsute insubordination. . . . Old people, clerks, and in general all so-called serious men shaved scrupulously from nose to gullet. Students who wore a beard or a moustache risked compromising their future. . . . Three-quarters of the population knew no other world besides what was enclosed by the girdle of the bastions. The opening of the railway between Milan and Monza was a colossal event, which seemed miraculous. Old people were heard to cry: Now that I have seen this wonder, I am content to die! And many, in fact, died.'

Prole eia forte piacquesi
Di cimentar la lede:
Conobbe Italia, e il nettare
Bette di sua melode.

All'ultima Donna es Silfina
Questo tributo onor:
Genti applaudite: applaudono
Con Voi le Grazie e Amore

73. Apotheosis of Maria Malibran. Engraving, 1836.
Malibran sang in the summer season, May–July, of 1836 in London. Then, while riding Lord Lennox's horse Comet in the Surrey countryside, she was thrown and dragged. Despite her injuries, she sang in *La sonnambula* on 23 July and in some concerts at the Manchester Festival. Bowing to the public's insistence, she agreed to sing an encore at the final concert. She was strongly advised not to, and her (second and adored) husband, Charles Bériot, wanted to make an announcement, explaining her condition. She refused: '*Non! Pas d'excuses! Je chanterai! Mais je suis une femme morte!*' ('No! No excuses! I will sing! But I am a dead woman!') After nine days of suffering, she died in the Mosley Arms Hotel on 23 September 1836. Gautier, hearing the news, wrote: '*Elle a eu le génie de mourir toute jeune*' ('She had the genius to die while young'). And she did indeed become a legend almost instantly, an operatic saint, as this 'apotheosis'—one of many pious, commemorative engravings produced at the time—clearly suggests.

Even musically, it was not a particularly happy time for Milan.
La Malibran was soon to die, la Pasta abandoned the stage at
this period. And Italy's greatest singers—Rubini, Lablache,
Tamburini, and their like—had emigrated to Paris and London,
where they were paid fabulous sums that La Scala's impresarios
could not offer. As Ghislanzoni goes on to report: 'In the boxes
of La Scala, during the opera performance, they played tarots and
at times they had supper. In the great theatre the benches in the
stalls were covered with a heavy, yellowish canvas; the stairs
were naked of carpets; the stage, gloomily lighted.'

Occasionally, during the performance of an opera—Donizetti's *Belisario*, for example—a patriotic sentiment expressed
on the stage would spark an anti-Austrian demonstration in
the audience. But, according to the librettist-historian, 'Men
who thought of Italy, who suffered under the foreign yoke, who
detested Austria, were very scarce. The majority were unaware
that Italy existed. And yet, some were acting in secret, some
were writing, some assumed the dangerous task of circulating the
papers of Mazzini. In those days there were terrible risks in
speaking of politics, even with the most intimate friends.'

Verdi, having completed his studies in Busseto, was in Milan
to apply for admission to the Conservatory. There were strong
arguments against accepting him: he was above admission age,
the Conservatory was over-crowded, and—coming from the
Duchy of Parma—he was a foreigner. His application was rejected. But Verdi had the loyal, unswerving support of a well-off
Busseto merchant, Antonio Barezzi, later to become his father-
in-law. Barezzi, also an enthusiastic and versatile amateur musician, had early recognized the boy's talents and had taken the
young Verdi into his home. Now he arranged for the boy to stay
on in Milan, where he could study privately. A teacher was
found: the composer-conductor Vincenzo Lavigna, an important
figure at La Scala and a leader of Milanese musical life. And Verdi
lodged with a friend of Barezzi's, Giuseppe Seletti, a native of
Busseto, now teaching in Milan. Though Seletti disliked his
apparently unruly young paying guest, he wrote to Barezzi regularly, reporting on Verdi's progress.

On 8 August 1832, he wrote: '[Verdi] has already received
five lessons, and all of them lasting an hour and a half. Lavigna
seems very interested, and in speaking both with me and with Dr
Frigerio, he declared that Verdi studies hard and he expects good
results. . . . No more fortunate choice could have been made for
a teacher, for he is a gentleman and for thirty years has been very
familiar with the successes and failures of scores when staged.
The Maestro has had Verdi subscribe to a music shop, and he
already has two scores at home which he is studying. The cost of
the subscription is three Austrian lire per month. When the
Theatre opens, moreover, he wants him to subscribe for every
night. Meanwhile he has made him write a Sinfonia, which he will
then have him perform in a private concert which is held every

76. Giulio Ricordi in later life.
The firm of Ricordi, founded in 1808 by
Giovanni Ricordi (1785–1853), was the
flourishing publisher of Rossini, Donizetti,
Bellini, and of the influential *La Gazzetta
musicale di Milano*, founded in 1842 (it
ceased publication only in 1902). The
business was continued by Giovanni's son
Tito (1811–88) and then, as Tito's health
declined in the late 1860s, by his son
Giulio (1840–1912). The firm's mainstay
for the second half of the last century was
Verdi, who dealt with all three generations
of Ricordis, not without moments of
tension and acrimony. Giulio was a fluent
writer, a graceful composer (under the
name J. Burgmein), a shrewd businessman,
and a skilled diplomatist (as he had to be, in
handling the prickly Verdi). Giulio was also
responsible for bringing the young, virtually
untried Puccini to the firm and for cleverly
and patiently guiding his career.

Sunday, where he has said he will introduce him. In short,
everything encourages hope in every way.'

Though Verdi remained by his own (and his landlord's)
definition a 'bear' socially, he met a number of prominent
Milanese, especially the leading musical amateurs. Lavigna sent
good reports back to Busseto and no doubt boasted also in Milan
of his gifted pupil. Years later, Verdi told his publisher Ricordi
(who wrote down the account) about his Milanese debut:

'In 1833 or '34 there existed in Milan a Società filarmonica
made up of good voices. It was directed by a certain Massini, a
man who, if not very learned, was at least tenacious and patient,
and so just what was needed for a society of amateurs. They were
organizing at the Teatro Filodrammatico the performance of an
oratorio by Haydn, *The Creation*. My teacher Lavigna asked me
if, for my instruction, I would like to follow the rehearsals, and I
accepted with pleasure.

'Nobody paid any attention to the youth modestly seated in a corner. The rehearsals were conducted by three maestri: Perelli, Bonoldi, and Almasio; but one fine day, by a strange twist of fate, all three conductors were absent from a rehearsal. The ladies and gentlemen were growing impatient, when Maestro Masini [sic], who did not feel himself capable of sitting at the piano and accompanying with the score, turned to me, asking me to serve as accompanist; and perhaps unconvinced of the knowledge of the young and unknown artist, he said to me: 'It is enough just to accompany with the bass.' My studies then were still fresh in my mind, and I certainly did not find myself in any difficulty, facing an orchestral score. I accepted, I sat down at the piano to begin the rehearsal. I well remember some little ironic smiles from the amateurs, ladies and gentlemen, and it seems that my youthful figure, thin and none too elegant in dress, was such as to inspire scant faith.'

The ladies and gentlemen soon stopped smiling. As the rehearsal progressed, Verdi warmed to his role, and after a while, still playing only with his left hand, he began to conduct the chorus with his right. In the end, he took charge, and 'when the rehearsal was over, compliments, congratulations on all sides,

77. Ricordi's publishing firm, c. 1840. The first piece of music published by Giovanni Ricordi in 1808 was a work by one Antonio Nava entitled *Le stagioni dell'anno in quattro sonate a solo per chitarra francese.* Dedicated to Napoleon, this was the No. 1 in a catalogue that was to run into hundreds of thousands of compositions. Ricordi's rise was rapid. He soon moved from the humble shop under the arcades in Piazza Mercanti. As his fortunes prospered, he had his headquarters in the building of La Scala itself, the part then called the Casino Ricordi. Later he moved to Via Omenomi, still in the vicinity of the Scala. There, the Ricordi establishment became a kind of salon, where distinguished visitors like Liszt and Thalberg performed, and Giovanni's son Tito, an accomplished pianist himself, accompanied singers like Pasta, Rubini, and Lablache.

and especially from Count Pompeo Belgioioso and Count Renato Borromeo.'

The three absent maestri had apparently lost interest in the unpaid job of conducting *The Creation*, so the preparation and performance of the concert was entrusted entirely to Verdi. The public performance at the Teatro Filodrammatico was such a success that it had to be repeated, privately, at the Casino de' Nobili, in the presence of the Archduke Rainer, the Austrian governor of the city, and his Archduchess, and of the social leaders of Milan.

Though he received no money for his work, which was also unreviewed, Verdi reaped other rewards. He was commissioned to write a ceremonial cantata (he was not yet the anti-Austrian patriot he would become a few years later), and he gained the grateful friendship of Massini, who then played an active role in the next, crucial step in Verdi's career. The Teatro Filodrammatico was—and is—next door to La Scala, just across a narrow street. How was Verdi to make that vital move?

First, on completing his studies with Lavigna, he had to go back to Busseto and assume the onerous position of village music-master and conductor of the local Filarmonici, the society of amateur musicians in which Barezzi was a leader. Verdi clearly was not keen to return to the town and to its factional quarrels, in which Barezzi and thus—against his will—Verdi himself would be involved. But he knew his duty. He left Milan and went back to Busseto; there he was able to marry Margherita Barezzi, who was to die only four years later.

In Busseto, Verdi composed the required Sinfonie and marches and occasional pieces, but like any Italian musician of his time, he thought only of a debut in the theatre. First he had to find a libretto, and here again Massini helped him, providing one from Milan: *Rocester*, by the journalist Antonio Piazza. Then, once the opera was written, there was the question of finding an impresario who would stage it.

He had hopes for a Parma production and made a special trip to the city, to meet the new impresario of the Teatro Ducale there. But the work was rejected. Then there was the possibility of an amateur performance, again at the Teatro Filodrammatico in Milan. But that hope also faded. In May 1838, Verdi went to Milan for a few days, to see what could be done (leaving Margherita, pregnant, behind in Busseto). During his annual September-October holiday he was in the city again. And from Milan he wrote to a Busseto friend: 'It [his opera] might be performed in the next Carnival season; but since it's a new opera, written by a new composer, to be staged in the leading theatre in the world, I want to think it over again thoroughly.' By now, Verdi was probably talking about *Oberto*, a text by Temistocle Solera, which he had set; the mysterious *Rocester* had vanished forever.

The pivotal figure in all this story was Bartolomeo Merelli, the

78. Giuseppina Strepponi as a young woman.

Clelia Maria Josepha Strepponi, known always as Giuseppina (1815–97), studied first with her father, the composer Feliciano, who died when she was seventeen, leaving his family in dire financial straits. With the help of a scholarship, Giuseppina continued her studies at the Milan Conservatory, then made her debut in 1834, perhaps pressed by the need to maintain her mother and siblings. Her career advanced rapidly. Her voice was sweet and expressive, but of limited power. She drove it—and herself— hard, and her health was further undermined by several pregnancies and miscarriages (the father of her illegitimate children has not been firmly identified, though the popular and handsome tenor Napoleone Moriani is a likely candidate). Giuseppina was instrumental in having Verdi's first opera, *Oberto*, performed at La Scala in 1839, and she created the role of Abigaille in his *Nabucco* (1842), the work that brought him real fame and success. Giuseppina's devotion to Verdi never failed, and she lived to share in his final triumphs as she had in his first.

friend of Donizetti, the man who had arranged for Bellini to open the Teatro Carlo Felice in Genoa. Verdi and Merelli had not yet encountered each other, but if Merelli was unaware of the composer's existence, Verdi certainly knew very well who Merelli was and what he could do.

In 1838, Merelli was forty-five years old and had been impresario of La Scala for only two years, though he had behind him at least two decades of experience, including the management of leading opera houses in Italy, as well as the Imperial Opera in Vienna and the Théâtre Italien in Paris, where he had commissioned—and supplied the libretto for—Rossini's monarchist cantata, *Il viaggio a Reims*.

Shrewd (and parsimonious) as he was, Merelli was willing to take a risk with unknowns, and for that matter, after the death of Bellini and the retirement of Rossini, established composers were scarce on the ground. In any case, the impresario liked to hedge his bets by hiring popular singers.

According to the story Verdi later told, Merelli one day at La Scala overheard two singers talking, with great admiration, about the opera score of a young man whom they knew only by name.

79. Lorenzo Salvi. Engraving by Kniehuben, 1830s.
The tenor Lorenzo Salvi (1810–79) made his debut at the Teatro San Carlo, Naples, in 1830, singing a small role in Donizetti's *Il diluvio universale.* But he was soon singing major roles, including Rossini's Otello, with Malibran in 1832 in Rome. He made his Scala debut in 1839 and that same season created the role of Riccardo in Verdi's first opera, *Oberto, conte di San Bonifazio.* This came at the end of the season, and the overworked Salvi did not sing well, although the opera was a success all the same. Salvi was also in the cast of the disastrous *Un giorno di regno* (1840), Verdi's second opera. In 1847, the tenor sang Verdi's *Ernani* at Covent Garden, in the famous performance when the contralto Marietta Alboni took the baritone role of the Emperor Charles V. Salvi sang in New York in 1850, and in 1851 he made an American tour with Jenny Lind, under the astute management of P. T. Barnum. He retired shortly afterwards.

The singers were the soprano Giuseppina Strepponi, a leading Donizetti interpreter and a Milan favourite, and the baritone Giorgio Ronconi, also a Donizetti specialist and a popular artist, well-launched on a long career. Strepponi and Ronconi were to have performed Verdi's *Oberto*, for a benefit in favour of the Pio Istituto, a popular Milanese charity; Merelli, who was enjoying a profitable season, had cancelled the benefit, however, without even examining the score. Hearing the singers' praise, he decided to take a look at it.

Verdi, though the performance had been called off, was still in Milan, but, as he told Ricordi, he 'was thinking of going back to Busseto. Then, one morning a servant from the Teatro alla Scala comes to me and quite brusquely says: "Are you that Maestro from Parma who was supposed to give an opera for the Pio Istituto? . . . Come to the theatre, because the Impresario wants you." "Is that possible?" I interjected, and the man replied: "Yes, sir, he ordered me to call the Maestro from Parma. . . . If that is you, then come." And I went. . . .

'I then introduced myself to Merelli, who promptly told me that, after the favourable report he had received about my music, he would like to give it during the coming season. If I were to accept, however, I would have to make some adjustments to the tessitura, since there would not be all four of the artists previously present. It was a handsome offer: young, unknown, I came upon an impresario who dared stage a new work without asking me for any kind of indemnification—an indemnification which, for that matter, I would have been unable to give. Risking, on his own, all the expenses of the production, Merelli simply proposed that we divide half-and-half the sum I would make if, in the event of success, I sold the opera.'

As it turned out, Merelli did not make a bad deal. Verdi's *Oberto, conte di San Bonifazio*, first given on 17 November 1839, was a fair success (fourteen performances before the end of the season), and the well-established publisher Giovanni Ricordi bought the rights for 2,000 Austrian lire (not an immense sum: a few years earlier Verdi had been paying eighty Austrian lire for a month's lodging).

Verdi's and Margherita's two small children, Virginia and Icilio (characteristic Roman republican names, derived probably from a drama of Alfieri), died between his 1838 visit to Milan and the opening of *Oberto*. Margherita herself died of encephalitis in June of 1840. The expense-sheet of her 'private, second-class, solemn' funeral survives, listing the cost for 'transportation from house to church', 'black drapes on the benches around the grave', 'cross in the cemetery'; the total expenditure was 522.12 Milanese lire.

When Margherita died, Verdi was engaged in writing his second opera, the comic *Un giorno di regno*, whose first performance, at La Scala on 5 September 1840, was a crushing failure. According to his later autobiographical conversation with Ricordi, Verdi, in his despair, meant to abandon the theatre at this time, though documents now show he was actually composing music for revivals of *Oberto* in other cities. In any case, once his understandable dejection began to lighten, Verdi returned to the opera house, and with *Nabucco* (Scala, 9 March 1842), he achieved real fame and an established position: first local, then international. The following year he went to Vienna, at Merelli's urging, to stage *Nabucco* there.

For the next decade or so, Verdi's life—in its public aspects— is the typical story of a successful composer of the time. In some ways, it resembles the story of Donizetti's career: operas composed rapidly, season after season, frequent demands from singers for new arias to be inserted in old operas, commissions from various theatres, all requiring the composer's presence. And, along with this professional activity, there was the social life of Milan, which even the 'bear' Verdi could not completely dismiss. Taken up by music-loving Contessas, he frequented salons, receptions, banquets. He sat for portraits, and was interviewed for the papers.

But there are significant differences between Donizetti's career and Verdi's. More than his older colleague, Verdi paid great attention to the choice of his libretto subjects and to the

81. Ignazio Marini. Painting by Giovanni Carnovali ('Il Piccio'). *c.* 1840.

The bass Ignazio Marini (1811–73) made his Scala debut in a benefit performance in 1833, and the following year sang Oroveso to Malibran's Norma. He was then on the Scala roster almost uninterruptedly until 1847. He created the title role in Verdi's debut-opera *Oberto* in 1839 (like the other singers in that cast he came in for some harsh criticism from the press). He also took part in the first Scala performances of Verdi's *Ernani* (1844) and *Attila* (1846), only a few months after their premières in Venice. He sang at Covent Garden in 1847–9 and New York in 1850, then in Havana and St Petersburg, where in 1862 he created a small role (the Alcade) in the première of another Verdi work, *La forza del destino.* He retired in 1864.

Giovanni Carnovali (1804–73), known as 'Il Piccio', was born in the province of Varese, studied at the Brera in Milan, and opened a studio in that city in 1835. He painted many mythical and Biblical subjects, in a free, romantic style, but was also known for his portraits.

80. (*Left*) Announcement of autumn season at La Scala, 8 August 1842.

Verdi's *Nabucco* had its première on 9 March 1842, and was repeated then for 65 evenings. It was revived at the beginning of the so-called autumn season, on 13 August, with a slightly different cast. Giuseppina Strepponi, creator of the role of Abigaille, was absent, replaced by Teresa De Giuli Borsi (1817–77, later to create the role of Lida in *La battaglia di Legnano*). In the title role, instead of Giorgio Ronconi, there was the less well-known baritone Gaetano Ferri (b. 1819), later to create Egberto in *Aroldo*.

shaping and writing of the text. Almost from the start, he took control of the dramatic scheme, even of the selection of words. Singers, indeed, demanded new arias, but most of the time Verdi refused to accede to these demands (at the request of Rossini, he did compose, on two occasions, a new aria for the tenor Nicola Ivanoff, Rossini's close friend and protégé). After his sudden celebrity and the almost ruthless exploitation (on his own part as well) of his renown and his genius, Verdi gradually slowed the pace and composed his operas at greater and greater intervals, until—in his last years—he could write only to please himself, without contracts or deadlines.

The clearest, most vivid picture of the early, feverish years is found in the letters of Emanuele Muzio. Born in Busseto in 1825, Muzio—like Verdi—came from a poor family, and, also like Verdi, he was discovered and encouraged by Antonio Barezzi. With Barezzi's help, the boy was sent to Milan to study with Verdi, as Verdi had studied with Lavigna (who had not lived to see his protégé's success). Muzio was Verdi's only pupil (except perhaps for some piano students during his village music-master days in Busseto); and to the lonely, taciturn widower, he was also a companion, a sounding-board, an errand-boy, and a source of unstinting, unalloyed devotion and admiration.

Muzio's letters to Barezzi constitute a virtual diary of Verdi's life in the mid-1840s, and indirectly give a picture of operatic life in Milan and elsewhere.

20 May 1844: 'The Signor Maestro has received a letter from Maestro Donizetti which says that, having heard he cannot go to Vienna to superintend the rehearsals and performance of his *Ernani*, he [Donizetti] begs the Signor Maestro to grant him the favour of allowing him to supervise the rehearsals and conduct the performance.'

11 June 1844: 'Oh, sir, if you had been in the house of the Signor Maestro Verdi the day that the news of the very happy outcome [of the Vienna *Ernani*] arrived, to see for a full hour, first one man arrive, to whom Donizetti had written, then another who had received the news from some Count, I don't remember the surname, and then another who had news from Merelli, and so many more, there was no end. . . .

'The same *Ernani* is being prepared in Florence and in Genoa. . . .

'The Signor Maestro is composing full blast, and never leaves the house until towards evening, at the dinner hour [dinner, in the nineteenth century, was usually eaten around 6 p.m.].'

24 June 1844: 'On Saturday a singer came, and she wanted the Signor Maestro to write a contralto part for her into the opera he's composing for Rome [*I due Foscari*]. He said the libretto was already finished, and he can't. No matter, this woman said, just one scene, one appearance, a cabaletta. . . . It was laughable: he couldn't shake her from her determination; afterwards she wanted him to promise that he would at least write a part for her in the Carnival season opera [*Giovanna d'Arco*]. The Signor Maestro, who was losing his patience, said: No, no. And she went away.'

Barezzi, after all, was a businessman; and Muzio realized the importance to him of Verdi's material success. The letters, therefore, contain a certain amount of financial information. Six days after the letter about the stubborn contralto, Muzio wrote: 'Just guess, Sir, to how many theatres Ricordi has already supplied the score of *Ernani*? More than twenty . . . the Signor Maestro drives music publishers crazy, he really does. The publisher Lucca at the moment is the craziest of all, because he can't have the ownership of an opera by the Signor Maestro, while he sees Ricordi making huge earnings, since just for the rental of the copies of the *Ernani* score (to say nothing of the numerous arrangements) he has taken in more than 30,000 Austrian lire.'

The following year Verdi finally wrote an opera for Lucca, *Il corsaro*, not, as it proved, a great money-spinner. Muzio naturally reported to Barezzi how Lucca had bought the score from the impresario Lanari for 13,000 Austrian lire, and added: 'The same

Lanari wants to sign up the Signor Maestro again for Rome; and today the Signor Maestro wrote him that he will not compose it for one centesimo less than *nine hundred* little gold Napoleons.'

Felice Romani had finally married Emilia Branca, in 1844; but her father's salon was still a centre of Milanese musical life, as it had been when Donizetti was in the city. Early in January 1845, Muzio reported: 'Next week, at the Brancas', they are having a historical-musical concert, beginning with Palestrina, Lillo, Lulli, etc., down to the greatest of modern pieces, the *trio of Ernani*, which will close the concert; the greatest artists and dilettantes of Milan will take part.'

Once in a while, Muzio sent Barezzi information, gossip or anecdotes not directly concerned with the Signor Maestro. Thus, on 6 March 1845, he reported the latest news from the opera house: 'At La Scala we also had a grand ballet, which people like very much, and it is staged with an amazing sumptuousness; in one act of the ballet the stage is converted into the Gran Teatro della Fenice, illuminated for a ball; with such a various number of costumes it's amazing. . . . Last night, when they were at the moment of unmasking, a piece of scenery fell as the beam supporting it broke, and three or four dancers were trapped under the canvas. People feared for their lives, but luckily they only bruised their backs a little. The curtain was rung down; and then they went on. The ladies witnessing the performance took a great fright; and it is said that one of them (in her fear) gave birth to a baby girl. It really was a frightening thing.'

In 1842 at its Scala première *Nabucco*—especially the chorus 'Va, pensiero'—had aroused patriotic enthusiasm; the following year, the choruses in *I lombardi* had produced the same effect. Nevertheless, describing the political situation in the city at this time, Massimo d'Azeglio wrote in his memoirs about: '. . . the subtle skill with which the Austrian authorities, themselves perhaps bent on making a comfortable bed in an agreeable, rich, fat and jolly city, knew how to dampen, to soften orders from Vienna and to allow (excepting, of course, any overt acts) the widest freedom to the Milanese to grumble, to taunt the *pollini* (police spies), to express their definitive opinions not only on the performance at La Scala but also on politics. It was enough not to yell too loud; with prudence you could say everything. And at the Caffè Martini they talked quite freely about the Government, the police, etc. But, it must be added, if meanwhile either Signor Bolza [chief of the Austrian police in Milan] or Signor Galimberti appeared, then the subject of conversation was promptly, radically changed.'

It was this mildness, no doubt, that permitted Verdi to express his—and his compatriots'—Italian feelings. And as his operas spread through the country, his music—and Verdi himself—gradually became synonymous with the spirit of the Risorgimento. Most of Italy, even fat, torpid Milan, began to press for freedom and unification. The election of Pope Pius IX in 1846,

82. Verdi in Paris in the 1850s. Photograph by André Adolphe Disderi.
Some time in the 1850s, while Verdi was in Paris, he went to the studio of the photographer Disderi and sat for a series of eight portraits, of which this is one. Verdi clearly was pleased with some of the results, for he gave prints of several of the portraits to his friends.

to succeed the reactionary Gregory XVI, briefly raised the patriots' hopes. Among Pius's first public expressions were the words, pronounced from the loggia of the Vatican: 'Gran Dio, benedite l'Italia!' They could have been taken from a Verdi libretto.

The Pope's amnesty, granted to political prisoners in the Papal States, also had a Verdian ring; Muzio wrote to Barezzi on 13 August 1846: 'In Bologna, on the occasion of the publication of the amnesty, they performed in the theatre the *Ernani* finale ('O sommo Carlo')—they changed the name from Carlo to Pio—and such was the enthusiasm that it was repeated three times. When they came to the words 'Perdono a tutti' [Pardon for all], cheers exploded on all sides.'

Even in the south of Italy, slower to stir in the cause of unification, the opera house was the focus of patriotism, despite more severe repression. In 1848, as Sir Harold Acton has written: 'Public demonstrations in Palermo resembled those in Naples except that loud cheers for independence were added. The first occurred during a performance of Donizetti's *Gemma di Vergy* at the Teatro Carolino. When the 'faithful slave' sang the moving aria: "Mi togliesti e core e mente,/Patria, Numi e libertà" [You took away from me my heart and soul,/Fatherland, Gods, and freedom], the whole audience rose automatically, waving handkerchiefs and shouting: "Long live the Pope, the King, and the Italian league!" Again, when the prima donna Parodi appeared on the stage with a tricoloured flag to sing "It is already the first dawn of the new year", a shower of leaflets fluttered over the pit and there were frantic cries of *Viva l'Italia*.'

Acton also quotes the journal of Lord Mount-Edgecumbe, who was present: 'Though universally and eagerly joined in by all classes from the highest to the lowest, they both [leaflets and cries] quickly terminated without the slightest violation of order, unless indeed the act of pelting with cushions one in authority at the theatre till he joined in the cry (having locked him up in his box), may be so termed; which it hardly can be, as immediately on his doing so, the greatest good humour was restored.'

In his early years in Milan Verdi had associated with members of the pro-Austrian nobility and had dedicated his fourth opera, *I lombardi*, to Napoleon's widow, Marie-Louise, then the Grand Duchess of Parma. (*Oberto* had been dedicated to her consort, Count Neipperg.) The composer had, however, certainly been influenced by the progressive, anti-clerical ideas of his patron Barezzi and of the whole Jacobin faction in Busseto that centred around the Filarmonici and the Barezzi living-room, a spacious and comfortable place for making music and also for discussing politics.

Verdi's choice of a libretto like *Nabucco* may have been inspired by its moving dramatic situations more than by its thinly-veiled nationalistic fervour. With *I lombardi*, the political motivation on Verdi's part was obviously deliberate. And, for some years afterwards, even in less political operas, some patriotic reference was almost always inserted, as the chorus 'O patria oppressa' in *Macbeth*.

If the obliging censors in Milan seldom made trouble, censors in other Italian cities were much more rigid and interfering. In Naples, the authorities were no longer chiefly concerned about avoiding offence to the deep religious sentiments of the sovereigns: now political matters also had to be strictly avoided. And the Papal censors in Rome were even more implacable. Thus, when Verdi's *Giovanna d'Arco*, after its Scala première in 1845, moved to the Teatro Argentina in Rome that same year, the libretto was completely re-cast, even though the heroine,

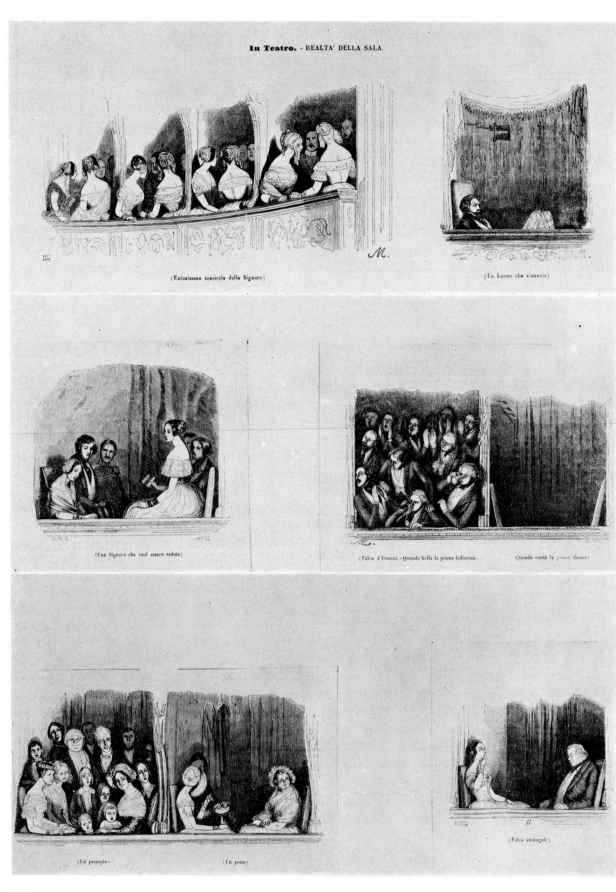

In Teatro. – REALTA' DELLA SALA.

(Entusiasmo musicale delle Signore)

(Un Leone che s'annoia)

(Una Signora che vuol essere veduta)

(Palco d'Uomini. - Quando balla la prima ballerina.

Quando canta la prima donna)

(Un presepio)

(Un pozzo)

(Palco coniugale)

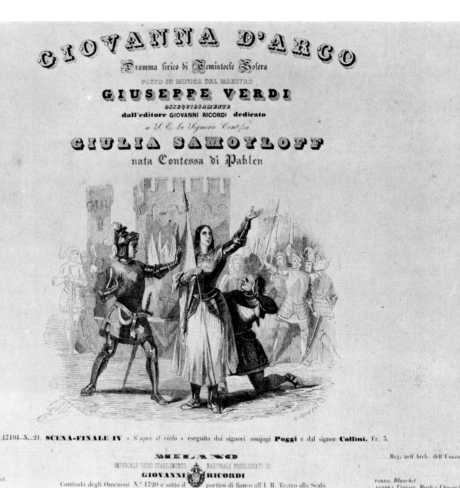

GIOVANNA D'ARCO

Dramma lirico di Temistocle Solera

POSTO IN MUSICA DAL MAESTRO

GIUSEPPE VERDI

ossequiosamente
dall'editore GIOVANNI RICORDI dedicato

a S. E. la Signora Contessa

GIULIA SAMOYLOFF

nata Contessa di Pahlen

17191-N.-21. **SCENA-FINALE IV** - *S'apre il cielo* - eseguita dai signori conjugi **Poggi** e dal signor **Collini.** Fr. 5.

Proprietà degli Editori.   MILANO   Reg. nell'Arch. dell'Unione.

IMPERIALE REGIO STABILIMENTO NAZIONALE PRIVILEGIATO DI
GIOVANNI RICORDI

FIRENZE, G. Ricordi e Jouhaud.   Contrada degli Omenoni N.º 1720 e sotto il   portico di fianco all'I. R. Teatro alla Scala.   PARIGI, Blanchet.
MENDRISIO, C. Pozzi.   LONDRA, Cramer, Beale e Chappell.

84. Verdi's *Giovanna d'Arco.* Frontispiece of vocal score, 1845.
The production of his *Giovanna d'Arco* at La Scala (where it opened on 15 February 1845) caused Verdi considerable anguish, and the situation backstage cannot have helped matters. The tenor Antonio Poggi, who was to create the role of Carlo, had also had a disagreement with Merelli and, further, was about to separate from his wife, the soprano Erminia Frezzolini (the first Giovanna), who was no doubt irked by her husband's notorious liaison with the rich and eccentric Countess Giulia Samoyloff (to whom Verdi, somewhat tactlessly, dedicated the score). However, *Giovanna d'Arco* was a success.

83. (*Left*) Three types of spectator. Cartoons from *Il mondo illustrato*, 1849. Opera audiences—like operas—have always been a fertile source of ammunition for cartoonists. Here, in 1849, a Milanese paper lampoons various types of opera-goer: (upper row) 'Ladies' musical enthusiasm' and 'A bored lion'; (middle row) 'A lady who wants to be seen', 'Men's box when the prima ballerina is dancing', 'The same, when the prima donna is singing'; (bottom row) 'A creche', 'A well' (the Italians refer to an omniscient person as a 'well of learning', and the older lady looking at the stage seems to fit the description), 'Conjugal box'.

Joan of Arc, was still seventy-five years away from canonization. Under the title *Orietta di Lesbo*, the opera was now set on the Greek island in an unspecified period, and Joan's passion to free her country from foreign servitude was altogether less impelling. Needless to say, all references to the Virgin in the original libretto were expunged, and, as usual, such exclamations as 'Dio' modified into the less dangerous 'Cielo'.

Verdi was to have still more serious conflicts with censors later, at the stage in his career which coincided with the final, most bitter and blood-stained phase of the Risorgimento. But, by then, the problems Verdi created for the authorities were not only political; they were also moral. Arousing fervent nationalistic spirits was bad enough; shocking the more and more predominantly bourgeois opera audience was almost worse. And the mature Verdi did both.

In these years, the 1840s and the early 1850s, Verdi was much concerned also with making money. He had been born into a poor family, his father a shopkeeper and small-scale farmer; it was a family, moreover, that had come down in the world. And Verdi was determined not only to make his own fortune, but also to recoup the position of the family. From the very beginning of his activity, he was to prove a good manager, a shrewd, even

sharp, businessman. In 1843, in dealing with La Fenice in Venice, where he had been invited to compose a new opera (it was to be *Ernani*) and supervise the Venice première of an 'old' one, presented earlier that year at La Scala, he wrote to the management: 'I will stage *I lombardi*, I will write the new opera, leaving the score entirely to the Management. I will have the libretto written at my own expense, and the Management or Society will pay me 12,000 (twelve thousand) Austrian lire. Or else the ownership of the score will remain mine, the other conditions being the same, and I will be paid 6,000 (six thousand) Austrian lire.'

At a certain point, in 1845, Verdi and his publisher Ricordi had some differences (they would have more in the future), and so Verdi offered his next opera to Lucca, Ricordi's rival.

'I commit myself,' Verdi wrote to Lucca, 'to compose for you an opera to be performed in an Italian theatre with a first-class company in the carnival season of 1848. . . . In compensation you will pay me 1,200 (one thousand two hundred) gold napoleons of twenty francs, in four instalments.'

At the same time, however, Verdi was writing to a friend: 'I cannot wait for these next three years to pass. I have to compose six operas, and then: farewell to it all.'

Verdi was, indeed, a clever manager, a great composer, but in this case, a poor prophet. His career was to continue for almost another half-century.

85. Teatro Gallo (Teatro di San Benedetto), Venice, *c.* 1850.
Venice was the first city to have—in 1629— a public opera house (until then opera had been the private entertainment of rulers and nobles). In 1821 the illustrious Teatro di San Benedetto was re-baptized the Teatro Gallo, when it was taken over by the impresario Giovanni Gallo. A later member of the same family, Antonio Gallo, was the impresario of the house a generation later. After the unhappy première of *La traviata* at the Fenice in 1853, Gallo was determined to revive the opera in his own theatre. The revised *Traviata* was presented at the Teatro Gallo on 6 May 1854, and was an overwhelming success, a vindication of Verdi and of the impresario. In 1868 the theatre changed names again and became the Teatro Rossini; it still stands, though subsequent remodellings have altered the appearance of the house almost totally since Gallo's day.

Chapter 7

VERDI made his first long trip abroad in 1847, when he was thirty-four. His destination was London, where he had been commissioned to write a new work, *I masnadieri* (The Bandits), for Her Majesty's Theatre. The metropolis he found was quite a different city from the Paris of Rossini, Bellini and Donizetti, which had also been the Paris of George Sand and Mürger. England's young queen and her consort had already firmly established the tone of their capital. Opera—which had been popular in London since Handel's day—was still an occasion of pleasure, but it was also a vehicle of culture. It is significant that on this occasion Verdi chose a libretto based on Schiller (*Die Räuber*) and had it written by a distinguished poet, Andrea Maffei, the composer's close friend and Schiller's Italian translator. Verdi's leading lady was to be Jenny Lind, that model of Nordic respectability, soon to be taken up by Her Majesty in person.

This was Lind's first London season, but like Verdi she was already internationally famous. Having sent Muzio ahead of him, the composer reached the city in mid-June. But the loquacious Muzio had already sent Barezzi his impressions of the city: 'Milan is nothing; Paris is something, compared to London; but London is a city unique in the world. Just imagine: almost two million inhabitants; then you can imagine what an immense city this is. To go from one end of the city to the other you have to pass three post-stations and change horses three times.'

Muzio complained that the English spoke no French (there is no evidence that, at the time, he spoke any himself), but fortunately 'the high society of the Lords' all spoke Italian, having been to Italy on pleasure tours. Knowing Barezzi's musical interests and competence, he also described the star soprano, giving at the same time an idea of the London repertory:

'I have heard la Lind in *La figlia del reggimento*, in *La sonnambula*, in *Roberto il diavolo*, and I must say she is an artist in every sense of the word. She is great in all three of the above-mentioned operas. In *Roberto il diavolo* she cannot be equalled. Her voice is a bit harsh at the top, weak at the bottom, but through study she has made it supple at the top so as to perform the most abstruse difficulties. Her trill cannot be surpassed; she has an unparalleled agility, and in general, to display the bravura

86. Marianna Barbieri Nini. Her obituary describes the soprano Marianna Barbieri Nini (*c.* 1820–87) in these terms: 'small and fat, ill-formed, with a huge head twice life size, she had a face that was hardly designed to win fondness at first sight'. Because of this physical handicap, she was said to prefer the role of Donizetti's Lucrezia Borgia, which allowed her to sing her opening scene wearing a mask. In any case, from about 1840 on, she was a star of the first magnitude in Italy. Verdi had originally written the role of Lady Macbeth in his *Macbeth* (1847) for Sophie Loewe, the first Elvira in his *Ernani* and the first Odabella in his *Attila*; but Loewe became unavailable and was replaced by Barbieri Nini, who—after taxing rehearsals under the martinet Verdi—enjoyed an overwhelming success.

of her singing she sings in fioriture, in gruppetti, in trills: things which pleased in the last century, but not in 1847. We Italians are not used to this style; and if la Lind were to come to Italy, she would give up this mania of hers for embellishments and would sing simply.'

Verdi arrived in London when the city was in the midst of an operatic war; his arrival, indeed, was part of a major campaign. The previous season, the conductor at Her Majesty's Theatre, Michele (later Sir Michael) Costa, had left the company, and had moved to the newly-reopened Covent Garden, now re-christened the Royal Italian Opera House. With him, Costa had taken an array of star singers, among them the tenor Mario, his wife the soprano Giulia Grisi, and the baritone Antonio Tamburini (of the 'Puritani quartet' a decade earlier), as well as many of the best players from the orchestra. They had been joined by the soprano Fanny Persiani (creator of *Lucia*) and the great Verdian baritone Giorgio Ronconi (creator of *Nabucco*). For its ballet troupe the Covent Garden company could boast the internationally famous Fanny Elssler.

88. (*Opposite, top left*) L'elisir d'amore, Paris, 1839.
After its première at the Teatro della Canobbiana in Milan in 1832, Donizetti's opera was given all over Italy. At the Naples première, in the spring of 1834, Fanny Tacchinardi-Persiani sang the role of Adina, which she repeated in Paris on 17 January 1839, when the opera opened at the Théâtre Italien. Here she is seen with the baritone Antonio Tamburini, her Belcore.

89. (*Opposite, top right*) Mario and Grisi in *Lucrezia Borgia* at Covent Garden, 1847.
The aristocratic Giovanni Matteo Mario, cavaliere di Candia (1810–83), sang under the name of Mario, simply. With his wife Giulia Grisi (1811–69), he performed often in Paris and also in London, where both husband and wife were immensely popular. Mario made his London debut, at Her Majesty's Theatre in 1839, as Gennaro in Donizetti's *Lucrezia Borgia*. He sang the same role, opposite Grisi, at Covent Garden in 1847, during the brilliant season when Verdi presented his *I masnadieri*, with Jenny Lind, at Her Majesty's, for the rival impresario.

90. (*Opposite, below left*) Jenny Lind in *The Daughter of the Regiment*, at Her Majesty's Theatre, London, 1847.
In her first London season, in addition to creating the role of Amalia in Verdi's *I masnadieri*, Jenny Lind also introduced Donizetti's *La figlia del reggimento* (Paris, 1840). As the impresario Benjamin Lumley says, in his *Reminiscences of the Opera*: 'The acting of Jenny Lind, as the simple-minded and impulsive *Vivandière*, struggling against the trammels of conventional 'fine-lady' life, again made a lively impression, whilst the warmth and feeling with which she sang . . . established the character as another of Jenny's triumphs.'

91. (*Opposite, below right*) Il trovatore in London, 1856. Lucy Escott, Henri Doughton, A. Brahm.
The first British performances of *Il trovatore* took place at Covent Garden in May, 1855. The work was immediately popular and was mounted in a production with British artists, illustrated here. The Leonora was Lucy Escott, who had been singing previously in Italy, especially in Naples, where she had become a friend, interpreter, and partisan of Mercadante. She left some amusing memoirs of the Mercadante-Verdi rivalry in Naples at that time.

87. (*Left*) Giulia Grisi as Donizetti's *Anna Bolena*.
This is the scene in Act II after the Queen's death sentence has been pronounced. 'Cease!' she says to Henry, who repeats his accusations of adultery: 'At this wicked charge, I recover my dignity', and she accuses him of lying.

92. Fanny Persiani as Lucia, 1835.
The soprano Fanny Tacchinardi-Persiani (1812–67) was the daughter of a popular tenor, Nicola Tacchinardi, admired interpreter of Cimarosa, Paer, and, finally, Rossini. Fanny's early repertory included Rossini's *Tancredi* and *La gazza ladra* and Bellini's *Il pirata*, *Beatrice di Tenda*, and *La sonnambula*. She sang Donizetti's *L'elisir d'amore* at La Fenice in Venice and at the Carcano in Milan, after which the composer selected her to create his *Rosmonda d'Inghilterra* (1834). The following year, at the San Carlo in Naples, she created the title role in his *Lucia di Lammermoor*, which she repeated in 1837 at the Théâtre Italien, where she sang almost every season thereafter until 1850. She also sang often in London, first (1838–46) at Her Majesty's, then—after the famous 'secession' of that theatre's artists—at Covent Garden, where her husband, the composer Giuseppe Persiani, was one of the impresarios (according to some accounts, he had as little talent for management as he had for composition). Her special repertory—Lucia, Adina, Rosina, Susanna, and Linda di Chamounix—was taken over by younger singers, forming virtually a distinct category, the 'soprano lirico leggero', whose later exponents were Adelina Patti, Amelita Galli-Curci, Toti Dal Monte, and others.

93. (*Right*) Luigi Lablache as Dr Dulcamara. Although Lablache did not create the role of Dulcamara in Donizetti's *L'elisir d'amore* at its première (Teatro della Canobbiana, Milan, 12 May 1832), he became one of its most celebrated interpreters. The character of the wily, wise quack doctor was ideally suited to the comic gifts of the great Neapolitan bass. He was not only a comedian, however. Verdi so admired his dramatic powers, especially in the role of Massimiliano Moor in *I masnadieri* (which Lablache created at Her Majesty's Theatre, London, on 22 July 1847) that he thought of Lablache for the title role in a *Lear* which he contemplated but never completed. Lablache's fame was international. Schubert dedicated three *Lieder* to him; he was invited to sing in the Mozart *Requiem* at Beethoven's funeral. Wagner praised Lablache's Leporello and wrote an aria for the bass to insert in *Norma* (Lablache politely declined). As he lay dying in Naples, he said to his daughter: 'Cecchina, I have no voice left; I die.'

At Her Majesty's, the manager, Benjamin Lumley, was obviously in trouble; but Lumley was of the resourceful breed of Barbaja and Merelli, and he fought back. In addition to commissioning a brand-new opera from Verdi (the first time the composer was writing a work expressly for a non-Italian theatre), Lumley took considerable pains to lure la Lind into making her British debut. And he also extracted a promise of an opera from Mendelssohn, a promise not kept, since the German composer had only a few months to live. From Lumley's old company, the great, indeed huge bass Luigi Lablache remained loyal. And for his ballet the impresario had not only Carlotta Grisi, cousin of the soprano, but also Marie Taglioni, both rivalling Elssler in reputation.

1859

FIGURINI dell' Opera RIGOLETTO del Maestro G. VERDI

Understandably, both companies—Her Majesty's and Covent Garden—did well (although Muzio gleefully reported some empty houses at the Royal Italian Opera). And so London enjoyed, for the next five years, the luxury of two excellent Italian opera companies.

The first 'cellist of Lumley's orchestra was the Italian musician Alfredo Piatti, who although only twenty-five years old was known throughout Europe. The Overture of *I masnadieri* thus includes an extended 'cello solo, making the piece virtually a small concerto for that instrument. With Lind in mind, Verdi also wrote some difficult, florid arias, giving the Swedish nightingale ample opportunity to show off her trills and gruppetti.

While waiting for his première (and completing the orchestration of his opera), Verdi went to Her Majesty's almost every night, since—as Muzio duly reported—'Lumley gave him a box in the row of the great nobility'. The composer was, no doubt, studying his singers; but the audience took the opportunity to study him. Even the Queen and Prince Albert trained their opera-glasses on him.

But Verdi and Muzio also followed the rivals' activity. Muzio wrote to Barezzi on 29 June 1847: 'On Saturday at Covent Garden they are doing *Ernani*, and la Alboni (contralto) will sing Carlo V. In London contralto and bass are the same thing.' Verdi would hardly have agreed with this substitution, but at that time he had no power to control productions of his earlier works.

The première of *I masnadieri* at Her Majesty's took place on 22 July, and Muzio wrote to his patron the very next day, showing a certain confusion about royal titles and relations: 'The opera created a furore. From the Prelude to the last-act finale there was nothing but applause, cheers, encores, and curtain-calls. . . . The Queen and Prince Albert, her consort [were present], the Queen Mother, and the Duke of Cambridge, the Queen's uncle, the Prince of Wales, the Queen's son, and all the Royal family, and infinite Lords and Dukes. . . . At four-thirty the door was opened, and people burst into the theatre with a fury never seen before. . . . The theatre's receipts were 6,000 lire, and it surpassed everything that they have taken in, including the evening when the Queen was there in grand gala.'

The Queen, that same evening, wrote privately in her journal: '. . . The music is very inferior & commonplace. Lablache acted the part of Maximilian Moor, in which he looked fine, but too fat . . . Gardoni acted the part of Carlo Moor & was beautifully dressed. Lind sang & acted most exquisitely as Amelia & looked very well & attractive in her several dresses. She was immensely applauded.'

Some years later, in writing his *Reminiscences of the Opera*, Lumley justified his Verdi commission: 'The opera was given with every appearance of a triumphant success: the composer and all the singers receiving the highest honours. . . . But yet the "Masnadieri" could not be considered a success. That by its

94. (*Page 132*) Veglione al Teatro alla Scala. Illustrated calendar, 1859.
Although 1859 was a year of tension and, finally, warfare, it was ushered in by the traditional *veglione*, or New Year's Eve rout, at La Scala. Milan had its share of left-wing revolutionaries, followers of Mazzini; but the city's major opera house was a gathering-place for the more moderate forces. Coincidentally, 1859 was also the year in which Verdi's *Un ballo in maschera* had its première, at the Teatro Apollo in Rome. This lithograph could also be an illustration of the opera's last scene.

95. (*Previous page*) Costumes for *Rigoletto*, 1851. These designs, for the first production of *Rigoletto* at the Teatro La Fenice on 11 March 1851, were published, at about the same time, by Ricordi, evidently to serve as a guide for the other opera houses which were prompt to mount the new work.

production I had adopted the right course, was unquestionable. I had induced an Italian composer, whose reputation stood on the highest pinnacle of continental fame, to compose an opera expressly for my theatre, as well as to superintend its production. More I could not have done. . . . To Her Majesty's Theatre the work was singularly ill-suited. The interest which ought to have been centred in Mademoiselle Lind was centred in [the tenor] Gardoni; whilst Lablache, as the imprisoned father, had to do about the only thing he could not do to perfection—having to represent a man nearly starved to death.'

Verdi, after conducting the third performance, left London for Paris, where he arrived on 27 July 1847. For just over a year the French capital was to be the composer's home: an important period, for it was during these months that he began to live openly with Giuseppina Strepponi. The soprano, now retired from the stage, was a successful voice teacher in Paris; Verdi had known her at least since the days of *Nabucco*, in which she created the role of Abigaille, and they had probably been lovers for three or four years. Now their relationship was sealed. Though they were not legally married until 1859, they lived together from now on, until Giuseppina's death fifty years later.

In Paris Verdi lived through the revolution of 1848 and the downfall of Louis-Philippe, and there he learned of the uprising in Milan, the *Cinque Giornate*, during which the Austrians were driven from the city. In August of that same year, however, the Austrians were back. Verdi, in Paris, had tried to arouse the republican government to support the Milanese, but his efforts—combined with those of other Italian expatriates—were in vain. And on the 24th of that August, he wrote to his old friend Countess Maffei, who had been forced to take refuge in Switzerland, along with her companion Carlo Tenca and other patriot friends:

'You want to know the opinion of France on Italian affairs? My God, what a thing you're asking of me!! Those who are not opposed are indifferent: I would further add that the idea of *Italian Unity* frightens these little men, these nullities who are in power. France will surely not intervene with arms, unless some event impossible to foresee drags her in despite herself. Franco-English diplomatic intervention can only be evil, shameful for France, and ruinous for us. . . . For that matter France is in an abyss, and I do not know how she will emerge from it. The inquisition being made on the events of May and June is the most base and revolting thing that exists. What a wretched, pigmy period! Nothing great: not even the crimes!'

Much as he hated writing occasional pieces, Verdi—at the personal request of Mazzini—wrote some music for an anthem with words by Goffredo Mameli, a Risorgimento hero, who was to die of wounds, in July of the following year, shouting 'Viva l'Italia'. Verdi's music reached Mazzini after the armistice and so served little purpose.

96. *Otello*, Act I. Set design. Carlo Ferrario (1833–1907) and/or Giovanni Zuccarelli (1846–97).

The story of the sets for the first production of Verdi's *Otello* is complex and confused. Originally, the designer was to have been Carlo Ferrario, who had worked regularly at La Scala for a number of years and had designed, among other things, the handsome sets for the revised versions of *La forza del destino* and *Don Carlos*. But at some point during the preparation of *Otello*, Ferrario had a quarrel with the Scala management and resigned his position. The younger Zuccarelli—also a Scala regular—was commissioned to take over. Verdi, however, admired Ferrario's work and insisted that he be called back. He was. The theatre programme for *Otello* tactfully credits both designers, though it seems likely that Ferrario was responsible for the actual realization of the sets, working from sketches made by Zuccarelli. This sketch differs, in fact, from the engravings of the first act as actually seen on the night of 5 February 1887. In the production, for example, the castle at left was somewhat less prominent, while the pergola—here barely visible, far left—was much larger.

97. (*Right*) Giovanni Battista Rubini in Rossini's *Otello*, Paris.

Half a century before Verdi's *Otello*, when Rubini appeared in Rossini's opera on the Othello story at the Italien in 1839, one of his critics was the twenty-nine-year-old Alfred de Musset, who wrote: 'With his admirable talent, [Rubini] is a divine singer, but too lazy as an actor.' But this defect, assuming Musset was right, did not lessen his popularity with the French audience. Admired as a technician, he concealed—according to the Escudier brothers—'the artifice of breathing so admirably that, in the longest phrases, it was impossible to tell the moment when he drew breath.'

98. Francesco Maria Piave.
Piave (1810–76) was born on the island of Murano, near Venice, where he spent his early life. He made his debut as a librettist with *Ernani* (1844) for Verdi, with whom he formed a fruitful working partnership and a close friendship. Piave was the docile junior partner in the team, and their friendship did not prevent Verdi from criticizing Piave severely on occasion. Still, when others attacked Piave's writing, Verdi loyally defended it; and the two men worked together on a long series of operas that included, after *Ernani*, *I due Foscari* (1844), *Macbeth* (1847), *Il corsaro* (1848), *Stiffelio* (1850), *Rigoletto* (1851), *La traviata* (1853), *Simon Boccanegra* (1857), *Aroldo* (1857), and *La forza del destino* (1862). In 1846, when the librettist Temistocle Solera left the text of *Attila* for Verdi unfinished, Piave completed it. He also wrote librettos for Balfe, Mercadante, Ricci, and others. In 1859 he moved from Venice to Milan, where he taught and also acted as stage director at La Scala. In 1869 he was paralysed by a stroke; Verdi then contributed to the support of the Piave family, even after the poet's death.

In that eventful summer of 1848, Verdi's thoughts were mostly political. 'It seems to me ridiculous to concern myself with . . . music', he wrote to his librettist Piave. But, in the same letter, he added: 'If I asked you to write me a libretto, would you do it?'

Whether the idea was ridiculous or not, the composer went on to expound his ideas to the poet: 'The subject should be Italian and free, and if you cannot find something better, I suggest to you *Ferruccio* [i.e. Francesco Ferrucci, 1489–1530, Florentine captain and patriot], a gigantic character, one of the great martyrs of Italian freedom. Guerrazzi's *L'assedio di Firenze* could supply you with great scenes, but I would like you to stick close to history. . . . I would like to have on stage the Priori, that is to say the Senate of Florence, and I would like Clement VII to take a drubbing, without having him appear, however.'

In the end the subject of Verdi's 'Italian and free' opera was not Ferrucci and the librettist was not Piave. The work was *La battaglia di Legnano*. The subject had been suggested some time earlier by the Neapolitan librettist Salvatore Cammarano, who had written the poem of *Alzira* for Verdi and was later to write *Luisa Miller* and *Il trovatore* (he had written librettos for numerous other composers, among them Donizetti, for whom he pre-

99. Salvatore Cammarano.
Salvatore Cammarano (1801–52) came from a remarkable Neapolitan family of writers, painters, and actors. He was a remarkable man himself, though noted for his vagueness and his reluctance to work. Still, he managed to produce a number of librettos and was much admired by critics and composers, including Verdi, for whom he wrote *Alzira*, *Luisa Miller*, *La battaglia di Legnano*, and *Il trovatore* (which he had nearly completed at his death). He wrote librettos also for other composers, among them Donizetti, for whom Cammarano prepared the text of *Lucia di Lammermoor*.

pared *Lucia*). Cammarano was a chronically slow (and over-worked) writer, and he completed the libretto only in October of 1848. On 20 December Verdi left for Rome, where the opera was to be staged early in the new year.

Unusually, Verdi had written this opera on his own initiative, without a contract for a specific theatre (the events of 1848 and the turmoil in Naples had allowed him to wriggle out of an unwanted commitment to the San Carlo). In May of 1847, long before the libretto was completed, Verdi had offered the opera to Ricordi for 12,000 francs (600 gold napoleons), plus 4,000 francs for the first season, and thereafter, for the next ten years, 300 francs for every season in countries where author's rights were respected, after which the opera would become Ricordi's property outright. Verdi had made another bold step forward in the control and exploitation of his work. At odds by now with the theatre that had seen his debut, Verdi added also a special condition: 'This opera will not be performed at the Teatro alla Scala without my permission.' He also decreed that no theatre was allowed to mutilate or change the opera in any way (even by raising or lowering the key of an aria—a condition impossible to enforce today, as it was then). Verdi was feeling the power of his fame.

100. (*Far left*) *Parsifal.* Chromolithograph
poster by Giuseppe Palanti.
For many years after Wagner's death, his
widow Cosima, respecting the composer's
wishes, prohibited any performance of
Parsifal outside the Bayreuth Festspielhaus,
for which it was composed. The copyright
did not expire until 1913, but in 1903 the
Metropolitan Opera in New York flouted
it, and a staged production was conducted
by Alfred Hertz. That same year Toscanini,
respecting Cosima's veto, conducted a
concert performance at La Scala of the
Prelude and Act III. This poster was issued
on that occasion. The protagonist of the
Toscanini performance was the Italian tenor
Giuseppe Borgatti, a great Wagner
interpreter in those days when German
operas were given in Italy always in Italian
translation.

101. (*Middle left*) *Cristoforo Colombo.*
Chromolithograph poster
Commissioned by the city of Genoa to
celebrate the four-hundredth anniversary of
the discovery of America, Franchetti's opera
about the city's most famous son, on a
libretto by Illica, was first performed at the
Teatro Carlo Felice on 6 October 1892.
Alberto Franchetti (1860–1942), a rich
eccentric, had an honourable career,
boasting several successes, among them
Germania (1902) and *La figlia di Jorio*
(1906, based on the D'Annunzio play of
1903). He is most frequently recalled in
histories of opera, however, for his
generosity in ceding the libretto of *Tosca* to
Puccini and that of *Andrea Chénier* to
Giordano.

102. (*Near left*) *La fanciulla del West* by
Giacomo Puccini. Chromolithograph poster
by Giuseppe Palanti.
Puccini's 'Far-West' opera, based on a play
by David Belasco, had its world première at
the Metropolitan Opera House, New York,
on 10 December 1910. Toscanini
conducted, and the cast was headed by
Emmy Destinn, Enrico Caruso, and
Pasquale Amato. The opera had its Italian
première, at the Teatro Costanzi in Rome,
the following June, when this poster was
published by Ricordi. *La fanciulla del West*
reached La Scala on 29 December 1912,
conducted by Tullio Serafin, with Ernestina
Poli-Randaccio, Giovanni Martinelli, and
Carlo Galeffi. The poster reproduces the
famous poker-game scene in Act II.

So now Verdi and Ricordi could decide for themselves which theatre was the right one to present the new work. Rome was the obvious choice. While the northern Italian cities, by the end of 1848, were once again under Austrian control, Rome was still in a state of revolution. Republican factions had assassinated Pellegrino Rossi, the much-disliked minister of Pius IX: he had been stabbed by the son of Ciceruacchio, as Angelo Brunetti was called, a hero of the Roman populace. The Pope, forced to disband his Swiss guards, had remained a virtual prisoner in his own city, until he managed to flee in November of 1848 and take refuge in the fortress of Gaeta, in the Kingdom of the Two Sicilies (twelve years later the last Bourbon king of Naples would spend his final days of quasi-rule in the same fortress).

And so, on 27 January 1849, a few days before the proclamation of the short-lived Roman Republic, *La battaglia di Legnano* had its première at the Teatro Argentina, the same cramped, dingy house where *Il barbiere di Siviglia* had been performed for the first time thirty-three seasons earlier. This, too, was a stormy occasion, but for different and not entirely musical reasons.

The work's reception was delirious. The proprietors of the boxes adorned them with tricoloured ribbons and patriotic mottoes. The men wore tricolour cockades in their buttonholes, and the ladies wore them in their hair. The capacity audience applauded every number of the work, often before it had come to an end. The entire fourth act had to be repeated. One officer, after yelling himself hoarse with cries of 'Bis, bis! Out with the flags!', threw his sabre, epaulettes and army greatcoat onto the stage, and would have thrown himself after them, if he had not been restrained, or rather, arrested.

The opera's subsequent fate was inevitably affected by the course of history. From exile, the Pope had called on the Catholic powers to save his reign. The Austrians, busy with the fractious Milanese and Venetians, could lend no help; but France, though a republic, was eager to assert herself on the peninsula. French forces laid siege to Rome; and despite the heroic resistance led by Garibaldi, the Roman Republic had to surrender on 30 June 1849. The Pope was brought back; and *La battaglia di Legnano* did not reappear in Rome for some years thereafter.

After the opening of his opera, Verdi had gone back to Paris. Having made his peace with the San Carlo, he was trying to get started on a new work. He and Cammarano had at first returned to the idea of Ferrucci and *L'assedio di Firenze*, prudently giving the projected libretto the unaggressive title *Maria de' Ricci*. But on 14 April Cammarano wrote to the composer: 'With great regret I am obliged to announce to you a dire event: the Authority in charge of these theatres asked for our outline of *Maria de' Ricci* and rejected it with a communication in the following terms: "Because of the unsuitability of the subject in the present situation of Italy and especially of Florence [Guerrazzi, author of the original novel, had actually headed the 1848 insurgence in Florence], it should be returned to the Management", and all efforts of the Management to have the veto repealed were in vain.'

Cammarano then suggested another subject, from Schiller's *Kabale und Liebe*; Verdi accepted the idea, and the opera eventually became *Luisa Miller*.

From Paris, Verdi continued to follow events in Rome; and on 14 July 1849 he wrote to his Roman friend, the sculptor Vincenzo Luccardi: 'For three days I have been impatiently awaiting your letters. You can well imagine that the catastrophe of Rome [the fall of the Republic] has plunged me into grave thoughts, and it is wrong of you not to write at once to me. Let us not speak of Rome!! What good would it do!! Force still rules the world! Justice! What use is it against bayonets!! We can do nothing but mourn our evil lot, and curse the authors of such misfortunes!

'Speak to me of yourself then! Tell me your news. What are you doing now? Tell me in short everything that our new masters allow you to say. Tell me also of my friends! Write me at once: do not delay a minute, for I am in hell.'

A few weeks later Verdi returned to Italy, to Busseto. In 1848 he had bought a farm some miles from the town, the property known as Sant'Agata, where his forbears had been lease-holders for many generations, from the mid-seventeenth century to the time of his grandfather, who had been born there. At first, Verdi's parents lived on the farm, and the senior Verdi sent his son regular reports on the farm's events ('almost all the cows have happily calved': 15 May 1849).

Verdi, on coming home, settled in another property of his, the Palazzo Orlandi, on the main street of Busseto. Giuseppina Strepponi came with him: a real proof of her devotion since, in the straitlaced community of Busseto, an unmarried woman (and one from 'the stage'), living with a famous widower, could only cause gossip. Eventually that gossip involved Verdi's beloved patron Barezzi, who apparently said something Verdi resented. After which, the composer wrote a characteristic letter:

'. . . I have no difficulty in lifting the curtain that veils the mysteries contained within four walls, and in telling you about my life at home. I have nothing to hide. In my house there lives a lady, free, independent, fond—as I am—of the solitary life, and with a fortune that guarantees her against all need. Neither she nor I owes an account of our actions to anyone; but, for that matter, who knows what relationship exists between us? What business matters? What ties? What obligations I have to her, and she to me? Who knows whether she is my wife or not? And if she is, who knows the personal reasons, the ideas behind keeping its publication silent? Who knows if this is a good or bad thing? Why could it not also be good? And if it is bad, who has the right to hurl anathema at us? I will say, however, that in my house she is due the same or rather greater respect than is due me, and no one

is permitted to fail in this; and she deserves it fully, I will say finally, both because of her demeanour and her spirit, and because of the special consideration she always shows others.'

In Paris, where Rossini had lived for years with Olympe before marrying her, Verdi and Giuseppina had encountered no obstacles; they could have gone on living happily in France. But Verdi was a man with deep roots, and if he chose to live in Busseto, he would live there, although—as he also wrote to Barezzi—'You, who are after all so good, so fair, and so great-hearted, must not let yourself be influenced and must not absorb the ideas of a town that, in my case—this must be said!—some time ago would not deign to have me as its organist, and now murmurs right and left about my affairs. This cannot last; but if it should, I am a man to make my own decisions. The world is so large, and the loss of twenty or thirty thousand francs will not prevent me from finding a homeland elsewhere.'

Verdi soon made it up with his beloved Barezzi, who had already succumbed to Giuseppina's charm, wit, and warm heart. But Verdi never made it up with the town of Busseto. He did not carry out his threat to settle elsewhere, but he had less and less to do with his fellow-townsmen (who liked to claim that Busseto had 'made' him, to which Verdi replied: 'Why don't they make another?'). In due course he moved from the Palazzo Orlandi to the farmhouse of Sant'Agata, which, over the years, he transformed into a handsome, comfortable villa, and he went into Busseto as rarely as possible.

Village gossip was a minor problem. Other problems were more serious. Although the revolutionary movements of 1848 had been in theory suppressed and the old governments, for the most part, restored, there was still widespread, clandestine ferment, and the censors were more alert than ever. Verdi made matters difficult for himself by choosing subjects clearly destined to provoke the reaction of the authorities and to shock audiences.

Gradually he was moving away from the patriotic-pageant operas that had won him his first popularity and fame. *La battaglia di Legnano* was really the last of these. With *Luisa Miller* (San Carlo, 1849) and, more, with *Stiffelio* (Teatro Grande, Trieste, 1850), he was turning to domestic drama, to private passions; his heroes—and especially his heroines—were no longer rebelling against an oppressor, an invader, but rather against society, against restrictive convention.

While *Stiffelio* was still unwritten, Verdi was already writing to its librettist Piave, on 28 April 1850: '. . . I would have another subject which if the [Venice] police chose to allow it would be one of the greatest creations of the modern theatre. Who knows? They allowed *Ernani*, they might allow this one too, and here there would be no conspiracies. [A theme particularly disliked by the police, who had real conspiracies to deal with at this time.]

'Try! The subject is great, immense, and there is a character in it who is one of the greatest creations of all countries and all periods. The subject is *Le Roi s'amuse*, and the character I am speaking of would be Tribolet who if [the baritone Felice] Varesi is under contract would be the best possible thing for him and for us.'

The first thing in the Victor Hugo play that had to be changed was the title: from *Le Roi s'amuse* it became *La maledizione di Vallier*, then *La maledizione*. Finally the work was called *Rigoletto*, the name that Piave and Verdi had given to Hugo's protagonist, the hunchback jester Triboulet. Other changes also had to be made, but, at Verdi's insistence, Piave left the basic situations as they were in Hugo's original.

In his original letter, Verdi had urged Piave to find 'an influential person who can obtain permission' for *Le Roi s'amuse*. Whoever the influential person originally found by the poet, his power apparently was insufficient. When Verdi was far along in the composition of the opera, it became evident that there was going to be trouble with the censors. Victor Hugo was a notorious republican, *Le Roi s'amuse* had been banned in France for 'immorality' after a single performance; the story dealt with a tyrannical, libertine monarch and an attempted assassination.

The Director of Public Order in Venice, which was again under Austrian domination, was a certain Martello, an admirer of Verdi's at heart. He made a number of suggestions to Piave for recasting the libretto in an acceptable fashion, and the obliging poet rewrote the text entirely, with yet another title: *Il duca di Vendôme*. The result was sent to Verdi, who fired off a furious rejoinder to the secretary of the Teatro La Fenice, where the opera was to be presented.

'Reduced in this way,' Verdi wrote, 'it lacks character, importance, and finally the scenes have become very cold. If it was necessary to change the names, then the localities should also have been changed, and he [the king] should have been made a Duke, a Prince of some other place, for example a Pier Luigi Farnese, or other, or else shift the action backwards in time, to before Louis XI, when France was not a unified kingdom, and make him either a Duke of Burgundy or of Normandy, etc. etc. In any event, an absolute ruler.'

Having discussed the character of the monarch, Verdi then went into greater, and smaller detail, scene by scene: 'In the fifth scene of the first act, all the courtiers' wrath against Triboletto makes no sense. The old man's curse, so terrible and sublime in the original, here becomes ridiculous, because the motive that impels him to curse no longer has the same importance and also because he is no longer a subject speaking so boldly to his king. Without this curse, what point, what meaning does the drama have?'

The censor had not only tampered with the political significance of the story; he had also adjusted the morals of the king or duke. Verdi complained: 'The Duke is a nullity: the

104. *Rigoletto*. Cover of quadrille arrangement by Charles d'Albert. 1853 (?). In pre-gramophone days, when the piano in the drawing-room was a source of family entertainment, arrangements of arias from popular operas were much in demand. An opera's popularity could virtually be measured by the number of adaptations it inspired, for voice or, often, for instruments or the most unlikely combinations of instruments. Thus Verdi's *Rigoletto* spawned endless offspring of dubious legitimacy. Charles d'Albert (1809–86) was the French-born father of the more famous German (but British-born) composer Eugen d'Albert. The senior d'Albert was a dancing-master and no doubt made this Quadrille for his own use, presumably at the time of *Rigoletto*'s first English production, at Covent Garden in 1853, with Giorgio Ronconi, Mario, and the soprano Angiolina Bosio.

RIGOLETTO

QUADRILLE,
PAR
CHARLES D'ALBERT.

LONDON, CHAPPELL & Cº 50, NEW BOND STREET.
PIANO FORTE WARE-ROOMS 13 GEORGE STREET, HANOVER SQUARE.

PRICE   3/-
DUET   4/-
SEPTETT   3/-
FULL ORCHESTRA 5/-

Duke must absolutely be a libertine; otherwise there is no justification for Triboletto's fear of his daughter's emerging from her hiding-place: the drama becomes impossible. Why, in the last Act, does the Duke go to a remote tavern alone, without an invitation, without an appointment?'

In the final act, the heroine's body is delivered, by her murderer, to her father, in a sack, ready to be thrown into the river. This scene also upset the censor, who altered it drastically. Verdi's counter-attack continued: 'I do not understand why the sack has been omitted! What does the sack matter to the police? Are they afraid of the effect on stage? Then allow me to say: why do they claim to know more than I about this? Who is the Maestro? Who can say this will be effective, and this not? There was a similar problem about Ernani's *horn*: well, who laughed at the sound of that horn? If the sack is omitted, it is unlikely that Triboletto would talk for half an hour to a corpse before a lightning flash comes to reveal that it is his daughter.'

But Verdi's real wrath and scorn were reserved for the modifications of the protagonist. The letter goes on: 'Finally I note that they have avoided making Triboletto ugly and a hunchback!! A hunchback who sings? Why not? . . . Will it be effective? I do not know; but if I do not know, then neither, I repeat, does the person who has proposed this change. Actually I find it very beautiful to portray this character externally misshapen and ridiculous, but inwardly impassioned and full of love. I chose this subject precisely for all these qualities, and these original features. If they are removed, I cannot write the music. If I am told that my notes will work also for this drama, I reply that I do not understand this reasoning; and I will say frankly that my notes, ugly or beautiful as they may be, are never written at random and that I try always to give them a character.

'In short, an original, powerful drama has been turned into something quite banal and cold. . . . In all conscience as an artist I cannot set this libretto to music.'

In the end a compromise was reached: the setting was shifted from the court of François I to the Mantua of an imaginary but absolute (and libertine) Duke; the sack was allowed; and Rigoletto remained ugly and deformed (at least for the first Venice production; in other Italian cities, the jester's hump was removed, the opera was radically toned down, and given such titles as *Viscardello*, *Lionello*, and even *Clara di Perth*).

With the public of La Fenice, *Rigoletto*, first given there on 11 March 1851, was an immediate, overwhelming success. The stories about the catchy aria 'La donna è mobile' being kept a deep secret until the première, to prevent the tune from being whistled and sung throughout the city, are certainly legends; but they indicate the opera's popular, almost folk quality, which complements its profound psychological insights and its dramatic intensity.

For the Venetian critics, however, *Rigoletto* was at first a be-

105. 'Ah, yes, thou'rt mine', from Verdi's *Il trovatore*. Lithograph by Brandard, 1855. When the Roman tenor Enrico Tamberlik (1820– 89) arrived in London for the 1850 season at Covent Garden, he was at the peak of his career, having already sung not only in Italy but also in Spain and Portugal. London liked him and he was invited back for successive seasons. On 10 May 1855, he was Manrico in the first London performance of *Il trovatore*. The cast included Jenny Ney as Leonora (seen here with Tamberlik), Pauline Viardot (Malibran's younger sister) as Azucena, and Francesco Graziani as Di Luna. The opera had a huge, immediate success—greater than any enjoyed previously by a Verdi opera—and its hit tunes were promptly heard on barrel-organs and sung in drawing-rooms. They were sung in translation—thus 'Ah sì, ben mio' became 'Ah, yes, thou'rt mine'—and some, especially 'Home to our mountains' virtually became folk songs, beyond any operatic context. Tamberlik continued to appear in London, at intervals, until 1877; and in the meanwhile he contributed to operatic history by helping persuade Verdi to write an opera for St Petersburg, where the tenor was regularly engaged. There Tamberlik created the role of Don Alvaro in this opera, *La forza del destino*, in 1862.

AH, YES THOU'RT MINE!
"AH, SI, BEN MIO!"
SUNG BY SIGNOR TAMBERLIK.
ITALIAN AND ENGLISH WORDS, THE LATTER BY
CHARLES JEFFERYS,
THE MUSIC BY
VERDI.

106. Felice Varesi, *c.* 1850.
Though he was short and somewhat bowed, the baritone Felice Varesi (1813–89) enjoyed a great success partly because of his vocal powers (which, however, declined prematurely) and, even more, because of his extraordinary ability as an actor. He made his debut in 1834 in Varese, in Donizetti's *Il furioso all'isola di San Domingo.* He sang in many other Donizetti operas as well as in works by Bellini, Mercadante, and the minor composers of the period, but he was particularly associated with Verdi, who wrote *Macbeth* (1847) with Varesi in mind. In 1851 Varesi was the first Rigoletto and in 1853 he created the role of Germont in *La traviata.* Whether because he was in bad vocal shape or because he considered the part beneath him, he sang poorly, was coldly received, and quarrelled with Verdi.

wildering experience. The review in *La gazzetta di Venezia* was typical, when it praised the 'wondrous orchestration', but then complained: 'The writing for the voice is less splendid. It departs from the style used till now, since there are no great ensembles.' Today, when the quartet from *Rigoletto* is perhaps, with the sextet from *Lucia*, the most famous ensemble in Italian opera, this criticism seems odd, but it was echoed, at that time, by the *Gazette musicale* of Paris, which said the score was 'lacking in melody and entirely without ensembles'.

With *Rigoletto*, Verdi's art reached a peak of inspiration, which he miraculously sustained, writing *Il trovatore* and *La traviata* immediately afterwards, in a period of less than two years. These years, these masterpieces, were also a turning-point in the composer's life. Having achieved this peak, Verdi could gradually begin to relax.

Chapter 8

THE history of Italian opera in the middle decades of the nineteenth century is largely the story of Verdi, his life and his works—largely, but not entirely. For one thing, Verdi—never very social—spent much of this time away from the cities, enjoying the peace and seclusion of Sant'Agata, or else he was outside Italy altogether, often in Paris, where the productions of his operas commissioned for the theatre there, *Les Vêpres siciliennes* (1855) and *Don Carlos* (1867), required his presence in the capital for extended periods.

In 1845, at the time of the première of his *Giovanna d'Arco* at La Scala, Verdi had quarrelled with Merelli, irritated at the impresario's cheese-paring productions and also at some underhand business dealing with the publisher Ricordi. Gradually, Verdi's quarrel with Merelli and La Scala, which continued long after Merelli had left the theatre, developed into a quarrel with Milan. The composer spent some time there in 1846 and 1847, paid the city a brief visit in 1848, then remained away from the musical capital of Italy for almost twenty years, the most productive years of his career.

This, for the most part, was not a period of great brilliance at La Scala. Verdi's operas—despite his attempt at boycotting the house—continued to be performed there, usually quite promptly after their premières elsewhere. And these operas, for a long time, were the mainstay of the Scala repertory, the theatre's chief drawing-card. In the late 1840s and the early 1850s, La Scala revived older works by Bellini, Donizetti and Rossini; the management even essayed a few brand-new pieces—by composers like Peri, Torriani, and the better-known Pacini—but they were almost unanimously unsuccessful. In the 1850s, the importation of the later, French works of Meyerbeer—*Le Prophète*, *Les Huguenots* (translated, of course, into Italian)—aroused the public's interest.

But the public of Milan, in those years, was more concerned with politics than with music (though the two often got mixed together). The anti-Austrian sentiment in northern Italy was coming to a head, growing into a movement; and the Milanese were in the eye of the coming storm.

Dissatisfaction with La Scala was probably not Verdi's only

reason for abandoning Milan. Although it had grown since his student days there, it was still, essentially, a small town, and like all small towns, gossipy. Verdi's relationship with Giuseppina Strepponi, who in her singing career had been particularly popular with Scala audiences, would not have gone unremarked or uncriticized, not least because Giuseppina's sentimental life, in the pre-Verdi days, had been far from blameless (she had borne several illegitimate children, of whom one survived, maintained, discreetly, at a distance).

After his departure from Milan, Verdi also broke with many of his friends there, especially the various Countesses who had lionized him in the first heady days of his youthful triumphs. But one friend remained steadfast: Countess Clara—or Clarina—Maffei, the now-estranged wife of Verdi's older friend, the poet and translator Andrea Maffei, librettist of *I masnadieri* for London. Married at eighteen to Maffei, who was almost twice her age, Clarina had soon established herself as a resourceful, charming and stimulating hostess. Her salon was a centre of Milanese artistic life, and in his last years in the city Verdi had been one of its ornaments, as Donizetti had been before him.

In 1847, the Countess and Maffei were legally, amicably separated. Clarina soon formed a lasting relationship with another writer, the critic and patriot Carlo Tenca, a year her junior. As Tenca's influence waxed, the character of the salon underwent a change. It became less artistic and more political, and the Countess began receiving significant Risorgimento figures like Anselmo Guerrieri-Gonzaga (who directed the foreign affairs of the provisional government of Milan in 1848), the future minister Cesare Correnti, whose publication *L'Austria e la Lombardia* helped to instigate the *Cinque giornate* of revolution, and the young Luciano Manara, who fought in the *Cinque giornate* and was later killed, in 1849, defending the Roman Republic.

The Countess's biographer, Raffaele Barbiera, unreliable about dates but credible when discussing the temper of the times, describes the atmosphere of 1848 in these terms: 'At the beginning of that year, a number of Milanese assumed an attitude decidedly hostile to the foreign masters: they refused to smoke any more cigars, a monopoly of the government; and then, on 3 January, groups of soldiers were sent into the streets, marching, and smoking with a defiant air. The populace booed them; the soldiers drew their sabres, lashed out blindly, and numerous citizens fell victims.'

If the populace and the intellectuals of Milan were against the Austrians, the aristocracy and the high society of the city had mixed feelings. Many of them had strong Austrian connections, even family ties. And, for that matter, after the 'cigar massacre', there were misgivings among the Austrians occupying the city. As Barbiera continues: 'Many Austrians . . . trembled at the danger to which their families would be exposed if there were reprisals. Countess Giulia Samoyloff [the one-time mistress of the composer Pacini, and a rich, eccentric Milanese hostess], though enemy of all political freedom and friend of the Austrian officers, closed her salon in horror and fled Milan.'

Inevitably, the dominant political sentiments of the moment were felt, and displayed, at La Scala. It so happened that, just at this time, the great ballerina Fanny Elssler was to dance at the theatre. She had already appeared there, as long ago as 1838, and had triumphed there again in the Carnival-Lent season of 1844–45, when the poet Giovanni Prati had hailed her as the 'tremendous angel' of the stage.

As Barbiera tells it: 'On 9 January of '47 la Elssler had again triumphed at La Scala in *La figlia del bandito*, a ballet by Jules Perrot on music by Cesare Pugni; and the whole city, more than ever, sang hymns to her elegant, slender figure, her beauty, her genius, her good heart. . . . But exactly a year later, what a change of scene! . . . The same enthusiastic admirers of '47 realized that she was . . . Viennese, and therefore she had to pay, in a single moment, for all the triumphs lavished on her over several seasons.

'Came the evening of 12 February 1848, and Fanny Elssler appeared in the romantic ballet *Faust*. Many liberal youths, gathered in La Scala, passed from hand to hand a satirical lithograph against Fanny; others had stayed away from the theatre, after an anonymous circular had been distributed, which said: "Another sacrifice, brothers! We must absolutely stay away from the theatre on the première of la Elssler. Leave room for the Germans, who will choose to applaud her in our name."'

The Austrian officers (who were, of course, great theatre-lovers and regular patrons of La Scala) did indeed applaud heartily, but the liberal youths drowned them out with boos, catcalls and jeers. Fanny Elssler fainted on stage.

The *Cinque giornate* came a little over a month later, 18-22 March 1848. After the revolution was suppressed, Countess Maffei and Carlo Tenca had to flee to Switzerland, along with many Lombard patriots. There, they met Giuseppe Mazzini and other heroes.

But in 1850 Clarina was back in Milan, established in a new flat at 21 Via Bigli, where she reopened her salon and kept it active for more than a quarter-century. In January of that year, Tenca began publishing his newspaper *Il crepuscolo*, which, at the outset, was firmly Mazzinian.

Police searches, arrests, trials, sentences, exiles, executions, terror in families, the weeping and suffering of mothers: this, according to Barbiera, is the picture of Milan in the years between 1850 and 1859. In 1850 La Scala reduced its annual programme to a single Carnival-Lent season, announcing only a few operas. The list of artists—with a few exceptions like la Gazzaniga and la Cruvelli—was undistinguished.

The life of the theatre reflected the life of the times. Early in 1857, with the aim of conciliating the fractious prov-

107. (*Left*) The Emperor Franz Joseph and the Empress Elisabeth of Austria at La Scala, 1857.
After an uprising in Milan in February of 1853, Austria decided to adopt a more conciliatory attitude in the management of the city, then still in its domain. In 1857 Franz Joseph appointed his younger brother Maximilian (future tragic emperor of Mexico) as governor, replacing the unpopular General Radetzky. The young Archduke arrived in the city with his new bride, Charlotte of Belgium, and the couple achieved a certain popularity. Franz Joseph himself, with the Empress Elisabeth, paid a state visit in 1857. Despite the enthusiasm depicted in this engraving of the period, there was deep-seated local opposition to Austria, and the second Italian war of independence broke out a short time later.

108. Giuseppe Verdi and Napoleon III. Verdi had mixed feelings about the French and, in particular, about Napoleon III, whose shifting (not to say shifty) policy towards Italy alternately aroused gratitude and contempt. But the composer enjoyed Paris, and visited the city repeatedly and with pleasure; and though he called the Opéra 'la grande boutique', he longed to have an authentic success there. His first and second attempts, with *Jérusalem* (1847) and *Les Vêpres siciliennes* (1855), were less than triumphant. In 1867 he tried again, presenting *Don Carlos*, with Napoleon III and Eugénie in the audience. The story goes that the pious Empress, displeased by the opera's anti-clerical tone, turned her back to the stage at one point. Verdi was already famous and popular in Paris, as this contemporary caricature, showing him with a pocket full of notes, suggests.

ince, the young emperor Franz Joseph visited Milan with his beautiful wife Elisabeth. Their coming had been preceded by an amnesty for political prisoners, including many of Countess Maffei's friends. The emperor's brother Maximilian, later to be killed in Mexico, was at this time the affable and lenient Viceroy of Milan. The local aristocracy was abundantly invited to the grand receptions and balls at the viceregal residence, but only the most die-hard pro-Austrian faction attended.

War was again on the horizon. And on 24 January 1859, when Verdi's *Simon Boccanegra* had its Scala première (it had been first performed two years previously, in Venice), there were loud cries of 'Viva Verdi', as the initials of the composer's surname were taken as a handy acrostic for Vittorio Emanuele Re d'Italia. (Vittorio Emanuele was head of the House of Savoy and, as King of Sardinia, a favourite candidate for the throne of a united Italy in the future.) Five days later, at a performance of Bellini's *Norma* with the celebrated Marchisio sisters, the Scala audience joined the chorus in the aggressive 'Guerra! guerra!' battle-cry. On 23 February, the crowd blocked the doors of the theatre, to prevent the evening's performance: a manifestation of public mourning

for Enrico Dandolo, a hero of the *Cinque giornate* and of the Roman fighting a decade before.

Finally, on 29 April 1859, Austria declared war on the kingdom of Sardinia and on France, now allied with the Italians, following secret concessions made to Napoleon III by Vittorio Emanuele's minister, Cavour. On 4 June the Austrians suffered a disastrous defeat at Magenta, and six days later Vittorio Emanuele and Napoleon III entered Milan. On 14 June, La Scala presented a gala programme consisting of Acts I and IV (and bits of II and III) of *Il trovatore* with, in between, the ballet *Rodolfo di Gerolstein*, subtitled 'an episode of the mysteries of Paris'.

In 1859, the Kingdom of Italy became a fact, even though Rome was not yet part of it. The capital, at first, was Turin; but Milan promptly asserted its own importance. And, as the heart of Milan, La Scala began to stir into new life. The 1859–60 season was longer than the immediately preceding seasons had been. It was also punctuated, on 26 February, by the performance of a special *Hymn* composed by Antonio Giuglini to honour Vittorio Emanuele, again visiting the city; and on 16 July during the summer pause, the double-bass player Giovanni Bottesini and the clarinettist Ernesto Cavallini gave a special benefit concert for the wounded in Sicily, where Garibaldi and his Thousand had landed in May.

The following season Gounod's *Faust*—then only three years old—was an outstanding success. But the significant event of these years was the performance of an opera entitled *I profughi fiamminghi* (The Flemish Refugees), which received a mere five performances at the end of the 1863 season. The librettist was a twenty-four-year-old poet, Emilio Praga, known in Milanese cultural circles for his cynical verses and his dissolute life; and the composer was the twenty-three-year-old Franco Faccio, a recent graduate of the Milan Conservatory, where his precocious brilliance had attracted attention.

His school-leaving piece at the Conservatory, performed in September 1861, had been a grandiose patriotic cantata, *Le sorelle d'Italia*, with a text by his fellow-student and bosom friend Arrigo Boito, then only nineteen. These two young men, iconoclastic, gifted, ambitious, had made both friends and enemies in Milan's artistic world, and their joint work was also a kind of banner for their rising generation.

The cantata's performance had been a success. And a writer in *Il pungolo*, an important paper of the time, commented: 'The success obtained by the *Mystery* of Boito and Faccio, far from putting the friends of these two distinguished students in a false and unpleasant position, put them instead in a very enjoyable position; as the audience came out, in the grip of emotion, those friends could show themselves in the authors' company, with pride and smug satisfaction at being somehow, as if by reflection, included in the halo of admiration, affection and curiosity that surrounds success, especially the success of the young.'

109. 'L'al di là' (The Beyond). Caricature by
Melchiorre Delfico, 1860.
Published in 1860 in the Neapolitan paper
L'Arlecchino, this view of the next world
shows, in the lower right section, the
recently deposed King of Naples, Francesco
II ('Franceschiello', as he was called),
surrounded by the Bourbon and Papal
courts, while the devil is cooking Calabrian
bandits—supporters of both regimes—on a
spit. Limbo is inhabited by vegetables,
Purgatory by laxatives. In the centre, a
puzzled angel is bearing Napoleon III and
saying, in Neapolitan dialect: 'Chisto nun
saggio addò cancaro l'aggio da portà!' ('I
don't know where the devil I'm supposed to
take this one!'). In Paradise, Garibaldi—
who had just defeated the Bourbons—
occupies the place of honour, flanked by
Cavour and General Cialdini. Verdi, at left,
and the cartoonist Delfico himself, at right,
are swinging thuribles. The violinist is the
Tuscan statesman Bettino Ricasoli.
Melchiorre Delfico (1825–95) was one of
Verdi's close friends in Naples; he made
many caricatures of the composer during
Verdi's several visits to the city.

Needless to say, Countess Clarina had already captured the
two young lions for her salon. And, in 1862, when, on leaving the
Conservatory, they set out on a travelling fellowship that would
take them to Paris, she gave them a letter of introduction to
Verdi. He was in the French capital, on his way back from Russia
(where his new opera *La forza del destino* had failed to be performed because of the soprano's indisposition; Verdi returned
some months later for the delayed première).

Verdi received the two young men cordially—as Rossini had
also done—and, taking advantage of Boito's presence in Paris, he
asked the composer-poet to supply the text for a *Hymn of the
Nations* commissioned by the International Exhibition in London. Boito, delighted, readily complied and delivered the verses
for this rare occasional composition of Verdi's. The older man
gave him a gold watch as a token of his appreciation.

When Boito and Faccio eventually returned to Milan, they
plunged into the thick of the cultural battle. In March of 1863, a
play jointly written by Boito and Emilio Praga, *Le madri galanti*,
was given in Turin: a resounding failure, it never achieved a
second performance.

Faccio's *Profughi fiamminghi* had a slightly better reception.
The work was meant quite consciously to be a major step in the
renewal of Italian opera (which the rebellious younger generation was proclaiming as overdue). In the audience on that opening night there was the publisher Giulio Ricordi, twenty-three
years old, who had just entered the family firm. The librettist and
critic Ghislanzoni was there, and so was the novelist Giuseppe

Rovani. Other composers were also in the audience, including Alberto Mazzucato, who had been Boito's and Faccio's professor at the Conservatory. Mazzucato, a conductor, had prepared the performance, which was then given under the baton of the young composer. The habitués of the Maffei salon, naturally, turned out in full force.

The anonymous critic of *La perseveranza* (probably the authoritative and progressive Filippo Filippi) was favourable, and took the new opera as a happy sign. 'We are faced', he wrote, 'by one of those painful gestations, through which art is transformed, struggling with a past that the public will not deny . . . we are in an embattled phase where it is possible only that, in accord with the historical tradition of every intellectual change, the new will subjugate the old, replacing the known with the unknown. . . . We dare assert that, at least for now, he [Faccio] is one of those most committed to the struggle, perhaps one of those who will share in the victory in times to come. Today the battle rages.'

Needless to say, if Faccio stood for the 'new' and the 'unknown', then Verdi represented the old and the known, the music to be subjugated. This sentiment was expressed, again indirectly, in other terms a short time later at a banquet given in Faccio's honour by a group of friends. Among the friends, of course, there was Boito, who was called upon to propose a toast. He recited (or, according to some reports, improvised) a sapphic ode, which he then published in a Milanese paper.

It was entitled *To Italian Art* (for 'art' read 'music'), and it began: 'Here's health to Italian art! May it escape for a moment from the bonds of the old and the foolish, to emerge young and healthy.' And later in the poem, obviously alluding to Faccio, the author said: 'Perhaps the man is already born who, on the altar, will set art erect again, chaste and pure: on that altar befouled like the wall of a brothel.'

Before the publication of the Ode and a few days after the performance of *I profughi fiamminghi*, Faccio—at Clarina Maffei's suggestion—had written to Verdi, asking, in effect, for the older man's blessing. At first Verdi did not answer. Then the Ode appeared in print. Verdi wrote first to the Countess, then to Faccio. To Clarina he said: 'I will tell you with my usual frankness that [Faccio] puts me in an embarrassing position. What can I answer him? A word of encouragement, you say. But what need is there of this word for someone who has already made his debut and established the public as his judge? Now it is a matter to be settled between them . . . .

'I know there has been much talk about this opera; too much, in my opinion. And I have read articles in the papers, where I found big words like *Art, Aesthetic, Revelations, Future*, etc. etc., and I confess that I, great ignoramus that I am, understood nothing.'

As Verdi's letter continues, it shows clearly that he had read

110. Verdi with scenes from his operas. Lithograph by Alessandro Focosi, 1851. One of the most popular illustrators of his time, Alessandro Focosi (d. 1869) engraved several portraits of Verdi. This one dates from 1851 (the array of Verdi's operas stops with *Il trovatore*, which had its première at the Teatro Apollo, Rome, on 19 January of that year), when the composer's fame had assumed international proportions. Note that the opera after *Il corsaro* (left side of the picture) is called *L'assedio di Arlem* ('The siege of Haarlem'). This was the title given to *La battaglia di Legnano* (1844) in one of its several censored versions; here the Germans of the original were changed into Spaniards, the Italians into Dutchmen, and Barbarossa into the Duke of Alba. The opera reached La Scala in its original form only in 1861, after the Austrians had been expelled.

Boito's poem and it had stung him: 'Arguments never persuade anyone; opinions most of the time are fallacious,' he wrote. 'Finally, if Faccio has found new paths, as his friends say, if Faccio is destined to place art again erect on the altar now *ugly as the stench of a brothel*, so much the better for him and for the public. If he is *on the wrong track*, as others claim, let him return to the straight and narrow, if he chooses to.'

Verdi also wrote to Faccio; a short, icy letter. 'If the public, that sovereign judge, has smiled on your first work and the reception, as you say, was good, then continue with confident spirit the career you have undertaken, and add to the great names of Pergolese [sic] and Marcello [composers mentioned by Boito in the Ode] another glorious name, your own. I wish the same for your friend Boito, whom I beg you to greet for me.'

Not content with the Ode, Boito also defended Faccio's opera in an article published in *La perseveranza*, where he called again for a renewal of Italian music. A short time later, in 1864, the *avveniristi* (from 'avvenire', future, in this case referring to 'music of the future', or 'Wagnerians') made another important conquest. In Milan, a group of musicians and music-lovers founded a Società del Quartetto, modelled on a similar society founded in Florence a few years earlier. Ostensibly, the society was intended to foster the performance of chamber music or symphonic music; but more profoundly, it was anti-opera, and hence anti-Verdi. The officers of the Società in Milan were leading figures from the Conservatory, except for the secretary, who was Giulio Ricordi. Boito was a charter member.

In Rome, too, there was a somewhat less vociferous anti-opera movement, led by Giovanni Sgambati, a pupil of Liszt, and also a composer, pianist, and seminal teacher. Sgambati, in Rome, was the centre of an admiring group of younger musicians. He tried to de-provincialize the city, fostering performances of foreign music, and actually conducted the Roman première of Beethoven's *Eroica*, in 1866. He composed a number of earnest symphonic works, as well as religious music and piano pieces.

The Società del Quartetto, in Milan, began the publication of a journal, which appeared every fortnight. Boito contributed several articles, including one on 'Mendelssohn in Italy', a pretext for talking about German music and for criticizing Wagner (an about-face on Boito's part, since a few years earlier he had been an ardent Wagnerian, and would become one again).

Boito's two ruling passions were for Dante and Shakespeare. The latter, at this time, was still a fairly exotic author in Italy, where Shakespearean tragedy had arrived in the theatre only a decade or so earlier. This passion inspired Boito's libretto *Amleto*, which he wrote for Faccio in 1862. Faccio set it rapidly, and it was performed in Genoa in 1864, with some success (although the enemies of the young group suspected the success of being manufactured by the large body of Milanese friends who journeyed to Genoa to applaud at the première). In 1871 *Amleto*

REGIO TEATRO DELLA SCALA

L'Impresa per aderire al desiderio di una parte del Pubblico ha creduto di provvedere meglio all'andamento dello spettacolo, lasciando luogo al Ballo e dividendo l'Opera in due sere, senza alterare l'integrità dello spartito il **MEFISTOFELE.** Perchè la divisione corrisponda al concetto poetico dell'Opera si darà una sera il prologo, il primo, secondo e terzo atto, che costituiscono la prima parte del Poëma di Goethe; l'altra sera si darà oltre il prologo, il quarto atto, l'intermezzo sinfonico ed il quinto atto che costituiscono la seconda parte dello stesso Poëma.

ORDINE DELLO SPETTACOLO

Prologo, primo, secondo e terzo atto dell'Opera indi il Ballo BRAHMA colla sig.ʳ *Ferraris.*

Domani si darà la Seconda parte dell'Opera suddetta, cioè: il prologo, quarto atto, intermezzo sinfonico e quinto atto dell'Opera ed il Ballo.

Prezzo del Biglietto serale L. **5** - Pei signori Militari (in uniforme) L. **3** - Pel Loggione L. **1. 50**

Per una Sedia distinta a bracciuoli L. **10** (oltre il biglietto serale) — Per una Sedia chiusa comune L. **5.**

Si aprirà la porta del Teatro alle ore 7

Milano, 7 Marzo 1868.   Tip. Pirola.   L'Impresa BONOLA e COMP.

111. Poster for second performance of Boito's *Mefistofele* at La Scala, 1868.
After the stormy first performance of Boito's *Mefistofele* at La Scala on 5 March 1868, the theatre's management thought to placate the irate public by dividing the excessively long work over two evenings, and issued this announcement to that effect. On the first of the two evenings the audience would see the Prologue and the first three acts of *Mefistofele*, together with the ballet *Brahma.* The next evening's programme comprised Prologue, fourth act, symphonic intermezzo, and fifth act of the opera, again with a ballet. As the announcement points out, the opera's division corresponds to the division of Goethe's *Faust*, on which it is based. Even in this divided version, however, *Mefistofele* did not please, and the opera did not survive the third night. The much-revised (and abridged) second version of *Mefistofele*, after its triumphant première at the Teatro Comunale, Bologna, 4 October 1875, was given with great success at La Scala on 25 May 1881, under the composer's supervision, and it was revived frequently in the seasons that followed.

reached La Scala, and failed; its failure marked the end of Faccio's career as a composer, just as his career as a conductor was taking wing—its splendid zenith came a decade or so later.

Boito had not forgotten that he too was a composer, and intermittently, in the early 1860s, he had been working first on the libretto, then on the score of *Mefistofele*, his ambitious adaptation of Goethe's *Faust* (Boito's title had obviously been chosen to avoid confusion with the Gounod opera, now firmly established in the Italian repertory). In January of 1868, Boito published the libretto, apparently intending it to be judged as a work of literature independently of the yet-to-be-performed opera.

Then, on Thursday 5 March 1868, *Mefistofele* was given at La Scala. The anticipatory hullabaloo was immense; expectations were feverish. At 6 p.m. that afternoon, two hours before curtain time, a huge crowd was waiting outside the theatre. Fifteen minutes after the doors were opened, the non-reserved seats in the gallery and stalls were packed. By 7.30, the ladies of Milanese society were already in their boxes—an unheard-of show of interest.

The young journalist Eugenio Torelli-Viollier, then of the *Gazzetta di Milano*, and later the founder and first editor of the *Corriere della sera*, described the scene.

'Around the benches in the stalls, at the rear, hundreds of spectators, on tiptoe, craned their necks to see over those ahead of them. . . . In the first row of boxes the aristocratic feminine beauties were all present, in the higher rows, male attire was predominant. Above them all: the gallery, the impatient and cynical gallery, easily aroused to enthusiasm, formidable in wrath, merciless in punishment, the gallery with its strong lungs and tireless hands, ready to hurl down from those heights— impartially, beyond all prejudice, alien to parties, factions, friendships, resentments—its thunderous ovations or its hydra hiss.'

Also in the audience was the young novelist Antonio Fogazzaro, then twenty-six (the same age as Boito). The next day he wrote to his mother-in-law: 'Mefistofele was finally performed last night, after long and hectic anticipation on the part of the audience, which for two weeks had seen postponed, for one reason or another, this great musical event, as Signor Boito's friends prophesied it would be. True, according to them, the libretto was also supposed to be a great literary event. . . . And true, too, many people, not bound to Boito by friendship or faction, considered the libretto's greatest achievement was its audacity in passing itself off as good poetry. But every accusation was met with the reply: wait for the music. . . . During the endless rehearsals there were murmured rumours of artistic miracles, ecstasy, enthusiasm.'

Boito himself conducted (his first experience on the podium, and enough to discourage him from a conductor's career). The Prologue was applauded, the first act had a mixed reception, and the next act went worse. The third act was an outright disaster. 'In the stalls, the gallery, the fifth row of boxes, they whistled like so many damned souls'—the description is that of another eye-witness, Leone Fortis of Il pungolo—'They were flushed, overheated, their eyes blazing; they seemed ready to tear the composer limb from limb. . . . The spectators below our box looked up at us, with two fingers stuck between their lips, and addressed at us, too, the violent gusts of their wrath, the angry imprecations of their fury. It was frightening.'

The performance, even according to the most favourable accounts, was bad; and the aggressive, provocative clapping of Boito's supporters in their boxes only exacerbated the situation. Debate raged in the square outside La Scala, where a crowd was waiting for the news from inside, delivered regularly at the end of each act. According to Torelli-Viollier, many people stayed up until four in the morning, arguing, discussing the great fiasco of Mefistofele. 'If a wing of the Teatro alla Scala had collapsed, its fall could not have produced a more profound sensation.'

The opera lasted until 1.30 a.m. Two days after the première, when the work was to be repeated, La Scala stuck up posters announcing that Mefistofele would be given in halves on two evenings. Each half of the opera would be punctuated, as was then the custom, by a ballet: Brahma. The Scala audience then seized the occasion to applaud heartily and polemically the music of Brahma, by Costantino Dall'Argine, who had been a classmate of

112. Amilcare Ponchielli. Painting by Eleuterio Pagliano, 1887.
Born in poverty, Amilcare Ponchielli (1834–86) won a scholarship to the Milan Conservatory at the age of nine and studied there for eleven years. His first operas, produced in his native Cremona, enjoyed only local success. And it was not until 1872, when a revised version of one of those operas, I promessi sposi, was mounted at the Teatro Dal Verme in Milan, that he attracted some attention. Giulio Ricordi commissioned him to write an opera, on a text by Antonio Ghislanzoni. This work, I lituani, had an encouraging reception at La Scala on 7 March 1874. Again at La Scala, in 1876, Ponchielli presented his next opera, La gioconda, libretto by Arrigo Boito (under the anagram-pseudonym Tobia Gorrio). The triumph was immediate and enduring. Ponchielli was offered the chair of composition at the Milan Conservatory, where his pupils included Mascagni and Puccini. But he was to enjoy his success only briefly. In 1886 he died of cancer.

The painter Eleuterio Pagliano (1826–1903) was as admired for his patriotism as for his art. After taking part in the Five Days of Milan in 1848, he rushed to defend the Roman Republic in 1849, accompanying his friend Luciano Manara, who was wounded there and died in Pagliano's arms. This portrait of Ponchielli, executed after the composer's death, is somewhat idealized, since the subject was physically unprepossessing, though much loved for his open, generous nature.

Boito's at the Conservatory, but whose music was anything but *avveniristica*. On the evening of 8 March, when the second half of the second performance was over, *Mefistofele* gave up the ghost. Nearly a decade later, completely revised, it was given in Bologna, and the new, more accessible version achieved a success and gained a somewhat slippery foothold in the repertory.

After the crushing failure of the first version, Boito's radicalism in art began to wane. He also wrote less and less music. Since 1859 he had been thinking of an opera set in Nero's Rome, and for many years, off and on, he worked at it. The libretto was published, production of the opera was announced, then postponed; and when Boito died, in 1918, the work was still unfinished, a chaos of sketches, variants, *pentimenti*. In the meanwhile, before the second *Mefistofele*'s success, Boito wrote librettos for other composers, often under the pseudonym of Tobio Gorrio, to make money.

Some of these other composers were new names, the musicians who were beginning to be mentioned as Verdi's younger rivals. One was Amilcare Ponchielli (1834–86), who for many years had made a modest living as band-master in some of the smaller northern Italian cities, including Cremona, near his birthplace. Finally able to move to Milan in the early 1870s, Ponchielli achieved his one genuine success, in 1876, with *La gioconda*, on a Boito libretto (which Ponchielli secretly disliked). Though Ponchielli was a composer of undeniable gifts, and a teacher of considerable influence—his pupils included Puccini and Mascagni—he was no rival for Verdi, and never considered himself one.

Meanwhile there was another, more curious entrant in the anti-Verdi stakes. In the early 1860s there arrived in Milan a twenty-eight-year-old Brazilian named Antonio Carlos Gomez (or Gomes, as the name is often written). The *Gazzetta musicale di Milano*, Ricordi's publication, described him thus: 'When Gomes walks through the streets—always alone and lost in thought—you would say he was a savage, transported abruptly and magically into the midst of our Milan. Gomes, with his way of walking, seems to suspect a precipice at every step, a betrayal; in every person, an enemy.

'This primitive tread, this frightened manner, this gaze so grim it seems sinister, make many consider him a misanthrope. Gomes is not that: he has a noble and generous heart, full of affection for his friends, of enthusiasm for his art. But he loves, adores, is roused to enthusiasm in his own way: like a true savage.'

Gomes was, in fact, half-Indian (his grandmother was a full-blooded Guarany); his father, a music-master, gave him his first instruction at the age of ten. At eighteen he was writing his first compositions, and in his early twenties he toured Brazil as a pianist. The Emperor Don Pedro had him admitted to the Conservatory, and then—after Gomes had composed two operas in Portuguese—offered him a stipend to study in Europe.

113. *La gioconda* by Amilcare Ponchielli. Cover of libretto, 1876.
Ponchielli's most successful opera was given its first performance at La Scala, on 8 April 1876, with Maddalena Mariani-Masi in the title role and the Spanish tenor Julián Gayarré as Enzo. The sets were designed by Carlo Ferrario. Though the opera was warmly received, Ponchielli was not content with it; he revised the score over the next years until he arrived at the version played today, first heard at La Scala in 1880, again with Mariani-Masi. This cover design of the first edition of the libretto does not depict a specific scene in the opera, but vaguely refers to the last act, entitled 'Il Canal Orfano', in which 'the lagoon and the piazzetta, festively illuminated' are supposedly visible.

A. PONCHIELLI

MARION DELORME

Melodramma in Quattro Atti di E. Golisciani

Prezzo netto L. una

Edizioni Ricordi.

He chose to settle in Milan, though the harsh climate made him suffer dreadfully. His Italian career began in the least likely fashion: he wrote the music for some revues in Milanese dialect. Then he began composing an opera with a Brazilian setting: *Il guarany*. Thanks to Countess Maffei (to whose salon he must have added an exotic note), the score was examined by the management of La Scala, and *Il guarany* had its première there on 19 March 1870. The baritone Victor Maurel made his local debut in what proved to be a spectacularly successful performance. Gomes, fearing failure, had climbed to the highest catwalk above the stage, planning to commit suicide if *Il guarany* was jeered. Fortunately the stage manager found him there, cowering, while the audience was clamouring for him to come out on stage. As the *Gazzetta musicale* commented, that audience 'could not have imagined that it had not only judged an opera,

116. Verdi, bust by Jean-Pierre Dantan
jeune, 1866.
In 1865 the sculptor and caricaturist Dantan
(1808–69) made a caricature of Verdi,
showing him as a lion, with his paws on the
piano. The composer was so pleased with it
that he gave some copies to friends and
kept one for himself in his bedroom at
Sant'Agata, where it still stands. The
following year—when Verdi was in Paris
for *Don Carlos*—Dantan made a formal bust
of him, which also won the subject's
approval. (This is a plaster version.) Verdi
gave a party for the sculptor, but as he
wrote to his friend Arrivabene, on 16
February 1866: 'Actually it was not a real
soirée, because I didn't send out invitations;
the other evening close friends came to my
apartment, to see this bust. There was talk
of having music, but I wouldn't allow it, to
avoid publicity. . . . To be sure with la Patti,
Fraschini, Dalle Sedie, Ronconi, etc. etc. we
could have made good music. The bust,
they all say, is really beautiful, but Dantan
surprised me with the caricature, which I
find even more beautiful.' The marble
version of this bust, now lost, stood in the
foyer of the Opéra. The romantic drapery is
not in character with Verdi's habitually
sober dress.

but had also saved the life of a noble and distinguished composer'.

The opera immediately went the rounds of the major Italian
theatres, which in the 1860s were producing the works of composers like Errico Petrella, Filippo Marchetti, Antonio Cagnoni
and Achille Peri, other would-be rivals of Verdi. The repertory
now included more frequent revivals of earlier operas; but
foreign works—except for Gounod and Meyerbeer—were still
few. And Verdi, however firmly he avoided Milan and La Scala,
continued to dominate the Italian stage, as he dominated Italian
cultural life.

Chapter 9

ON 29 April 1859 Austria invaded Piedmont, and Italy's Second War of Independence began. A few weeks later, on 21 May, Giuseppina Strepponi wrote to the Verdis' friend Cesarino De Sanctis in Naples: 'We are at Sant'Agata . . . we thank you and thank, for us, our friends for their affectionate concern. We are in good health, without fear, but worried about the gravity of events. This morning at eight the drawbridges were raised and the gates of Piacenza closed, which is eighteen miles from us. Part of the Franco-Piedmontese Army is moving down to attack that fortress and tomorrow, or perhaps this evening, we will hear the rumble of cannon. Everything is being made ready to turn this into a war of giants. Verdi is grave, serious, but calm and confident in the future.'

The retreating Austrians, a short time later, actually blew up the fort of Piacenza (and the sound of the explosion must, indeed, have reached the peaceful oasis of Sant'Agata). The war was also brought close to home by some personal encounters. As Verdi wrote to Clarina Maffei, on 23 June: 'The day before yesterday a poor priest (the only right-minded man in this whole countryside) brought me the greetings of [the patriot Giuseppe] Montanelli, whom he had run into at Piacenza, a private soldier among the volunteers! That is beautiful, sublime! Oh, if my health were different, I would be with him too! I say this to you, and in great secrecy; I would not say it to another, for I wouldn't want it to be thought vain boasting. But what could I do, incapable as I am of a march of three miles?'

The armistice of Villafranca, in July, annexed Lombardy to Piedmont; it allowed Venice, however, to remain in Austrian hands, and this offence to Venetian patriotism plunged Verdi into despair and revived all his dislike of the French and of Napoleon III. But it also led to his serious involvement in politics. On 4 September, the citizens of Busseto chose Verdi as their representative in an assembly of the provinces of the Duchy of Parma. Forgetting temporarily his feud with the town, Verdi attended the session, and on the 12th of that month he voted, with the majority, for the annexation of the Duchy to Piedmont. Three days later he was in Turin, where he was received by King Vittorio Emanuele II.

By this time Verdi was a monarchist, although in his youth he had been a Mazzinian and a republican, much influenced, no doubt, by the liberal, free-thinking circles of Busseto and of the Barezzi household. In his evolution towards monarchy (a process undergone by many Italians at the time) and in his generally more conservative outlook, his improved social position played a role. But also important was his profound, uncritical admiration for Camillo Cavour. Although Cavour came from an aristocratic background quite different from Verdi's, the two men had much in common: their pragmatism, for one thing, and, more specifically, their interest in modern farming methods and in improving Italian agriculture (Verdi made a habit of inspecting the farm machinery sections of the various International Exhibitions he attended, and he introduced new methods at Sant'Agata).

Two days after his meeting with the King, Verdi went to Livorno Ferraris, near Vercelli, to meet Cavour. The meeting made a deep impression on him. At this time, Cavour was temporarily out of power, but he and Verdi met again, in January 1861, when the statesman was once more Prime Minister; and it was at Cavour's insistence that the composer stood as candidate for the first national Italian Parliament. Verdi's reluctant candidacy caused him some trouble with the other local candidate, a professional politician.

Needless to say, Verdi was elected, and on 14 February 1861 he went to Turin to attend the inaugural session. The composer's parliamentary career was not distinguished, but until Cavour's death the following June, Verdi dutifully sat through debates and, according to reports, always voted exactly as his mentor did. Verdi mourned Cavour's death as a personal loss and as a national tragedy, which it was. Afterwards, his attendances in the Chamber became much rarer.

His dedication to the idea of national unity, however, was as ardent as before. On 19 March 1861, from Turin he wrote to De Sanctis in Naples: 'Consider that if the great idea of the Unity of Italy were not to be achieved it would be all your fault [i.e. the fault of the Neapolitans, who were showing signs of wanting to remain separate from the North], for there is no doubt about the other parts of Italy. If because of miserable notions of local pride Italy were to be divided in two (God forbid), she would always be at the mercy and under the protection of the other great powers, and therefore poor, weak, without freedom, and half-barbarian. Only Unity can make her great, powerful, and respected.'

International respect for Italy, recognition of the new, unified country's culture, was now a constant concern of the composer. If, as he himself admitted, he was not a good representative of Busseto in the Parliament at Turin, he was a conscious and prestigious representative of Italy abroad. Although he detested writing occasional music and, even as a young man, frequently refused invitations to compose ceremonial anthems on important occasions, he did write—with Boito, as we have seen—the *Inno delle nazioni*, to represent Italy at the London Exhibition of 1862. And in 1860–1, at a time when he had talked about giving up the writing of operas, he was easily persuaded to accept a commission for *La forza del destino*, no doubt because it came from the imperial court of Russia (the handsome fee, needed for the renovation of Sant'Agata, was also a powerful argument). That foreign première was followed by two others, of equal éclat: *Don Carlos*, for the Paris Opéra at the time of another great International Exposition in 1867; and *Aida*, written for the new Khedival Theatre in Cairo, and performed there—after a delay caused by the Franco-Prussian war and the siege of Paris, where the costumes and sets were being prepared—in 1871, after the Unification of Italy had become complete.

One question that arose in Parliament in the 1860s did stir Verdi's profound interest, as well as his active, constructive participation. This was the matter of international copyright and authors' rights in general. Previously, as a citizen of the Duchy of Parma, which had no treaties covering these matters with foreign countries, Verdi had suffered considerably. His works were not protected abroad, and when, in 1856, he sued Torrivro Calzado, impresario of the Théâtre Italien, for staging an unauthorized production of *Il trovatore*, Verdi lost the suit. Finally, Italy passed a new law on 25 June 1865. As a result, the publisher Ricordi promptly secured the rights to Rossini's operas as well as Verdi's.

Verdi had other things that bothered him in those years: the development of the Società del Quartetto, the gradual penetration of Italian opera houses by the foreign repertory, and—greatest of all these musical concerns—the rising tide of Wagnerism, culminating in the Italian presentation of Wagner's operas.

Italy's Wagnerians were more obstreperous than numerous, but they had a valuable leader in Giovannina Lucca, who was Wagner's Italian publisher and, as such, the composer's agent in Italy. Born Giovannina Strazza in 1814, she was the daughter of a Milanese shopkeeper who sold cooked food. In her twenties she married Francesco Lucca, twelve years her senior and already an established music-publisher, bitter rival of Ricordi. Francesco died in 1872, but even before his death the vigorous, enthusiastic, notoriously uncultivated Giovannina had taken over the management of the firm. In his early days, Verdi had written a few works for Lucca (*Attila*, *Il corsaro*, *I masnadieri*); but he never liked the couple, and in later years would have nothing to do with them. Their partisanship of the Wagnerian cause was not calculated to lessen his dislike.

The Luccas also owned the Italian rights to works by Gounod, Halévy, Meyerbeer, Goldmark, and other foreign composers. But Wagner, whom Giovannina familiarly called 'mio Wagner', after 1868, became the firm's chief interest, its emblem. Taking advantage of a rupture between Verdi and his one-time close

CHI VA IN TEATRO
(Studi sociali di **Camillo**.)

Questo va in Teatro perchè è abbonato — un uomo di buona società deve per lo meno essere abbonato alla Scala.

Quello va in Teatro.... per forza.... è un giornalista!

Questi vanno in Teatro perchè.... la loro guida li consiglia di andarci.

Egli va in Teatro colla speranza di criticare la musica, o la commedia, che non sia sua, o degli amici.

Questi vanno in Teatro, per il Teatro, per provare l'emozione della scena. Ce ne son pochi, ma qualcheduno ce n'è.

Questi vanno in Teatro colla scusa di divertire i bimbi.... ma un po' anche per divertirsi loro.

friend, the conductor Angelo Mariani, Signora Lucca succeeded in arranging a production of *Lohengrin* at the Teatro Comunale in Bologna, where Mariani was the permanent conductor. The opera, by now, was almost a quarter-century old, and hardly a revolutionary work (Wagner, in the meanwhile, had written and presented *Tristan* and *Meistersinger*, and had almost completed the *Ring*); but in Italian musical circles, this performance represented an epoch-making event.

The première of *Lohengrin*, in Italian translation, at the Teatro Comunale in Bologna took place on 1 November 1871, only a few weeks before the world première of *Aida* in Cairo, which was to be followed by the European première at La Scala. Critics, music-lovers, Wagnerians—and Verdians—flocked to Bologna from all over Italy. Wagner himself, invited by the city's mayor, Camillo Casarini, a devotee, was unable to come, but he wrote a long letter beforehand to Mariani, encouraging him in his task. The contents of the letter immediately became common knowledge.

Among those who travelled to Bologna for this *Lohengrin* was Arrigo Boito who, on the return trip to Milan, according to a

117. *Chi va in teatro?* ('Who goes to the theatre?') Caricatures published in *Il trovatore*, 21 October 1869.
In 1869 La Scala was becoming the expression of the new Milan, prosperous and staunchly bourgeois, the nation's 'moral capital' as it was to be called, referring to the sobriety and industry of the Milanese. The spectators described by the cartoonist Camillo are, top, left to right: 'He goes to the theatre because he's a subscriber. A man of good society must at least be a Scala subscriber'; 'This man goes to the Theatre perforce—he's a journalist'; 'These (foreign tourists) go to the Theatre because . . . their guide advises them to go.' Bottom row: 'He goes to the Theatre in the hope of criticizing the music, or the play, provided he or his friends didn't write it'; 'These go to the Theatre for the Theatre, to feel the emotion of the performance. There are few of them but there are some'; 'These go to the Theatre with the idea of entertaining the children . . . but they also entertain themselves a bit.'

younger fellow-composer, Antonio Smareglia, displayed his excitement and enthusiasm by hanging his long legs out of the window of the train. When reproached by the guard, Boito is supposed to have replied: 'I offer Wagner everything I have, including my legs.'

The leading Bolognese critic, Enrico Panzacchi, was also a fervent Wagnerian. Later, he wrote a long, somewhat novelized account of that dramatic evening: 'Stalls, stools, seats, boxes, galleries: all crammed. Everyone was in his place; almost all the men in full dress and white tie, the women décolletées, very elegant. In the ten minutes of waiting, the house . . . resounded with a subdued, deep hum, like a giant beehive; up in the top gallery every now and then a more rude grumbling escaped, a burst of laughter, a shout: Viva Verdi! Viva Rossini! But it was only for a moment!'

Another observer, Count Gino Monaldi, wrote: 'On that evening . . . the two thousand or more people who occupied the vast and beautiful hall of the Teatro Comunale in Bologna never imagined, on entering the theatre, that they would leave it with the profound conviction of having heard a musical masterpiece. They began to have a presentiment of that conviction with the Prelude. . . . The conviction became ecstatic bliss at the wondrous wave of supreme sonority reached by the amazed cry of the throng at the appearance of the magic swan.'

Although the first act went well and was enthusiastically received, the second began to tire the gala audience. But then the third—according to Monaldi and others—sealed the success of the evening. Mariani wrote an account of the triumph to Wagner, who wired him in reply: 'Evviva Mariani'. Boito also wrote to Wagner (whose *Rienzi* he had translated), and the composer sent him a long answer, later published as *Brief an einen italienischen Freund*. The letter concluded: 'Perhaps a new marriage is necessary between the genius of peoples, and in this case we Germans could not have a happier choice of love than one which would mate the genius of Italy with the genius of Germany.

'If my poor *Lohengrin* should prove the herald of this ideal wedding, it would truly have performed a wondrous mission of love.'

Verdi, who knew Wagner's work only from printed scores, went to a later performance of *Lohengrin*, on 19 November, travelling to Bologna by train. He wanted to remain incognito, but he had bad luck. First he encountered Mariani, face-to-face, at the railroad station. Then he had to sit in the box of the local agent of Ricordi's, a man not good at keeping secrets. So there were more cries of 'Viva Verdi' in the Comunale, while the composer sat grimly in the rear of the box, invisible to the crowd, ignoring its acclamation.

Verdi had brought a piano score of *Lohengrin* along with him, and during the performance he held it open on his knees, as he pencilled copious and merciless comments in the margins. The

singers, aware of Verdi's presence in the house, were understandably nervous, and the performance was not their best.
Verdi's scrawled remarks make his impatience clear: 'too loud',
he wrote at the very first bars of the Prelude, and then at the
bottom of the page, 'cannot be understood'. He also made a note
of Mariani's numerous cuts, which began with the elimination of
more than a page of the Prelude itself. Later in the act, he wrote:
'chorus off pitch', and then: 'whole scene badly performed'.

But he also recorded occasional words of praise, like 'beautiful', for Wagner, for Mariani and the interpreters. The approving
annotations, however, are outnumbered by his criticisms of the
tempi, his notation of mistakes, and interjections like 'ugly',
'bad', 'a mess'. Summing up, at the end of the score, Verdi wrote:
'Mediocre impression. Music beautiful when it is clear and there
is thought. Action flows slowly, like the words. Hence boredom.
Beautiful instrumental effects. Abuse of sustained notes, becomes heavy. Mediocre performance. Much *verve*, but without
poetry and refinement. In the difficult moments, always bad.'

Wagner had made his entry onto the Italian stage. Eventually
he would become familiar to Italy's opera audiences, but not
without difficulty. The following year the Comunale of Bologna
and Mariani presented an Italian *Tannhäuser*, which had no more
than a *succès d'éstime*. And when, during that same season,
Lohengrin was given at La Scala, on 20 March 1873, the evening
was a miserable fiasco, due not so much to the performance
(conducted by Faccio) as to publishers' rivalry and to the
chauvinistic jealousy between Milan and Bologna. *Lohengrin*'s
first Roman performance, in 1878, was not warmly received,
though it starred the popular Teresa Brambilla and was conducted by her husband Amilcare Ponchielli, composer of *La
gioconda*.

For a decade or more after that first Bologna *Lohengrin*, only
Wagner's early operas were considered performable in Italy:
Lohengrin and *Tannhäuser* were followed by productions of
Rienzi and *The Flying Dutchman*. One or another of these was
given, between 1871 and 1888, in Venice, Trieste, Florence,
Turin, Rome, Genoa and Naples, besides Bologna and Milan,
and even in smaller cities like Parma, Treviso, Verona, Novara,
and Mantua. Then, in 1888, Bologna made another bold step
with the Italian première of *Tristan und Isolde* (or rather, *Tristano
e Isotta*, in Boito's translation). The following year *Meistersinger*
reached La Scala, conducted by Faccio; and in 1891 *Die Walküre*
was performed. Later, as Arturo Toscanini's career developed,
first in Turin and then at La Scala, and as his taste began to
influence Italian operatic life, Wagner became a vital part of the
Italian repertory.

Verdi, meanwhile, was making his peace with Milan. Giuseppina led the way by paying a visit to the city in May of 1867,
ostensibly to buy furniture for the Verdis' new winter quarters in
Genoa. While in Milan, she called on Clarina Maffei, whom she

had never met; and the two women immediately became fast friends. As a mark of this sudden, but deep friendship, Clarina took Giuseppina to meet her friend and neighbour, the great writer Alessandro Manzoni. To Giuseppina, Manzoni said that he would be happy to see Verdi, if the composer were ever to come to Milan.

Though Verdi was certainly sceptical, even cynical about human relations, he was also, incongruously, a hero-worshipper. He had revered Cavour, for example; and he adored Manzoni. As Verdi wrote to Clarina after Giuseppina's return to Sant'Agata with the surprising account of her Milanese stay: 'You know how great my veneration is for that Man, who, in my opinion, has written not only the greatest book of our day [*I promessi sposi*], but also one of the greatest books ever produced by the human brain.'

Verdi sent Manzoni a signed photograph and said to Clarina, who was to deliver it: 'Tell him ... that I respect him and venerate him as much as one can respect and venerate on this earth, both as a man and as the most lofty and true honour of this, our always most tormented country.'

The prospect of meeting Manzoni was a strong incentive for Verdi to interrupt his long boycott of Milan, but still it was over a year before he finally went to the city. Afterwards, he wrote a letter to his French publisher Léon Escudier: 'Last week I was in Milan. It had been twenty years since I last saw that town, and it is now completely transformed. The new Galleria is really something beautiful. A truly artistic, monumental thing. In our country there is still the sentiment of the *Great* connected with the Beautiful.'

The Galleria, then an elegant arcade of shops and cafés and a popular meeting-place for artists, was only a short walk from Manzoni's house. Verdi's letter continues: 'There I visited our great *Poet*, who is also a great citizen, and a sainted man! Absolutely, in our Great men there is a certain naturalness, not found in the great men of other countries.'

After this reconciliation with Milan came Verdi's reconciliation with La Scala: he gave the theatre permission to stage *Don Carlos*, which had had its world première in Paris just over a year before. Verdi did not supervise the production or attend the performances, but their success obviously gave him great pleasure. He wrote to his friend Count Opprandino Arrivabene: 'Ah yes, *Don Carlos* went really well in Milan, and the Impresario's receipts said the same thing, because the till was always full, even for the last two, non-subscription performances. Indeed, the poor people had to pay five lire to get in and fifteen to sit down!'

For the rest, La Scala was going through one of its bad spells, and Giulio Ricordi—with a financial interest in the fortunes of the house—hoped to arouse Verdi's concern. The theatre proposed to mount *La forza del destino*, but the composer wanted to revise it, and set a condition (which secretly delighted Ricordi) that he, Verdi, 'attend and direct rehearsals of the new numbers and of the whole opera, which will perhaps be retouched in some places.'

The librettist and critic Antonio Ghislanzoni managed to adjust the text to Verdi's satisfaction (Piave, the original librettist, was now half-paralysed and unable to work); Verdi wrote the new pieces, revised the opera throughout, and then journeyed to Milan to oversee the preparations of the production. Though he had at first insisted that he would not be present at the première (27 February 1869), in the end he did stay and thus was able to observe the work's success (marred by one, isolated whistle at the end of the first act). There were fourteen performances of *Forza* that season.

But costs were rising steeply, and impresarios were in perennial difficulty. Verdi, on his return to Sant'Agata, wrote about the problem to his friend Giuseppe Piroli, a member of Parliament: 'The success of *Forza del destino* was good. Excellent performance. . . . Orchestra and chorus went divinely. What fire! what enthusiasm! . . . Too bad, too bad that the Government so pitilessly abandons this art and this Theatre that still has so many good things about it.

'You will say: why can't it get on without the support of the Government? No, that is impossible. The Teatro alla Scala has never been so busy, so filled as this year. Nevertheless, if the Impresarios cannot manage to have fifteen performances of *Forza* with more than five thousand lire from the box office every night, they are lost. I believe this is impossible to achieve, and so the Theatre must close.' As it happened, the theatre did not close, at least not then; but financial problems were to be a crucial question from now on.

The last musical event of that season, on 23 April 1869, was a performance of Rossini's *Petite messe solennelle*, commemorating the death of the composer in his villa at Passy, outside Paris, on 13 November 1868. Verdi, who had seen the older composer often during his own stays in Paris, was moved by this loss of another of Italy's great men. In his emotion, Verdi had conceived the noble but impractical idea of a *Requiem* to be composed, collectively, by Italy's leading musicians. Almost immediately he ran into trouble: those who had been left out were offended; those who had been included were displaying temperament, or being dilatory. Among the excluded was Angelo Mariani, who fancied himself as a composer as well as a conductor. Verdi exploited this occasion to quarrel with Mariani, whose mistress, the soprano Teresa Stolz, had already attracted Verdi's attention. It seems unlikely that, after all, there was a physical relationship between Verdi and la Stolz; but they did become friends, and their friendship made Giuseppina temporarily very unhappy and made the breach between Verdi and Mariani permanent.

The Rossini *Requiem* project was abandoned, but not until

118. *L'edera* ('Ivy'). Painting by Tranquillo Cremona.
Born in Pavia, Cremona (1837–78) worked chiefly in Milan, where he was a leader of the 'scapigliatura' movement. His studio in Corso Porta Nuova was a meeting-place for fellow-painters and also for writers and musicians. In this portrayal of hopeless romantic love, the composer Alfredo Catalani (1854–93) served as model for the desperate young man. The haughty lady rejecting him is a portrait of Cremona's sister-in-law Lisetta Cagnoli, and not of Teresa Junck, the real-life object of Catalani's passion. Completed in May 1878, a month before Cremona's death, the painting was acquired by Teresa's husband, the wealthy art patron Benedetto Junck.

Gve Doré 1860

Verdi had composed the two sections assigned, by lot, to him (the 'Requiem' and the 'Libera me'). He put the music aside, but did not forget it; and in 1873, when Manzoni died, the composer took these pieces out of the drawer and developed them into a full-scale work.

In theory, Verdi's *Messa da Requiem* does not belong in a story of Italian opera; but its composition and performance represented another stage in Verdi's return to Milan, where the success of the *Requiem* at its first performance, in May of 1874, was also an opportunity for the Milanese to demonstrate their warm devotion to the composer. By now Verdi had got into the habit of visiting the city and staying in the Grand Hotel Milan which—though he never gave up his Genoa residence— gradually became a second winter home.

In 1879, Verdi came back to Milan to conduct a special benefit performance of the *Requiem* for victims of some terrible floods that had wracked Italy. Teresa Stolz and the mezzo-soprano Maria Waldmann, who had taken part in the work's first performance, came out of retirement for this solemn occasion. At the end of the performance (which raised an immense sum for charity), the orchestra and chorus of La Scala serenaded Verdi in Via Manzoni, beneath the windows of his suite in the Grand Hotel.

While still basking in the gratifying warmth of this homage, Verdi, in great good humour, dined with Giulio Ricordi and Franco Faccio. The shrewd publisher, eager to lure his prime musical property back to the theatre, steered the conversation to Shakespeare, a favourite author of Verdi's since the composer's childhood. Then Ricordi started talking about *Othello* and about Arrigo Boito, whose youthful irreverence and

121. Riccardo Zandonai, *Francesca da Rimini*. Poster by Giuseppe Palanti, 1914. Tito Ricordi personally adapted D'Annunzio's steamy drama *Francesca da Rimini* for the young composer Riccardo Zandonai, whom Tito was grooming to be the successor of Puccini. The opera, first performed at the Teatro Regio in Turin on 19 February 1914, was an immediate—if not enduring—success. Tito's evident predilection for the work led to a temporary coolness between Puccini and the firm.

122. (*Right*) *Iris*. Chromolithograph poster by Leopoldo Metlicowicz.
The Trieste-born Metlicowicz (1868–1944) who joined the art department of Ricordi i 1892, was strongly influenced by the Jugendstil movement. His poster for the opera of Pietro Mascagni, presented in 1898, aptly illustrates its *fin de siècle* exoticism. Luigi Illica's libretto was based on a Japanese legend, *The Maid who Loved Flowers*; the opera was first performed at the Teatro Costanzi in Rome, starring Hariclea Darclée, the Rumanian soprano who was to create the part of Tosca in Puccini's opera two years later.

IRIS

MUSICA DI P·MASCAGNI
LIBRETTO DI L·ILLICA
G·RICORDI & C· EDITORI

OFFICINE G·RICORDI & C· MILANO

Jago:

. . . .

—Credo in un Dio crudel che m'ha creato
Simile a sè, e che nell'ira io nomo.
~~E che nell'ira io nomo.~~
—Dalla viltà d'un germe o d'un atòmo
Vile son nato;
Son scellerato
Perchè son uomo,
E sento il fango originario in me.
— Sì! questa è la mia fè!
— Credo con fermo cuor, siccome crede
La vedovella al Tempio,
che il mal ch'io penso e che da me procede
Per mio destino adempio.
— Credo che il giusto è un istrion beffardo
E nel viso e nel cuor,
Che tutto è in lui bugiardo,
Lagrima, bacio, sguardo,
Sacrificio ed onor.
— E credo l'uom giuoco d'iniqua sorte
Dal germe della culla
Al verme dell'avel.
— Vien dopo tanta irrision la Morte!
— E poi? — La Morte è il Nulla,
E vecchia fola il Ciel.

182

123. (*Left*) Iago's 'Credo' in Verdi's *Otello*.
Autograph of Arrigo Boito, 1884.
Some time in late April 1884, while Boito
and Verdi were working on *Otello*, the
librettist conceived the idea of a 'wicked
Credo' for the opera's villain. Verdi had
asked the poet for a scene that would not
be lyrical, in a more 'broken-up' form, and
Boito felt this text filled the bill. Verdi
liked the idea and set the words as Boito
had written them, without any changes.

124. (*Right*) Arrigo Boito. Pastel by Arturo
Rietti, 1909.
The Trieste-born Arturo Rietti
(1863–1943) was a sought-after portrait
painter in Milan in the last decade of the
nineteenth century and the first decade of
the twentieth. In addition to Boito, he
painted Toscanini, Giordano, and Puccini
(all three portraits, like this one of Boito,
are in the Museo teatrale alla Scala). By
1909, when this portrait was made, the
rebellious young Boito had become a sober
conservative, who sat on committees and
made commemorative addresses. In 1901
he had published the text of his *Nerone*, the
opera he had been working on all his
mature life and would never finish. In 1912
he was named Senator of the Realm.

125. (*Overleaf*) La folla dei curiosi ('The
crowd of the curious'). Chromolithograph
by A. Fumagalli.
A gala night at La Scala has always been an
important event not only for the people
fortunate enough to have tickets, but also
for the whole city. Crowds like those in this
magazine illustration gather outside just to
watch the audience arrive or, after the
performance, to see the artists leave, often
to a salvo of cheers (and occasionally jeers).

126. (*Page 185*) La discesa dai palchi ('The
descent from the boxes').
Taken from a popular magazine, this
illustration shows the smart audience at La
Scala around the turn of the century. The
composition of the public, however, was
changing. In 1891 the fifth row of boxes
was eliminated to make room for a larger
gallery, and as Boito wrote to Verdi: '. . .
an excellent decision. The theatre is freed
from a section of the audience that, by long
tradition, was distracted, bored, and
turbulent; and in their place it puts a great
gallery of bourgeois spectators who will pay
little and, when the opportunity arises, will
enjoy themselves greatly. The public of the
gallery is the best audience at La Scala.'

Wagnerismo were now past. Verdi seemed to show an interest in
all this discussion.

The next day Faccio—with whom Verdi was now on good
terms, since Faccio had conducted the splendid Scala première of
Aida, as well as other Verdi works—brought Boito to the Grand
Hotel. The poet-composer had a sketch for an *Otello* libretto with
him: obviously he had worked fast. Verdi was hesitant at first. He
left Milan for Sant'Agata, and Boito sent him the libretto there.
Verdi tried to parry, but the temptation was too great. He was
caught. And for the next seven years of his life, *Otello* was to
remain his chief musical concern, until its première on 5 February 1887.

The première was given at La Scala: Verdi's return was complete. This was the first presentation there of a new Verdi opera
since *Giovanna d'Arco* in 1845. It was a sensational international
event, an occasion that gave the measure of Verdi's position in
the world—and not only in the musical world. But that world was
still changing rapidly, its musical life was beginning to turn in a
new direction, and in some ways Verdi was a magnificent sur-
vivor from a past that was already history.

Chapter 10

'MILAN is rich, and loves to hear itself called rich, especially now, when being broke seems the order of the day. Milan is rich, which is to say there is no shortage of richly-bedecked carriages.' This was an editorial comment in the *Gazzettino* in 1867, at about the time Verdi made his return to the city and wondered at its marvels, its Great and Beautiful things. But a few months later the same newspaper ran a headline: 'People Still Starve to Death!' And in March 1868, it printed the story of a father of eight children who hanged himself because of poverty. Another article published at the time was entitled 'Social Differences', and it said, at one point: 'In this immense society that we call civilized and whose triumphs are praised every day, along with its genius and its glory, there is such a mass of incongruities, of contradictions, inequities, absurdities, which the social laws protect and the conventions sanction, that any idea of the just and the unjust, the honest and the dishonest becomes confused.'

Politically, by 1870 Italy was united. But Unification did not turn out to be the fulfilled dream that idealists and even hard-headed men like Verdi had cherished; with Unification, Italy's tremendous problems became evident. They were generally referred to as 'the social question'. For the most part, the rising middle class wanted to ignore them, but they stared the country squarely in the face.

Gradually, painfully, Italy was becoming a modern country: in 1879 elementary education was made obligatory; in 1882 a new electoral law increased the number of voters from 600,000 to 2,500,000. In 1892, against strong opposition, the Italian Socialist Party was officially born.

In the early winter of 1880, Giacomo Puccini arrived in this new, rich Milan. He was almost twenty-two, a bit old for the Conservatory, but—unlike Verdi almost fifty years earlier—he was admitted. And on 18 December, four days before his birthday, Puccini wrote home to his mother in Lucca: 'Yesterday I had my second lesson with [the composer and director of the Conservatory Antonio] Bazzini, and it is going very well. For the present that's the only course I have, but on Friday I begin Aesthetics. I've worked out the following schedule: in the morn-

ing I get up at half-past eight; when I have a lesson, I go to it; otherwise I practise the piano a while. I don't need much, but I do have to practise. . . . At half-past ten I eat breakfast, then I go out. At one I come home and study for Bazzini for a couple of hours; then between three and five back to the piano, and a bit of reading of classical music. . . . At present I am going through Boito's *Mefistofele*, which a friend has lent me. . . . At five I go to my frugal (extremely frugal!) meal, and I eat a Milanese minestrone, which to tell the truth is very good. I eat three bowls of it, then some other concoction; a bit of cheese with *bei* [i.e. *bachi*, or worms; Puccini probably meant gorgonzola, a Lombard speciality which would have seemed foreign to a Tuscan like himself],

128. *Nerone* by Arrigo Boito. Set design by
Lodovico Pogliaghi.
Arrigo Boito's posthumous opera, *Nerone*,
had its gala première at La Scala on 1 May
1924, conducted by Arturo Toscanini.
Aureliano Pertile sang the title role, with a
cast that included the baritone Carlo
Galeffi, the bass Marcel Journet, and the
soprano Rosa Raisa. The opera was staged
by Giovacchino Forzano, referred to in the
programme as 'direttore di scena' (the terms
'director' and 'producer' had not yet come
into use). The designer was Lodovico
Pogliaghi, active at La Scala since 1909.

129. (*Right*) Giacomo Puccini, Pietro
Mascagni, Arrigo Boito, Ruggero
Leoncavallo. Colour prints by 'Aroun al
Rascid' (pseudonym of Umberto
Brunelleschi).
Brunelleschi (Pistoia 1879–Paris 1949)
designed sets, but was also a caricaturist.
These four portraits belong to a special
number, entitled 'Nos musiciens', of the
French satirical publication, *L'assiette au
beurre*, dated 27 September 1902. The brief
texts are not so much satirical as simply
offensive. Thus Boito (1842–1918) is called
'a Milanese who clumsily imitates Germany
and spoils his macaroni with sauerkraut'.
Puccini (1858–1924) is granted 'a certain
theatrical vivacity', but his most famous
opera up to that point is called *La Vide
Bohème*, and he is criticized for his
'instrumental vacuousness'. Leoncavallo
(1857–1919) is responsible for a *L'avide
Bohème* of his own, and *Pagliacci* is called
'ignoble'. The youngest of the quartet,
Mascagni (1863–1945), fares no better.
This 'megalomaniac' is accused of 'silly'
imitation of early Verdi.

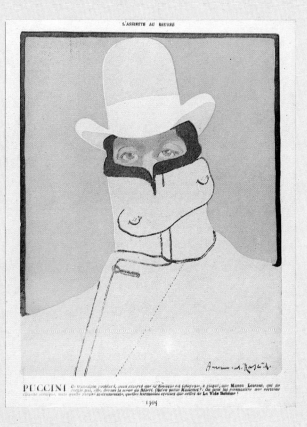

PUCCINI *De transition poétard, sous réserve une «*musique au fatoyeuse, a gagné, une* Manon Lescaut, *qui ne réussie pas, elle, devait la seule de Halévy. (Adieu pensé* Massenet?) *On peut lui reconnaître une certaine vivacité scénique, mais quelle verqbe instrumentale, quelles harmonies acides que celles de* La Vido Bohême!*

1305

MASCAGNI *Il musique à tour de bras les* Iris, *les* Rantzau, *sans retrouver le triomphe de* Cavalleria Rusticana. *Ivre de son propre (?)* Piccolo Spumante, *ce négligemment s'intitule « chef » du* Verismo « *alors qu'il patauge dans la première manière de Verdi, niaisoidment. Si bon « verismo, » heudt* Trovatore.

1298

BOÏTO *Les poètes content sa musique, les compositeurs louent ses vers, mais le* Néron, *l'*Orestiade, *et même le* Mefistofele *de* Tobia Gorrio — *anagramme — que me veut-tu? — décodent un* Milanais *qui pastiche gauclement l'Allemagne et rate ses morceaux à base de choucroute.*

1300

LEONCAVALLO *Napolitain besogneux, Musique une façon d'autobiographie,* L'avide Bohême, *et d'ignoble* Paillasse, « *a soldati, dont l'*Opéra *à l'aplomb d'annoncer le nouveaux étalage. Ce sous-Puccini travaille présentement, avec l'*Empereur Guillaume, *à un* Roland berlinois. *Chacun d'eux imprime son collaborateur. Tous deux ont raison.*

1301

with a half-litre of wine. Afterwards I light a cigar and go off to the Galleria for a stroll up and down, as usual. I stay there till nine and come home with aching feet. When I get home I do a bit of counterpoint, but don't play because we can't play an instrument at night. Afterwards I slip into bed and read seven or eight pages of a novel.'

What were the novels Puccini read, in 1880? He was never an intellectual, so it is possible that he consumed the popular fiction of the time, like the horror stories of Carolina Invernizio (author of such hair-raising works as *The Madwoman's Revenge*, *The Crime of a Mother*, *The Corpse in the Po*). But Puccini, at least later in his life, was also interested in keeping abreast of cultural events, so he may have read the works of some of the rising younger writers, like the Neapolitan Matilde Serao, the Milanese Emilio De Marchi, the Ligurian Edmondo De Amicis, or the young Antonio Fogazzaro, from Vicenza. Another writer who might have attracted him was Giovanni Verga, a Sicilian then resident in Milan, at the outset of his career.

Countess Maffei still received, and some of these writers frequented her salon, but it was quite different now from the Risorgimento days, when its gatherings had been a fiery hotbed of clandestine patriotism, or from the brilliant 1860s, when the bold young Boito and his friend Faccio had brightened—and sometimes shocked—the assembly. There were other salons as well, now, and soon Puccini began to be seen in them. Shy, taciturn, provincial, he was still welcome, for his talent— immediately evident—served as his passport.

One of the hostesses who took Puccini up was Signora Giovannina Lucca, who introduced him to Boito, Gomes, and other musicians, and also encouraged him to study the music of Wagner (which he could now hear in the theatre as well). In 1884, the firm of Lucca published Puccini's *Capriccio sinfonico*. This had been his 'school-leaving' piece at the Conservatory, performed at the final concert—conducted by Faccio—and warmly received, with a good review from the authoritative Filippo Filippi.

But the *Capriccio* was not Puccini's first publication. In October of 1883, the weekly magazine *La musica popolare*, published by the firm of Sonzogno, had issued as its musical supplement a little song of Puccini's entitled *Storiella d'amore*, composed the previous summer. An earlier number of the same magazine, the 1 April issue, in fact, had announced a competition for a new one-act opera.

Puccini had seen the announcement and, after considerable trouble, had procured a libretto by the poet, journalist and playwright Ferdinando Fontana. Working against a tight deadline, Puccini completed the work and entered the race.

Sonzogno were a long-established publishers, dating back to the late eighteenth century. In 1866 they founded the newspaper *Il secolo*, the most popular daily of the time, and they also

130. Giacomo Puccini and Ferdinando Fontana, 1884.
When Puccini completed his studies at the Milan Conservatory in 1883, his first thought was to write an opera. But in order to do so, he had to have a libretto and he lacked the money to commission one. Through the intercession of his teacher Amilcare Ponchielli, composer of *La gioconda*, Puccini made the acquaintance of the playwright-poet-journalist Ferdinando Fontana (1850–1919). A member of the Milanese 'scapigliatura' (literally 'dishevelled') Bohemian movement, Fontana had been the Berlin correspondent of the *Gazzetta piemontese*, had had two Milanese dialect plays performed, and had also written some librettos. For Puccini he produced *Le Villi*, originally called *Le Willis* (1884), and *Edgar* (1889). Both librettos came in for criticism, and Puccini then turned to other poets. An ardent republican, Fontana took part in the Milanese uprising of 1898 and had to go into exile in Switzerland, where he remained until his death.

launched a series of cheap editions of literary and scientific works, encouraging self-education among the ambitious poor. The spirit of Horatio Alger or Samuel Smiles was strong in post-Unification Italy, and their Italian equivalent was to be found in a widely-read and praised book entitled *Volere è potere* (rough translation: 'Where there's a will, there's a way'). This collection of inspirational biographies, assembled by Michele Lessona, a zoologist and senator, told how many leading Italians—including Verdi—had gone from rags to fame, if not always riches.

In 1874, under the guidance of Amintore Galli, music critic of *Il secolo*, Sonzogno had launched a collection of cheap piano scores, price one lira each; soon Galli began publishing new works, rivalling Ricordi and Lucca. The firm also secured Italian rights to a number of foreign operettas (including those of Offenbach), then to works by the leading French composers, from Ambroise Thomas's *Mignon* and *Hamlet* to Bizet's *Carmen*. As the activity of Giovannina Lucca waned (she finally sold out to

Turandot

Atto III.

G. Puccini

Turandot

BRUNELLESCHI

131. (*Left*) *Turandot* by Giacomo Puccini. Costume sketch by Umberto Brunelleschi. At his death, in 1924, Puccini left his opera *Turandot* unfinished. The final scene was then written, by Franco Alfano, on the basis of Puccini's sketches; and the première of the work took place at La Scala on 25 April 1926: a gala, international occasion. The cast included Rosa Raisa in the title role, Maria Zamboni as Liù, and the Spanish tenor Miguel Fleta as Prince Calaf. The sets were designed by G. Chini, the costumes by Brunelleschi.

132. Teatro Dal Verme, Milan: interior, 1872.
Built in 1864 by Gaetano Ciniselli, a famous equestrian, who performed there with his troupe, the theatre was at first called the Politeama Ciniselli. The owner also leased the house to other impresarios, for popular seasons of opera and drama. Finally the house was bought by Count Francesco Dal Verme, who tore down the original wooden construction and built a handsome opera house, to which he gave his name. It opened on 22 September 1872, with a performance of Meyerbeer's *Les Huguenots* (in Italian, *Gli ugonotti*). On 31 May 1884, Puccini made his operatic debut at the Dal Verme with his *Le Willis* (later *Le Villi*) and in 1892 Leoncavallo's *Pagliacci* had its première in the house. In 1930 the theatre changed hands again and became a cinema.

Ricordi in 1888), Sonzogno's musical domain expanded. And as Verdi's career moved towards its inevitable end, his publisher's energetic rival aimed at discovering the next Verdi.

The first Sonzogno competition, which had this aim in mind, ended badly for Puccini and, in the final analysis, badly also for Sonzogno. The jury included Galli, Faccio, and Ponchielli (Puccini's composition teacher); it picked two operas from among the twenty-eight submitted, but neither of these two was the Puccini score. For one thing, the manuscript—copied and submitted in haste—was practically illegible (Puccini's writing remained a barely decipherable scrawl to the end of his career).

The right people, musically speaking, in Milan knew all about Puccini's participation in the contest, and—all of them familiar with his talent—they were surprised when he failed to win. The librettist Fontana was appalled; his indignation spread to other influential figures, and soon the city's cultural leaders were convinced that Sonzogno and his jury had made a dreadful mistake.

Marco Sala was a friend and contemporary of Boito's—both men were now in their forties—and a critic of some standing, as well as a fair amateur violinist and a composer of popular dance music. In Sala's house, Fontana arranged for a private hearing of Puccini's opera, *Le Willis*, as it was then called. Boito was there, along with Signora Lucca, the composer Alfredo Catalani, and

LA FACCIEIDE.

1. Prima di incominciare. — 2. All'ora precisa. — 3. A solo di oboe. — 4. Adagio cantabile. — 5. Con sordini.
— 6. Piano delicatissimo. — 7. Passo di bravura del flauto. — 8. Attacco dell'allegro. — 9. Più mosso. —
10. Allegro furioso. — 11. Savoia!!! — 12. A solo di violoncello. — 13. Smorzando. — 14. Stretta finale.

133. 'La Facceide' (The Faccio-aeid).
Caricatures of Franco Faccio conducting,
1882. Published in *Il Guerrin meschino*,
Milan.

In the 1860s, when he had just finished his
studies at the Milan Conservatory, Franco
Faccio (1840–91), like his bosom friend
Arrigo Boito, was considered an *enfant
terrible* (as well as *prodige*), a Wagnerian, a
leader of the iconoclastic avant-garde. His
operas, *I profughi fiamminghi* (1863) and
Amleto (1865), the latter on a Boito libretto,
were hailed by his partisans as a new path
in Italian music. Verdi, naturally, viewed
both young men with suspicion. But Faccio
and Boito gradually abandoned their
revolutionary ways and eventually turned
into pillars of the establishment, Boito
becoming Verdi's librettist and Faccio
proving to be his favourite conductor. After
the failure of a revival of *Amleto* at La Scala
in 1871, Faccio gave up composing and
dedicated himself entirely to conducting.
He was responsible for the Italian première
of *Aida* (1872) and the world première of
Otello (1887), both at La Scala. He also
conducted symphonic concerts and, in one
of them, included the first significant work
of Giacomo Puccini, the *Capriccio sinfonico*
which the composer wrote in 1883 as a
school-leaving piece from the Conservatory.
As this series of caricatures implies, Faccio's
podium manner was eccentric. The final
picture, lower left, entitled 'stretta finale',
showing the conductor's head exploding, is
tragically ironic: Faccio went mad in 1890
and died in an asylum the following year.

others. The verdict, this time, was unanimously favourable; and a
subscription was initiated, to underwrite a performance of the
work. Boito signed his name at the head of the list, with fifty
lire; Marco Sala also put himself down for fifty; and other
contributors included the prominent publisher Emilio Treves,
Duke Giulio Litta (his wife was a famous salonneuse and friend
of Boito's), the music critic Aldo Noseda, and several important
members of the rising Milanese business community, among
them the industrialists Vimercati and Biraghi.

Puccini's *Le Willis* was then performed on 31 May 1884, at the
Teatro Dal Verme, and this operatic retelling of the *Giselle* story
was a considerable success. Sonzogno's defeat was compounded
when Giulio Ricordi immediately bought the score and commissioned Puccini to write another opera, for which the advance
would be paid in the form of a monthly stipend, enabling him to
devote himself entirely to composition.

Puccini, at twenty-six, was launched, even if somewhat
precariously—and somewhat belatedly, if one thinks of his predecessors (Rossini's first opera was staged when he was eighteen;
Donizetti made his debut at twenty-one, Bellini at twenty-two;
Verdi, a late-comer, made his at twenty-six, like Puccini). His
next opera was written more slowly, and during a period of
private unhappiness and problems: his mother died in 1884, not
long after the première of *Le Willis* (Puccini was in time to bring
to her death-bed the laurel wreath he had been given at the
opera's final performance); and—to complicate his situation still
further—he had begun living with Elvira Gemignani, wife of a
tradesman from Lucca, whom she had abandoned for the composer. Their son, Antonio, was born in 1886, on 23 December,
the day after Puccini's birthday.

Puccini's second opera, *Edgar*, was not performed until 21
April, Easter Sunday, 1889; and its première, at La Scala under
Franco Faccio, was less than happy. Ricordi's Board of Directors,
at a meeting after the event, wanted to rescind Puccini's subsidy
(since it was clear that *Edgar*'s earnings would not make up for
the advance); but Giulio—now in command of the firm, after the
death of his father, Tito, the previous year—insisted that
Ricordi's support of Puccini should be continued. He staked his
reputation and his position on this young man, and the Directors
were forced to bow to his will.

If, a decade or so earlier, the musical cognoscenti had been
looking for rivals for Verdi, now they were engaged in the game
of spotting Verdi's heir. The race for the succession was wide
open, but Ricordi—more from instinct than from evidence, at
that time—was convinced Puccini was the one who would take
over. Though, in 1877, Verdi had presented *Otello* at La Scala,
thus showing that, at seventy-four, he was still full of life, and
though, six years later, he would astonish the world with the
vitality of his *Falstaff*, there was no allaying the speculation.

Earlier stars had set. Boito was now engaged in the endless task of *Nerone*, the never-finished opera that was already becoming a legend (and a source of jokes). Faccio, after *I profughi fiamminghi*, had produced his *Amleto*, on a Boito libretto, which had failed to make the rounds of the theatres. Gomes, after *Il guarany*, had written other fairly successful operas, but he was spending less and less time in Milan and more and more in Brazil, where he had become the national composer. Ponchielli, a more credible contender, had died, at fifty-one, in 1886.

There were other, more eccentric attempts to seize the popular imagination and—with it—Verdi's crown. In 1873, the always adventurous Teatro Comunale in Bologna presented *I goti* (The Goths), the first work of a twenty-one-year-old composer, Stefano Gobatti, who seemed to have appeared from nowhere. The public, perhaps influenced by Gobatti's poverty and obscurity, decreed a thunderous reception; and the composer—to Verdi's annoyance—was immediately hailed as the new Verdi. After its sensational success in Bologna, *I goti* was given all over

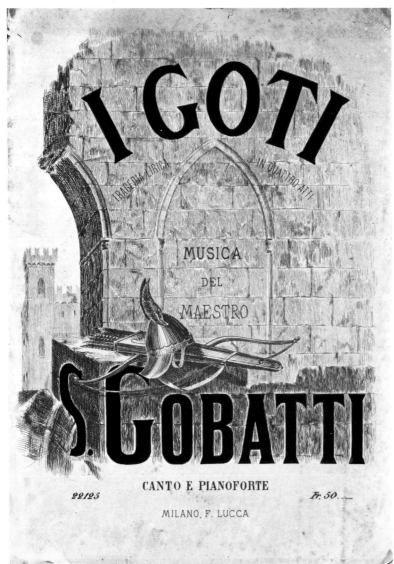

134. Stefano Gobatti, *I goti*. Cover of vocal score, 1873.

Born in the village of Bergantino (Polesine), in the Po valley, in 1852, Stefano Gobatti studied in Mantua, then in Bologna, and finally at the Naples Conservatory. In 1873, when still only twenty, he returned to Bologna with the manuscript of an opera, *I goti* (The Goths); and after making a contribution towards the expense of production, he persuaded the impresario of the Teatro Comunale in Bologna to produce it. A writer of the time described the atmosphere surrounding the opera's preparation: 'It was all people talked about, and the sad legend circulated: this young musician, who had arrived in Bologna, had sacrificed everything, with his worn-out shoes, single shirt which he had on his back, threadbare jacket of black corduroy, suffering hunger and hardships of every kind to raise the six thousand lire the impresario had demanded, felt downcast, lost, without hope.' On 30 November 1873, at the closing of the season, *I goti* was finally given and was—to provide the sad legend with a suitably happy ending—an unheard-of triumph. Gobatti was hailed as the new (and better) Verdi—an opinion which irritated the old Verdi considerably. But the enthusiasm was short-lived. Gobatti's next operas were abysmal failures, and he died in obscurity in 1913.

Italy; but Gobatti's next two works failed abjectly, and the composer's career ended while he was still in his thirties.

Another, less improbable candidate was Alfredo Catalani. Born in 1854, he came from Lucca, like Puccini, whose uncle Fortunato Magi had been Catalani's teacher (uncle Fortunato had also been Giacomo's first music-teacher but had given the boy up as hopeless). Also like Puccini, Catalani came from a family of musicians. After studies in Paris and at the Milan Conservatory, he had been taken up by Clarina Maffei and by Giovannina Lucca, who soon became his publisher. His first opera, *La falce* (The Sickle), another school-leaving piece, was given at the Conservatory in 1875; its librettist was Boito, one of Catalani's firmest supporters at this stage of his career.

A man of considerable culture, Catalani soon became closely linked with the 'scapigliatura' or 'dishevelled' movement, a generation of writers and painters who prided themselves on their iconoclasm (they not only declared God dead: they criticized Verdi and even Manzoni). Catalani frequented the studio of the painter Tranquillo Cremona, a leader of the movement, and the salon of the rich young patron of the arts Benedetto Junck, whose wife Teresa was to become Catalani's mistress.

Despite the chronic poor health that led to his death at the age of thirty-nine, Catalani was fairly productive. After his student work, he wrote *Elda* (produced in 1880), *Dejanice* (1883), *Edmea* (1886), and finally his best works: *Loreley* (1890, a reworking of *Elda*) and *La Wally* (1893, a few months before his death).

But though his music was recognized as exquisitely, tastefully fashioned, and though he enjoyed loyal support (including that of the young, but already dynamic Arturo Toscanini), Catalani failed to catch on. His naturally reserved character, his gradual embitterment, and his illness seemed to separate him from the mainstream of Italian music and from the musical public.

His bitterness is evident in a letter he wrote to a friend in the summer of 1889: '. . . Now there are "dynasties" also in art, and I know that Puccini "has to be" the successor of Verdi . . . who, like a good king, often invites the "crown prince" to dinner!' In 1889, the crown prince Puccini had produced only two operas, the more recent a failure; but Ricordi had invested his money wisely, even if more years had to pass before he—and Puccini—would begin to see real returns.

 Chapter 11

IN 1870, when the troops of King Vittorio Emanuele II made a breach in the walls of Rome and entered the city through Porta Pia, the capital of the Papal States was still the small, provincial, backward town that Leopardi, Rossini and Massimo d'Azeglio had known half a century or more earlier. It was also a beautiful city. Within its walls there were vast parks and villas; there were small farms, and groves of olive trees. The population was half that of Naples, about 200,000.

To many Northerners, Rome was an alien city. Manzoni never saw it, nor did Cavour, nor—obviously—did Vittorio Emanuele, until 1870. Verdi had stayed there a few times for strictly professional reasons, for the preparation of the first productions of *I due Foscari*, *La battaglia di Legnano*, *Il trovatore*, and *Un ballo in maschera*; but it was not a city he particularly liked. Actually, Rome was most admired by foreigners—Stendhal, Keats, Shelley, and their successors.

Henry James, coming to Rome not long before the arrival of Vittorio Emanuele's troops, found it in many respects the same city that Hawthorne and William Wetmore Story had known a generation before. Artists still gathered at the Caffé Greco in Via Condotti and dined cheaply at the Trattoria Lepri opposite it (Melville had dined there in 1857 for nineteen cents). But by 1871, when, after a plebiscite whose conclusion was foregone, Rome was chosen to be the nation's capital, the city was beginning to change; and the change would become rapid and profound.

A national government needs ministries; a king needs a palace. For the latter, the royal family, at the government's insistence, took over the Quirinal, the former summer palace of the Popes. Pius IX, of course, had withdrawn inside the Leonine Walls and had become, as he was popularly called, 'the prisoner of the Vatican'. For the ministries, there were other palaces and convents. The convent of San Silvestro became the Ministry of the Interior (it is now Rome's Central Post Office); Palazzo Braschi was assigned to the Ministry of Agriculture. The Medicis' former Roman residence, the Palazzo Madama, became the Senate House; and Palazzo Montecitorio, designed by Bernini, housed the Chamber of Deputies.

Some of these were only temporary solutions. And there were other problems: housing, for one. Rome had few hotels and a limited number of empty palazzi (whose patrician owners, often pro-Pope, were not eager to let floors or apartments to the quasi-foreign Piedmontese, who were beginning to flock to the city in the wake of the government and the Parliament). Developers, speculators and builders accordingly appeared on the scene; and one by one, some of the most beautiful of Rome's centuries-old gardens vanished. The Villa Ludovisi, for example, near what is now the Via Veneto, was one of the first to be developed into housing for the city's newcomers.

Augustus Hare, long an admirer of Rome and one of its most charming guides, wrote in horror of the new turn of events: 'The absence of Pope, Cardinals and monks; the shutting up of the convents; the loss of the ceremonies; the misery caused by the terrible taxes and conscription; the voluntary exile of the Borgheses and many other noble families; the total destruction of the glorious Villa Negroni and so much else of interest and beauty; the ugly new streets in imitation of Paris and New York, all grate against one's former Roman associations. And to set against this, there is so very little.' And he continued, writing in 1882: 'Twelve years of Sardinian [i.e. Savoy] rule have done more for the destruction of Rome, with its beauty and interest, than the invasion of the Goths and Vandals. The whole aspect of the city is changed, and the picturesqueness of old days must now be sought in such obscure corners as have escaped the hand of the spoiler.'

In 1870, not long after the breach at Porta Pia, Rome suffered a terrible flood, and the Tiber overflowed its banks, as it had often done before. The damage and hardship were vast; and shortly after the Unification, Garibaldi came to the city in an attempt to persuade the government of the necessity of regulating the river (the old hero's plan included altering the Tiber's course and creating a sea port).

Many dismissed Garibaldi's project as fanciful, and in some respects it was. But work did begin on the Tiber embankments (another imitation of Paris), which were finally completed in 1900, having meanwhile saved the city from the disaster of another flood. These embankments were certainly an improvement, but they came at a cost: the destruction of many buildings, including the glorious old Teatro Apollo, which had housed, among many other world premières, the first performance of *Il trovatore* in 1853. The last performance at the Apollo was given on 31 January 1888: Ambroise Thomas's *Hamlet*, starring Victor Maurel (creator of Verdi's Iago and, five years later, of his Falstaff).

In the meantime, a new theatre had risen in Rome, the brainchild of one of those spoilers—or builders, depending on one's point of view—who were changing the face of Rome. This new opera house (where legitimate plays were also given) was the

Teatro Costanzi, named after its constructor, Domenico Costanzi.

Costanzi, born in 1818, came from Macerata, in the Marche, part of the Papal States. As a young man, he acted as a courier and guide, accompanying distinguished and rich foreign visitors to Italy. In the course of his journeys, he learned French and German, developed a fondness for the arts, and—as he travelled abroad—gained a shrewd insight into the nascent tourist business.

In 1851 he married and settled in Rome, where—conscious of Rome's deficiencies in the tourist sector—he took up his father's profession: building. And he began constructing, and operating, hotels. These included the Albergo Roma, where, in 1865, the Empress Charlotte received Pius IX, and the handsome Hotel de Russie (still standing) in the Via del Babuino, near the Piazza del Popolo. Later, as Rome began to spread, he built the Albergo Costanzi, near the Piazza Barberini (Boito stayed there), and the Locanda del Quirinale (also still standing) in the new Via Nazionale.

In the same neighbourhood he built himself an impressive palazzo at Via Urbana 11 (now 167), and around 1875 he retired from the hotel business, selling the Albergo Costanzi to the Jesuits. And it was at this point in his life that the music-loving Costanzi decided to construct a great theatre, a symbol of the new Rome and, in effect, a monument to himself.

The so-called 'Third Rome', successor to the Rome of the ancients and the Rome of the Popes, was developing eastwards, moving—not accidentally—away from the Vatican. The Pope may have been a prisoner there, but his presence was deeply felt throughout the city. One of those most conscious of it was Vittorio Emanuele himself. When urged to visit the capital's poor, in Trastevere, virtually in the shadow of St Peter's dome, the king flatly refused, for fear that the clamour of his reception might reach the ears of Pius.

The Rome of Vittorio Emanuele (almost a contradiction in terms, since he hated the city and escaped from it whenever he could) focused around the Quirinal Palace and the Termini railroad station. Between them the old Via Pia was turned into Via XX Settembre (commemorating the date of the breach at Porta Pia), intended to be lined with ministry buildings. Parallel to this street ran the Via Nazionale, completed in 1868, shortly before the arrival of the troops, by one of the Pope's ministers, Monsignor de Merode, himself no mean spoiler.

The Via Nazionale was meant to be the street of theatres, hotels, and cultural buildings, like the pompous Palazzo delle Esposizioni. Here, too, was built the American church, St Paul's-within-the-walls, the first Protestant church ever to be constructed in Rome. It was the work of the British architect G. E. Street, who shortly afterwards built the English church in Via del Babuino.

135. Teatro Costanzi, Rome, 1884.
In 1879 the builder Domenico Costanzi and
the architect Achille Sfondrini initiated the
construction of an opera house which was
first to be called the Teatro Costanzi, then,
under Mussolini, the Teatro Reale
dell'Opera, or Royal Opera House. After
the fall of Mussolini and, with him, the
Italian monarchy, the theatre became
simply the Teatro dell'Opera. The interior
(seen here as it was in its early years) was—
and is—capacious and elaborately
decorated. After it opened, on 27
November 1880, its first big event, in
the 1884 season, was a pirated performance
of the first act of Wagner's *Parsifal*. In
1890, at the Costanzi, Mascagni's *Cavalleria
rusticana* was given its epoch-making
première; and three years later Verdi paid a
memorable visit to the house for the Rome
première of his *Falstaff*, with the same
artists who had created the work a short
time before, at La Scala.

The construction of these Protestant churches obviously
shocked many of the old Romans. When Costanzi submitted his
plan for a new theatre to the Works Department of the new
Rome, an obscure building inspector, probably a left-over from
the old regime, commented: 'Though a new theatre is one of
those sores that afflict the city, like Protestant chapels and such
things, nevertheless, having carefully examined Sig. Costanzi's
plan, as to the arrangement, the comfort, the sturdiness of the
building, I can find nothing to note against it.'

Costanzi's architect was the Milanese Achille Sfondrini, who
had already designed theatres for Padua and Rieti. Sfondrini had
problems with the site, and the result was a somewhat cramped
building, less grandiose than Costanzi would have liked. The
contractor dreamed of a great National Theatre, the capital's
official opera house. But the Teatro Costanzi did not assume that
role until long after its founder's death. In the 1920s, when
Mussolini wanted to enhance the theatre's prestige and, with it,
the lustre of his regime, he turned Sfondrini's building over to
Marcello Piacentini, the Albert Speer of Fascism, for remodel-
ling.

In 1880, when it was inaugurated, the Costanzi was still far
from the centre of the city; and when the Apollo was closed in
1888, to be demolished, it was the old Argentina that was
officially re-named the Municipal Theatre of Rome. In this guise,

it began its new life just four days after the Apollo's final performance. The renewed Argentina's first offering was *Carmen*, and Queen Margherita was in the audience. Unlike her husband Umberto I and most of the Savoy family, she actually loved music and cultivated the arts.

On 27 November 1880, the night of the Costanzi's inauguration, the Queen had also been present, with her husband. Actually, the royal couple arrived halfway through the first act of the opera, which was Rossini's *Semiramide*, so the orchestra had to stop the music and play the bumpy, vulgar Marcia Reale. King Umberto then left before the last act (there were four, in the version being used). But the Queen stayed on to the end, and the opening was a huge success. The theatre was described, by one enthusiastic critic, as 'one of the most notable, not only in Italy, but in Europe'. Costanzi and Sfondrini received ovations along with the opera's interpreters. The lighting system was particularly advanced, even revolutionary, and was much admired (the supernatural events in *Semiramide* offered the lighting director great scope).

In its first years, the Costanzi did not present a very daring repertory. The big event of its first decade was in 1887, when, shortly after the Scala première of *Otello*, the entire company, with the Scala orchestra and chorus, travelled by special train to Rome and repeated the opera at the Costanzi. The theatre's first operatic milestone, however, came three years later.

Although his first competition, in 1883, had managed not to discover Puccini, Edoardo Sonzogno still believed in encouraging the composition of new operas. In 1888 he announced a second competition, and this time he struck gold. There were seventy-three entries, and the winner was Pietro Mascagni's *Cavalleria rusticana*, which had its world première at the Costanzi on 17 May 1890.

Mascagni, born in Livorno in 1863, the son of a baker, had studied briefly at the Conservatory in Milan, where for a time he had also shared lodgings with Puccini (their japes and hardships are supposedly portrayed in *La Bohème*). But Mascagni's explosive, touchy personality was not suited to institutional life, at least not then (later, in the years of fame, he was director of the Pesaro Conservatory, where he was apparently a good administrator). After a quarrel with the head of the school, he left Milan, joined a travelling operetta troupe as its conductor, and led a vagabond life, mostly in southern Italy, for several years. Then, in the remote town of Cerignola, he found a position as municipal music master. He settled down, started a family, and made a humble living by giving piano lessons, conducting local groups and playing at functions. Mostly he suffered and slaved over what he meant to be his initial masterwork, a complex, romantic four-act opera called *Guglielmo Ratcliff*, based on a Heine play in the Italian translation by Verdi's old friend and collaborator Andrea Maffei.

136. Mascagni's *Cavalleria rusticana*, 1890.
When the young Mascagni's first opera,
Cavalleria rusticana, won a sensational
success at the Teatro Costanzi in Rome on
17 May 1890, it not only launched the
hitherto-unknown composer on his career,
it also brought the *verismo* movement in
opera to prominence, prompting a series of
'lower depths' operas, aping Mascagni's
work and the naturalist writers in fiction
and drama. Actually, the Sicilian peasants of
Mascagni's work, as they are depicted in the
libretto by Menasci and Targioni-Tozzetti,
are far removed from the reality of Sicily,
especially as it was in the late nineteenth
century.

When Puccini's *Le Villi* (as the longer, revised version of *Le Willis* was entitled) was given in Naples, early in 1888, Mascagni made the journey from Cerignola to greet and congratulate his older and more successful friend. Puccini, who knew all about the tormented composition of *Ratcliff*, urged Mascagni to set the big work aside and compose, as his first effort, a work that would be easier to produce and more commercial.

Mascagni took Puccini's words to heart. With the Sonzogno competition in mind, he wrote to a young friend back in Livorno, Giovanni Targioni-Tozzetti, and asked him to prepare a libretto. The librettist suggested *Cavalleria rusticana*, a story by Verga, who had also made a dramatization performed in 1884 in Turin, with Eleonora Duse as Santuzza. Mascagni had seen the play, and was enthusiastic about the idea. Time was short, however, so Targioni-Tozzetti called in another young writer, the twenty-one-year-old Guido Menasci, to lend a hand.

The opera was finished barely in time. Mascagni himself spent an entire day locked in his study, making the fair copy of the libretto. The jury first picked three operas, all of which would be performed; the final winner would be officially announced only after the three performances. But from the public's reaction to *Cavalleria rusticana* it was clear that this was the victor. On 19 May, two days after the première at the Costanzi, Mascagni wrote to his father: 'I still haven't recovered from the emotion and the confusion. I would never have imagined such en-

thusiasm. Everybody applauded. In the stalls, in the parterre, they were all standing; the orchestra also rose to its feet and gave me a colossal demonstration. All the ladies, including the queen, applauded.'

The critics soon began to point out that Mascagni's opera—whatever its enduring musical merits—represented a new path. In 1891 the opera was given in Vienna, where the redoubtable Eduard Hanslick wrote: '. . . The dramatic action in *Cavalleria* is conducted according to concepts that are absolutely modern. Its music springs and spreads solely from the situation, and not according to the old pattern of construction on the *aria*.'

At about the same time, the work was given in London and received with rapturous praise. George Bernard Shaw, or Corno di Bassetto as he signed himself, felt obliged to stem the tide of 'laudatory extravagances', and he wrote: 'Already I have read things about Cavalleria Rusticana which would require considerable qualification if they were applied to Die Meistersinger or Don Giovanni.' Shaw nevertheless praised the work as 'lively and promising'.

Hanslick, in his review, underlined the rapidity with which young Mascagni's first opera had crossed the Alps (and, one might add, the Channel). Rossini had written a dozen operas before *Tancredi* made him known outside Italy; and Bellini, Donizetti, and Verdi were already established composers at home before *Il pirata*, *Anna Bolena*, and *Ernani*—respectively their first exported works—made them known in foreign houses.

Later, in reviewing another Mascagni opera, Hanslick, referring back to *Cavalleria*, wrote: '. . . We were impressed especially by the extraordinarily happy choice of subject. Beyond doubt, the text of the libretto stimulated the most fervid side of Mascagni's talent . . . all was well-motivated, natural, realistic.'

Mascagni may not have invented *verismo* in opera, but it was unquestionably he who made the opera public aware of the trend. The naturalistic movement in literature, following the example of Zola and Maupassant, was already under way in Italy, thanks not only to Verga, its most distinguished exponent, but also to his fellow-Sicilians Luigi Capuana and Federico De Roberto. Verga had moved, tentatively, from fiction into the theatre (he soon returned to fiction), and his friend, the Piedmontese Giuseppe Giacosa—after some elegant, far from realistic verse plays and historical dramas—had presented some early examples of bourgeois, Ibsenesque realism in plays like *Tristi amori*, which was to be followed by his best work, *Come le foglie*. And, in the dialect theatre, Carlo Bertolazzi had begun his series of dramas of Milanese life, culminating in *El nost Milan* (1894–95), while Luigi Illica was about to produce his moving, humble story *L'Ereditaa del Felis*. Similarly, in Naples, the poet Salvatore Di Giacomo had presented the first of his plays, some of which were to inspire later composers of *verismo* operas (notably Umberto Giordano, who set *Il voto* and *Il mese mariano*).

Only a short time before the première of *Cavalleria rusticana* the audience of the Teatro Costanzi had witnessed another opera based on the same Verga story: *Mala Pasqua* by Stanislao Gastaldon, now remembered only as the composer of the once-popular salon song 'Musica proibita'. So *verismo* was in the air: the musical, as well as the literary air; and for that matter, there is an easily-perceived connection between *Cavalleria* and *Carmen* (fifteen years its senior), which in its day had also shocked audiences with its frank depiction of passion and life among the lower orders.

Verga's Sicilian peasants, even when played by a company

205

Attacco.   Moderato.   Andantino.

Andantino agitato.   Grazioso.   Allegro.

Adagio.   Pianissimo.   Scherzoso.

138. (*Left and right*) Pietro Mascagni conducting, *c.* 1900.

When he abandoned the Milan Conservatory in 1883, after a quarrel with the director, Mascagni earned a precarious living by conducting a touring operetta company in southern Italy. Later, when he had achieved fame, he conducted not only his own operas but also the works of others. In 1898 he was conductor of the Società Orchestrale in Milan and in 1913 conductor of the symphonic concerts of the Scala orchestra. This 'staged' series of photographs, published in *L'Illustrazione italiana*, suggests that Mascagni had a somewhat histrionic podium manner, which, for that matter, would be in keeping with his notoriously explosive personality.

speaking proper Italian, had seemed amazing to their first, northern Italian audiences. For Mascagni's opera, the librettists radically altered the language of the characters, making them speak an involuted, poetic, high-flown Italian, more familiar to operatic heroes and heroines than to remote Sicilian villages.

Santuzza, Mamma Lucia, and Turiddu were not the first peasants to be seen on the operatic stage; but their predecessors had been viewed in an idyllic, pastoral light. They were the merry farmers resting in the shade at the beginning of *L'elisir d'amore*, or the simple and festive mountaineers of *La sonnambula*, or the heroic rustic patriots of *Guillaume Tell*. The peasants of Mascagni, even with their unlikely vocabulary and syntax, talk of military service, hauling wine, going to Communion, adultery: events of everyday life.

If Mascagni had predecessors, he also soon had imitators. Within a few years there were numerous operas about the poor, rural and urban. Neapolitan slums were a favourite milieu: *A*

Santa Lucia by P. A. Tasca in 1892, Giordano's *Mala vita* that same year, and then *A basso porto* by Spinelli, *Maruzza* by Floridia, and *Festa a Marina* by Cornaro. The *verismo* bandwagon was on the move.

But the only important imitation was *Pagliacci* by Ruggero Leoncavallo, who, by his own admission, had Mascagni's success firmly in mind when he sat down to compose his one-act piece. He had also written its libretto, based on a village crime with which his father, a magistrate, had dealt. First performed in 1892, under Toscanini, *Pagliacci* was given the following year at the Costanzi, paired with *Cavalleria* on a double-bill, establishing a musical union that has endured ever since.

But *verismo*, in the strictest sense, lasted only those few years. As long ago as 1923, the Tuscan critic Giannotto Bastianelli wrote that in the opera immediately following *Cavalleria*, the romantic *L'amico Fritz*, Mascagni was certainly not presenting 'a continuation of his presumed *verismo* ideals . . . *verismo* was

given to *Cavalleria* purely and simply by chance.' And Bastianelli pointed out, with acumen, how *Fritz* contains elements typical of the new Italy, including 'a strange erotic sadness'.

The term *verismo* came, fairly soon, to be applied generically and almost meaninglessly to the music of the young composers, Puccini and Mascagni and their contemporaries, and to their immediate successors Giordano and Cilea. The operas they wrote were not always about poor peasants and were seldom naturalistic, but these musicians did have some qualities in common, qualities that distinguished them clearly from Verdi and the composers who paralleled the middle years of his career.

First, these younger musicians shared a strong interest in local colour. The exotic novel—in the vein of Pierre Loti, Pierre Louÿs, and so on—was popular in Italy, and had its Italian branch. There was also a growing school of travel writers, headed by Edmondo De Amicis. Their influence is perceptible in the librettos of Luigi Illica, especially in the ones he wrote without

the collaboration of the more sober Giacosa. In a libretto of the 1850s or earlier, stage directions would be terse, not to say laconic: throne-room, corridor, garden. Only the indispensable scenic elements were indicated: doors, windows, balconies; or, if the scene were outdoors, a fountain, a tree. Illica and his epigones, on the contrary, would write page after page, describing the time of day, the furniture, even the character traits and physical aspects of the *dramatis personae*.

Operas of the so-called *verismo* composers quickly dropped the peasants and criminals of Italian dialect drama and returned to the grander or, at least, more singular characters of earlier opera. The new works, however, shared with the earlier ones like *Cavalleria* and *Pagliacci* a taste for violence and exacerbated passions. Violence and passion had, of course, existed in the operas of Verdi and Donizetti, where there had been duels and poisonings and murder. But there was a difference between, say, the execution of Manrico in *Il trovatore* and the torture of Mario Cavaradossi in *Tosca*: both events take place off stage, but in the case of Puccini's hero, the torture is prolonged and the audience actually hears realistic howls of pain (sometimes extended, beyond realism, by tenors determined to make their presence

felt even from the wings). In the Puccini opera—and in other operas by his contemporaries—there is a strong element of sado-masochism. And this 'erotic sadness' reaches a peak in the final duet of *Andrea Chénier*, when the lovers, en route to the guillotine, sing ecstatically 'long live death, together!'

If the borders of *verismo* are difficult to trace, the significance of the movement is easy to grasp. Verdi's world, the straightforward moral values of that world, had been superseded (even though Verdi himself was still alive and, at the time of *Cavalleria*, still composing). Italian opera, while losing none of its popularity

142. Ruggero Leoncavallo playing *scopone* with friends, 1915. Photograph by Mario Nunes Vais.
Ruggero Leoncavallo (1857–1919), after the phenomenal success of his *Pagliacci* in 1892, had a chequered career as a composer and was often embittered by his failures (and perhaps by the successes of his colleagues). But, by all accounts, he was a man of great personal charm, guileless and winning. One of his solaces was the popular Italian card game *scopone*.

143. Francesco Cilea, c. 1900.
Cilea (1866–1950) is sometimes associated
with the 'young school', though
temperamentally he was far removed from
the violence and garishness that
characterized the most typical *verismo*
works. He studied at the Naples
Conservatory, and while there produced a
little opera, *Gina*, which came to the
attention of the publisher Sonzogno, always
alert to new talent. Sonzogno commissioned
Cilea to write another opera, *La Tilda*
(1892), which was briefly successful. It was
only with *L'Arlesiana* (1897), however, that
Cilea found his authentic, lyrical vein,
which became even more distinct in
Adriana Lecouvreur (1902), the single opera
of his that endures, to some extent, in the
repertory. With *Gloria* (1907) he ended his
operatic career, though he lived for almost
another half-century.

144. (*Below*) Giordano's *Andrea Chénier*, Act
III. Engraving by Bonamore for
L'Illustrazione italiana, 1896.
Giordano's most famous opera had its
première at La Scala on 28 March 1896,
with Giuseppe Borgatti in the title role, the
thirty-year-old Spanish soprano Avelina
Carrera (in her only Scala season) as
Maddalena, and Mario Sammarco as
Gérard. The conductor was Vittorio Vanzo.

at home or abroad, was conforming to the new Italy, officially united but still riven by powerful undercurrents of dissension, of struggle between the emerging classes. In his time, Verdi had been at the heart of the struggle for Italian freedom. Now, in the new struggle, many artists preferred to withdraw, to separate their art from life. The first works of *verismo*—the peasants talking, or rather singing, about fetching wine—had been misleading. If Turiddu and Alfio had debated about land reform or organization of farm workers, that would have been another thing. But Italian composers now preferred to write about the Middle Ages or the French Revolution or even, in Puccini's case, the Wild West; and the drama was sentimental, not political or social.

145. Verdi and the 'young school'. This imaginary group, dating from the 1890s, shows Verdi, the 'grand old man' of Italian music, in a box with some younger composers. In the background, standing, is Arrigo Boito. Seated beside Verdi is the 'crown prince', Giacomo Puccini, who with *Manon Lescaut* (1893) had established himself as the leading Italian opera composer of his generation. Other members of the so-called *giovane scuola* are also portrayed here: Pietro Mascagni, Ruggero Leoncavallo, standing, and, in the foreground, the youngest of the group, Umberto Giordano. The fact that none of the composers is looking at the others is significant. Except for Verdi and Boito, few of them were very close friends by this time.

Chapter 12

ON 1 February 1893, Puccini's *Manon Lescaut* had its première at the Teatro Regio in Turin; the opera enjoyed a warm success, and with it, the composer's career was, at last, securely launched.

Turin was a wise choice for the opera's presentation. Close enough to Milan to attract that city's leading critics, publishers, and connoisseurs, Turin was also enjoying a specially happy period, as far as the theatre was concerned. In the early years of the century, the Piedmontese capital had been something of a musical backwater. The reigning house of Savoy was not much interested in opera, or else was interested for the wrong reasons. Lady Morgan, writing in 1820, gave an idea of the situation:

'[The opera in Turin] is exclusively set aside for the noblesse; the Queen presiding over the distribution and prices of the boxes. Her list decides the number of quarterings requisite to occupy the aristocratic rows of the first and second circles, and determines the point of *roture*, which banishes to the higher tiers the *piccoli nobili*.'

Of course, good singers performed in Turin (la Marcolini, the great interpreter—and sometime mistress—of Rossini, was a special favourite in her time); and major works, censorship permitting, were given. But it was only in 1868, after the capital of Italy—and the Savoys—had moved to Florence (in preparation for the later move to Rome) that the Regio became nationally important and the theatre in Turin began to flourish.

By Puccini's time, though the city had only 350,000 inhabitants, there were twelve theatres running almost the entire year round. One, the Teatro Scribe, had a resident French company for operetta. Besides the Regio, the Vittorio Emanuele and the Carignano had opera seasons. There were regular concert series, including one sponsored by the Double Quintet Society.

When the composer-conductor Carlo Pedrotti took over the artistic direction of the Regio in 1868, that theatre began to move into the vanguard of the Italian operatic world. For one thing, the Regio was now municipal, giving it a financial stability that theatres in other Italian cities did not yet have. Pedrotti was able to transform the orchestra and enliven the repertory.

Then, in 1876, Giovanni Depanis became general manager of

146. Cesira Ferrani, 1893.
The first interpreter of the title role in
Puccini's *Manon Lescaut* (Teatro Regio,
Turin, 1 February 1893) was the soprano
Cesira Ferrani (real name Cesira Zanazzio,
1863–1943), seen here in her costume for
the second act. Puccini called her the 'ideal
Manon, in appearance, talent, and voice'.
The voice was small, but the singer had
great temperament. In the course of her
career she sang *Manon Lescaut* about three
hundred times. She also created the role of
Mimì in Puccini's *La Bohème*. She had made
her debut in Turin (her native city) in 1887
as Micaela in *Carmen*. Her repertory
included operas of Verdi (*Ernani, Simon
Boccanegra*) and Wagner (*Lohengrin*), as well
as works of Gounod, Massenet, and others.
She sang Mélisande (or rather Melisanda) in
the first Italian performance of Debussy's
Pelléas et Mélisande at La Scala under
Toscanini (2 April 1908), a legendary
occasion. The following spring, at the
Teatro Costanzi in Rome, she bade her
farewell to the stage in the same role.

the Regio, which entered its period of glory, to culminate in the
brilliant Toscanini seasons towards the end of the century.
Depanis was an enlightened industrialist, a good amateur musician, and a friend of the Piedmontese intellectuals of the older
generation (he and Massimo d'Azeglio had been close). His son
Giuseppe Depanis, who had trained as a lawyer but never prac-
tised, was an equally important cultural figure: a music critic, he
was a member of the Circolo d'Artisti, where he associated with
writers like Giuseppe Giacosa and Giovanni Camerana (one of
the *scapigliati*), the sculptor Davide Calandra and his brother,
the novelist Edoardo.

In his first seasons at the Regio, the older Depanis brought the
theatre's repertory up to date, with productions of *Mefistofele*,
Lohengrin and *Carmen* and the Italian premières of Massenet's *Le
Roi de Lahore* and Goldmark's *Die Königin von Saba*. He also
introduced new Italian operas and young composers, notably his
son's close friend Catalani, whose *Elda* Depanis mounted in
1880. A decade later, the same opera's second, more successful
version, *Loreley*, was also presented at the Regio.

147. Ruggero Leonvacallo with the first interpreters of his *Zaza*, 1900.
Ruggero Leoncavallo himself conducted the première of *Zaza* at the Teatro Lirico, Milan, on 10 November 1900. He is shown here with the first interpreters, the tenor Eduardo Garbin and the soprano Rosina Storchio to his right, a comprimaria and the baritone Mario Sammarco to his left. The opera was Leoncavallo's most popular, after *Pagliacci*, and remained in the Italian repertory for several decades.

It was the successor of Depanis, Luigi Cesari, who was responsible for the première of *Manon Lescaut*. Puccini was already known to the Regio audience, which had previously heard the première of the second, extended version of *Le Villi* in 1884 and, with less enthusiasm, *Edgar* (three years after the work's Scala première). *Manon Lescaut*, therefore, was a seed that fell on carefully prepared soil.

The opera's success inspired long articles in all the papers. It had a run of fifteen performances, and—a week after the opening—there was a great banquet in Puccini's honour at the Albergo Europa, with speeches, toasts, and a long, fulsome poem by the lawyer Carlo Nasi, organizer of the festivities. There was, however (as Alberto Basso has indicated in his history of the Regio), a story-behind-the-story, which is far from pleasant and yet typical of the music-publishing world of the period.

There had been some talk of giving Catalani's new opera, *La Wally* (which was to prove his last), that same season. Because of Giovannina Lucca's retirement from the field, the opera now belonged to Ricordi, as did, of course, *Manon Lescaut*. Giulio Ricordi, however, was determined to push Puccini, his chosen Crown Prince; and it would have been, in his view, a tactical mistake to risk two new operas in the same period. The Regio tried to insist on including Catalani, but Ricordi threatened to raise the rental fees on the other operas scheduled for that season (*Meistersinger*, *Aida* and *Rigoletto* among them): all his property. In fact, as Basso points out, in those years at the end of the century, the publishers' power was so great that opera seasons were often arranged more by Ricordi and Sonzogno than by the official managers of the various houses.

Editorial rivalry became front-page news a short time after the *Manon Lescaut* première, when Puccini, returning from Turin, arrived in Milan. It was 19 March 1893. Perhaps recalling his foot-sore student days, Puccini went for a stroll in the Galleria, where he naturally ran into some acquaintances. Among them was Ruggero Leoncavallo, whom Puccini had known for several years. Leoncavallo had been one of several writers involved in the libretto of *Manon Lescaut* (its authors were so numerous that Ricordi finally published the work with no librettist's name at all).

What happened next has been told many times and from various, conflicting points of view. One thing is sure: Puccini mentioned to his colleague that he was already at work on his next opera. It was going to be *La Bohème*, based on Murger's *Scènes de la vie de Bohème*. Leoncavallo was astonished and indignant; he revealed that he was also working on a *Bohème* opera and reminded Puccini that he, Leoncavallo, had first offered him a libretto on the subject months before, but Puccini had rejected it. After this rejection, Leoncavallo had decided to set the story himself.

Leoncavallo was published by Sonzogno, who was also proprietor of the daily paper *Il secolo*. The next day, the paper ran an announcement by the composer to the effect that he had been working for some months on an opera, *La Bohème*, to his own libretto, drawn from Murger. He was claiming prior rights: a moral claim only, since the Murger volume was in the public domain. The following day Puccini wrote a Letter to the Editor, which appeared in the *Corriere della sera*, saying, in effect: What difference does it make? Let Maestro Leoncavallo write his opera, and I'll write mine, and the public will decide between them.

Puccini, despite his assertions, had probably not written a note of his *Bohème* at the time. The libretto was in the very first stages of gestation, and Illica had just given Giacosa a rough draft of the text. But the competition with Leoncavallo was useful to Ricordi, who made it a pretext to spur on the usually dilatory Puccini. All

148. Giacomo Puccini, caricature by Caruso.

As a young man, before he thought of becoming a professional singer, Enrico Caruso (1873–1921) seriously considered studying art. Nothing came of this idea, but throughout his life, the tenor amused himself—and his friends—by drawing countless caricatures. The Italian-American journalist Marziale Sisca, who published many of these drawings in his humorous paper *La Follia di New York* and then collected them in a volume, wrote: 'A keen sense of observation, a talent for penetrating the deepest recesses of minds and hearts, a profound understanding of human foibles . . . these were the rare gifts that enabled Caruso to appear on the scenes in an interpretation of characters which was . . . realistic, masterful . . . These same gifts enabled him to bring to life, on paper, in a few lines, those subjects which awakened his interest. Although I often watched him work, my amazement never ceased as I witnessed his drawing, in a few minutes, of either a caricature or a sketch which embodied all of the characteristic traits of the individual who was the object of his keen eye.'

One series of Caruso caricatures was inspired by Puccini's New York visit of 1907, when the composer attended the United States première of *Manon Lescaut*. A second series derives from Puccini's later New York visit in 1910, for the world première of *La fanciulla del West*. Caruso was the tenor lead on both occasions.

Milan was soon talking about the rival operas: gossip was abundant. Ricordi even tried to keep the proofs of the opera secret, when they were ready, and refused to let copies of the libretto circulate until the very last moment.

The young Arturo Toscanini was now musical director of the Regio, and its orchestra had been improved still further. In addition to playing for the opera, it also now gave regular concert seasons. With proper contracts and decent wages, it was the first permanent orchestra in Italy. And its bravura was evident at the opening of the season, on 22 December 1895, when it partici-

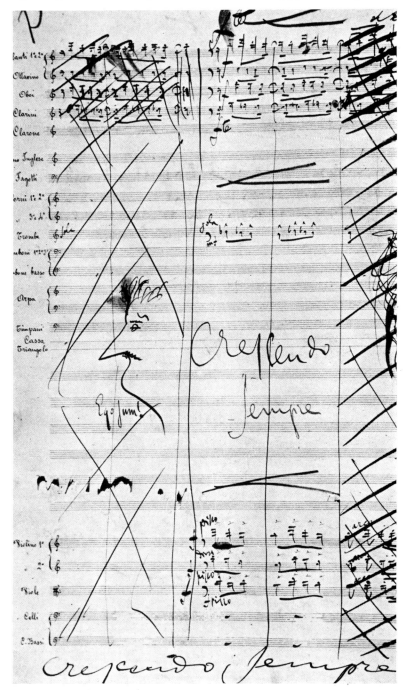

149. Autograph of Schaunard-Colline mock duel in Puccini's *La Bohème*, Act IV, 1895–6.
The composition of Puccini's *La Bohème* took place over a period between 1893 (the time of the composer's Milan encounter with Ruggero Leoncavallo, also engaged in composing a *Bohème* opera) and January 1896, when Puccini's opera went into rehearsal in Turin. In October of 1895 Puccini was writing to the librettist Luigi Illica, asking him to reduce the length of the last act. A long solo of Schaunard's was thus cut. Similarly, a Brindisi, which had been much discussed, was reduced to a few lines. But, as Puccini wrote to Giulio Ricordi, in October 1895: 'I am putting the greatest gaiety into the herring dinner and the dance. Musetta rushes in at the height of the racket.' This mock duel, which follows the dance, is the height of the racket, in fact, which Musetta interrupts with the news of Mimì's illness. This almost illegible writing was characteristic of Puccini from beginning to end of his career.

pated in a new production of *Die Walküre*: a personal triumph for Toscanini, whose work of preparation had been heroic.

But the applause had hardly died away before the conductor was at work preparing the season's other major event: the première of *La Bohème*. This time, Puccini had not wanted a Turin opening: he disliked the Regio's acoustics and he was unfamiliar with Toscanini. When he arrived in the city for rehearsals, he was also disappointed in some of the singers. But at rehearsals he found Toscanini—as he wrote to Illica— 'gentilissimo' and those days in Turin saw the beginning of a long, if not always smooth friendship.

The first performance of *La Bohème*, on 1 February 1896 at the Regio, was not a complete success. Many of the critics were at first hostile. The opera soon found its audience, however, and Puccini established himself not only as the heir of Verdi, but as the chosen bard of the now potent Italian middle class. Mimì became everybody's sweetheart, the operatic equivalent of a Mary Pickford or of the long-suffering heroines of the current popular fiction.

Tosca

The Italian middle class, however, was in for some shocks. The closing years of the nineteenth century, for Italy, were unhappy ones. First there was the doomed invasion of Abyssinia and the humiliating defeat of the Italian army at Adua on 1 March 1896, a month after *La Bohème*'s première. Then there were Socialist riots, uprisings, urban and rural disorders. In 1898 violence became prevalent. The unemployed peasants in Apulia began the demonstrations. In April there were riots in the Marches, in Romagna, and in Tuscany. Civil government was suspended and replaced by martial law in one province after another. Finally, in Milan, the army, under General Bava-Beccaris, fired on the crowd, killing almost a hundred civilians and wounding several hundred more (two soldiers were also killed).

Verdi, by now a staunch conservative, approved of the General; and so did Boito, who wrote to his friend, the French critic Camille Bellaigue, in Paris: 'Verdi is fine, both in spirit and body. He witnessed the uproar of the past few days like an old mastiff observing some yapping poodles, he who remembers the generous struggles of '48. Do not believe that this was a riot for bread (Milan is a rich and hard-working city), they have enough of that. The aim of this uproar was rather jam, but thank God, their leaders (almost all Deputies) were defeated and are now reflecting on the difficulties of a social revolution in the underground cells of the Castello sforzesco. We are still in a state of siege, a state which is not without its charm. It offers, first of all, the illusion of a return to the Middle Ages. One has to be home before midnight, one encounters patrols, the bicycle has vanished, the automobile as well. For myself, I am enraptured by it and feel rejuvenated by four centuries.'

Puccini, during this period of turmoil, was in Paris, to supervise the preparation of the French première of *La Bohème* and to discuss, with the dramatist Victorien Sardou, the final act of his play *Tosca*, which Giacosa and Illica were already adapting into a libretto. Only one of the composer's published letters—to his friend and fellow-Lucchese Luigi Pieri, now living in Milan—refers to the riots and the shooting, and the tone is even more casual than Boito's. But then, unlike Verdi, Puccini had little interest in politics, and his political positions, when he assumed any, were most often dictated by immediate personal or economic concerns.

152. Casa di riposo 'G. Verdi', Milan. The *Casa di riposo* opened its doors on 10 October 1902, on what would have been the composer's eighty-ninth birthday (some people, including Verdi, thought he was born on 9 October, however). The first guests were five men and four women, mostly retired singers. Since then hundreds of other guests, some formerly famous, others obscure, have enjoyed Verdi's posthumous hospitality.

Chapter 13

ON 14 May 1900 Verdi signed his last will and testament, a matter of twenty clauses and two codicils. He left bequests to various charitable institutions and to his servants, according to the length of their service to him. He left funds to support two promising students—of agriculture, not music—for a four-year course. To the Casa di Riposo per Musicisti, the home for aged and needy musicians which he had founded and had seen constructed the previous year, he left his royalties and some investments; and he left the bulk of his property, including Sant'Agata, to his heiress, a cousin, Maria Verdi, whom he had taken into his house as a child and had brought up. Now she had married the son of his Busseto legal adviser Carrara and had started the family whose descen-

dants still live in the Villa Verdi and handsomely maintain it.

Verdi was getting ready to die. 'Oh! an old man's life is truly unhappy!' he wrote not long afterwards to a friend: 'Even without specific illnesses, life weighs upon you, and you feel that your vitality and strength are diminishing more each day. This is what I feel within me, and I lack the courage and the strength to occupy myself with anything.'

On 29 July, King Umberto was assassinated. The widowed Queen Margherita wrote a Prayer for her husband, which the Italian press published with due prominence. Verdi's old friend Countess Giuseppina Negroni Prati Morosini—daughter of one of his hostesses in the *Nabucco* days—wrote to him, suggesting he set the Queen's words to music. Verdi demurred; but some weeks later, on re-reading the widowed monarch's *Orazione*, he scrawled a few, inconclusive lines of music. Those were the last notes from his pen.

In mid-December he left Sant'Agata, planning to spend some time in Milan, in his regular quarters: a comfortable, first-floor suite in the Grand Hotel. He was apparently in good health and in good humour, and his Milanese friends visited him constantly, so he had no cause to feel alone. But he may have been somewhat distressed by the programme of La Scala, of which Toscanini was now musical director. In the last year of Verdi's life, only one of

153. Verdi on the construction site of the *Casa di Riposo*, Milan, 1898–9.
In March of 1896, during a brief stay in Milan, Verdi deposited a large sum in the Banca Popolare, the amount set aside for the construction of a rest-home for aged and needy musicians. He had already bought the plot, then on the wooded outskirts of the city, the previous year. The architect was Camillo Boito, older brother of Verdi's librettist and friend Arrigo. Work began in 1898 and advanced slowly. In his last years Verdi visited the construction site on several occasions. Here he is seen with Giulio Ricordi (left), Arrigo Boito (behind Verdi's umbrella), and the contractor, Signor Noseda (right).

his operas was given there: *Otello*. Wagner, on the other hand, was represented with *Siegfried* and *Lohengrin*; and Puccini, the heir apparent, was included with *Tosca*, fresh from its Roman première.

On the morning of 19 January 1901, planning to go out for a carriage ride, Verdi was dressing. Suddenly he slumped on his bed, as his maid cried out for help. The composer had had a cerebral haemorrhage: his left side was paralysed, and he was unconscious.

The city of Milan was virtually paralysed as well. While Verdi lingered on, unaware of the outside world, daily bulletins were issued by the doctors. Straw was spread on the Via Manzoni, beneath the dying man's windows, to muffle the noise of traffic. Artists, including Adolfo Hohenstein, who had designed the sets and costumes for *Falstaff*, came and made final portraits of the composer. One of Milan's most famous priests, Don Adalberto Catena, who had assisted at the demise of the devout Manzoni, came to the room of the unbeliever Verdi and, as the composer lay in a coma, administered the Last Sacraments. Other visitors were Boito, Giulio Ricordi, Verdi's lawyer Campanari, Teresa Stolz, as well as relatives and specialists. Fortunately room 108 of the Grand was capacious.

Months later, recalling those last hours, Boito wrote to his friend Bellaigue: 'He put up an heroic resistance. The breathing of his broad chest sustained him victoriously for four days and three nights. The fourth night still his breathing filled the room, but the effort . . . poor Maestro! How good and beautiful he was to the last moment!'

The last moment came at 2.50 in the morning of 27 January 1901.

Verdi's instructions for his burial had been characteristically precise and emphatic: no ceremony, no music, everything to be carried out quietly, discreetly, at dawn. And in the first morning light on 30 January, the coffin was taken from the Grand Hotel to Milan's Cimitero Monumentale and lowered into the earth beside the coffin of Giuseppina, which had been there for almost three years.

This burial, however, was temporary. The composer had also made careful arrangements for his and Giuseppina's remains to be placed permanently in the chapel of the Casa di Riposo, when it was finished. And so, a month later, on 27 February, the two coffins were moved again, for the last time. Now there was no preventing a solemn, grandiose ceremony. All Italy, including the House of Savoy, was there to pay homage. Toscanini had arranged the orchestra and the chorus of La Scala on the steps of the central building of the Monumentale; and as the cortège moved out through the streets of Milan, he conducted the chorus that, from the days of *Nabucco*, had remained Italy's unofficial national anthem: 'Va, pensiero.' It had been twenty years since *Nabucco* had last been performed at La Scala.

154. Crowds waiting to buy tickets for *Siegfried* at La Scala, 1899.
In 1871, when the first Italian performance of a Wagner opera took place—*Lohengrin* at the Teatro Comunale in Bologna—Wagner was a curiosity for many Italians, a mania for a few, and a matter of indifference for most. But rapidly, thanks to the devotion and bravura of a few interpreters (notably the conductors Angelo Mariani, Franco Faccio, and then Arturo Toscanini), the Wagner cult expanded, and the composer's operas became a welcome and regular part of the repertory. Toscanini, who had opened the Scala 1898–9 season with *Meistersinger*, inaugurated the following season, on 26 December 1899, with *Siegfried.* In accordance with the custom of the time, both operas were given in Italian translation (thus becoming *I maestri cantori di Norimberga* and *Sigfrido*), and with Italian casts. This newspaper illustration of the time indicates the popularity of Wagner and refers to *bagarinaggio* (scalping), revealing that there was a black-market demand for tickets.

Verdi's death cannot properly be called the end of an era, for his era had already ended, with *Falstaff*, or perhaps—if that final, comic opera can be considered a sport—with *Otello*. The crowd that joined the Scala chorus in singing 'Va, pensiero' was a different breed of Italian from those who had sung the inspired, patriotic words sixty years earlier. This was the rich city Boito had described to Bellaigue; these were the people who wept at the death of Mimì and thrilled at the passionate love of Tosca and Mario (and perhaps at the sadistic lechery of Scarpia).

In March 1902, a little over a year after Verdi's death, another important event took place in the Grand Hotel. The tenor Enrico Caruso, who had just taken part in the world première of Baron Alberto Franchetti's *Germania* at La Scala, made a series of ten recordings for the Gramophone Company, including two arias from the Franchetti work and two from *Mefistofele*. Opera records were not a new invention, and, for that matter, these were not Caruso's first recordings. But the high artistic quality (despite the primitive conditions under which the piano-

155. (*Right*) Verdi as an old man, outside La Scala, Milan.
In the summer of 1868 Verdi visited Milan for a few days, his first stay in the city since the late 1840s. It was the beginning of a *rapprochement* which continued the following year, when La Scala presented the revised version of *La forza del destino*. In 1872, Verdi supervised the European première of *Aida* at La Scala, and in 1874 he conducted the first performance of his *Requiem* in the Milanese church of San Marco. Gradually Verdi spent more and more time in the city, and after Giuseppina Verdi's death in 1897, he stayed for longer periods in their regular rooms at the Grand Hotel et de Milan, a short walk from La Scala. Despite his advanced age and the infirmities connected with it, Verdi—as this photograph suggests—kept abreast of the news (which increasingly dismayed him).

GUISEPPE VERDI

*'Cento baci per te e Tomma
Divertiti'. La tua*

*Tanti baci da Luigia Irene e tutti.
Genova 31-7-904*

accompanied pieces were recorded) and the peculiar 'phonogenic' nature of the Neapolitan tenor's voice made these discs
an international success. The product of the improvised
recording studio, set up in a room of the Grand, brought opera
even closer to the public. Various composers—including Leoncavallo and Puccini—wrote songs specially commissioned for
gramophone records.

The Milanese throng, at the Cimitero Monumentale and the
Casa di Riposo, in burying Verdi had been burying the past. The
present was now Puccini. In those same last days of February
1901, he was deciding on the subject of his next opera, which was
to be *Madama Butterfly*, based on an American play he had seen
the previous summer in London, where he had gone to attend
the British première of *Tosca* at Covent Garden.

The director of the play, David Belasco, was also the co-author
(he signed the piece together with John Luther Long, who had
written the story on which the dramatization was based). Belasco
was known as a master of realistic effects and stage tricks: ideal
for a spectator like Puccini who understood no English.

At about this time, rumours were going around that Puccini
would write an opera in collaboration with Gabriele D'Annunzio,
with whom he had first had some discussions in 1894, after
Manon Lescaut. A few years Puccini's junior, D'Annunzio was
now approaching the peak of his career, having published his
'Roman' novels *Il fuoco* and *Il trionfo della morte* and, at the
instigation of Eleonora Duse, whose lover he then was, having

156. Giuseppe Verdi and his birthplace at
Roncole. Early 1900s.
By the time he died, early in 1901, Verdi
had become an Italian national hero. After
his death, he was virtually canonized. Thus
this postcard, circulated at the time,
romanticizes the simple, stark building in
which he was born.

157. (*Right*) Toscanini conducts La Scala
orchestra and chorus at Verdi's burial, 27
February 1901.
In his will Verdi specifically directed that
his funeral was to be simple, private, and
without music or singing. So on the foggy
dawn of 30 January 1901, his body was
taken to the church of San Francesco di
Paola, and then to the Cimitero
Monumentale, where the remains were
placed in a grave beside those of
Giuseppina Strepponi Verdi, who had died
in 1897. This arrangement, however, was
temporary; and less than a month later, the
two coffins were moved, for permanent
burial, to the chapel of the *Casa di riposo*
that Verdi had built. On this occasion the
terms of Verdi's will no longer applied, and
a solemn public demonstration was possible.
On the steps of the Monumentale Arturo
Toscanini conducted 'Va, pensiero' as the
cortège set off.

turned his talents to the theatre with works like *La città morta*. But to the febrile intensity and the verbal sumptuousness of the 'image-fashioner' (as D'Annunzio styled himself), Puccini preferred the easier and more sensational 'wizard of Broadway'.

Work on *Butterfly* was delayed when Puccini was badly injured in an automobile accident (child of his time, he had a passion for motor cars and motor boats). But finally the new opera was presented at La Scala on 17 February 1904. It was an overwhelming fiasco, all the more shattering as Puccini had been confident of success—so confident, in fact, that he had, exceptionally, invited his beloved sister Ramelde and her little daughter Albina to the première. Only a few hours after the curtain mercifully fell, Ramelde dashed off a letter to her husband:

'We are more dead than alive! I don't know what I'm writing. We're in bed, it's four a.m. We went to bed at 2, and I can't close my eyes. . . . The public was hostile from the start. We realized that at once. We never even saw Giacomo, poor thing, because we couldn't go back-stage. We reached the end, God knows how; I couldn't hear the second act at all. . . . Disgusting audience, abject, base. Not one sign of respect. . . . Mascagni and Giordano were there: imagine their fun!'

The reference to Mascagni is not casual. Many people present at the *Butterfly* première—Puccini among them—were convinced that the fiasco was organized, inspired by Sonzogno and his composers, Puccini's rivals. The effect on the composer was predictable; as he wrote the next day: '. . . It was a real lynching! Those cannibals didn't listen to one note. What a horrible orgy of madmen, drunk with hate! But my *Butterfly* remains what it is: the most deeply-felt and imaginative opera I have conceived!'

158. Enrico Caruso recording, self-caricature.
As the Italian critic and historian of singing Rodolfo Celletti wrote: 'Caruso enjoyed an immense popularity, which the development of the gramophone record greatly helped. In his turn, however, it was Caruso who gave records their first real achievements.' Caruso's voice was particularly phonogenic, and even with the primitive techniques of the period, he managed to convey the quality of his singing and the reality of his art. His first significant recordings were made in 1902, in Milan, for Zonophone, and then, that same year, an even more important series was recorded in a room of the Grand Hotel et de Milan, for the Gramophone and Typewriter Company. From 1904 until 1919 he recorded exclusively for the Victor Talking Machine Company, first in New York, then in their Camden, New Jersey, studios. In December 1920, he suffered a severe haemorrhage just before a performance of *L'elisir d'amore* in Brooklyn. He sang anyway, and also sang at the Metropolitan in the ensuing weeks, until he was forced to stop. After an operation, he returned to Italy to convalesce, but died in Naples on 2 August 1921.

159. Gabriele D'Annunzio at 'La Capponcina', 1906. Photograph by Mario Nunes Vais.

Gabriele D'Annunzio was a close friend of the broker-photographer Nunes Vais, for whom the poet posed often, especially in the years between 1898 and 1910, when he was living at La Capponcina. There D'Annunzio wrote, among other works, *La gioconda, Francesca da Rimini, La figlia di Jorio* for the theatre, and the novel *Il fuoco*, based on his clamorous affair with Eleonora Duse. At about the time of this photograph, Puccini visited D'Annunzio to discuss the possibility of their collaborating on an opera. The poet made several suggestions, including *La Parisina* and *La Rosa di Cipro*, neither of which finally convinced Puccini. Mascagni eventually set *La Parisina* (1913); other D'Annunzio texts were set by Alberto Franchetti, Ildebrando Pizzetti, Riccardo Zandonai, Italo Montemezzi, and G. F. Malipiero.

Actually *Butterfly* did not remain what it was. Puccini, who was accustomed to tinkering with his works even after performance, made some radical changes (and the hostile Milanese public was not entirely wrong; the opera's original interminable second act was clearly a test of endurance). Three months later, the revised opera was hailed joyously in the provincial theatre in Brescia, under Toscanini.

Now the intervals between one Puccini opera and the next grew longer; the composer's crippling spells of indecision worsened, as he became attached first to one text then, fickle, abandoned it for another. Six years went by before *La fanciulla del West* (1910), then seven and eight before *La rondine* and *Il trittico* (1917 and 1918); after this he became absorbed by *Turandot*, which was to occupy him until his death.

Old Giulio Ricordi and, even more, his brilliant, difficult son Tito were already looking around for the next Crown Prince. Sonzogno had snapped up Mascagni and Giordano (whose *Andrea Chénier* in 1896 and *Fedora* the following year had put him in the forefront of the 'young school'), and then Francesco Cilea, a slightly younger member, who made his mark in 1897 with *L'Arlesiana*, followed in 1902 by *Adriana Lecouvreur*.

PINKERTON (Caruso) SHARPLESS (Scotti) TOGO (Bada') CIO-CIO-SAN (**Farrar**)

While Puccini was working on his Far-West opera, in 1907, Giulio was introduced, by Boito, to a young man from the province of Trento, Riccardo Zandonai. The aspiring composer had arrived in the city with a sheaf of his music and some letters of introduction. His work impressed both Boito and Ricordi, who promptly signed him up and gave him a libretto: *Il grillo del focolare* ('The cricket on the hearth', from Dickens). The opera, given in Turin in 1908, encouraged Ricordi's to continue helping the composer; and after his father's death, in 1912, Tito worked closely with Zandonai on *Francesca da Rimini*. Tito himself dealt with D'Annunzio and skilfully adapted the poet's long play to libretto dimensions. Tito also staged the opera—in 1914—and contributed to its flattering success.

The firm's interest in this young composer did not escape the sensitive Puccini's attention, and it led, at one point, to a brief separation between Casa Ricordi and their most important living property. As a result, Puccini's light opera, *La rondine*, written at this time, was published by Sonzogno. But a further result of the dissension was Tito's eventually leaving the firm (obviously the directors were not pleased with the autocratic younger Ricordi—whose regal manner earned him the nickname of 'Savoia'—since he had alienated the house's great asset).

160. Puccini's *Madama Butterfly*, New York, 1907. Caricature by Enrico Caruso. In 1907, Heinrich Conried, general manager of the Metropolitan Opera, planned a special season of Puccini operas, including the first Met performances of *Manon Lescaut* and *Madama Butterfly*. For the occasion Conried offered Puccini a fee of 8,000 dollars to come to New York and supervise the productions. He did supervise, to some extent, the *Butterfly* rehearsals (although he had not arrived until the première of *Manon* was under way). Caruso—who recorded the preparation of the opera in a number of caricatures—was Pinkerton; Geraldine Farrar, idol of the American public, Cio-cio san; Antonio Scotti, Sharpless; Louise Homer, Suzuki. Arturo Vigna conducted. A week after the opening, Puccini wrote to Tito again: 'La *Butt.* went well for the press and the audience, "but not for me". A performance without poetry. I don't like Farrar much; she sings sharp, and her voice doesn't carry in the big hall. I had to fight for two complete rehearsals, including the dress!' To his London friend Sybil Seligman, a Caruso fan, Puccini was also critical of the tenor: 'lazy and too pleased with himself'.

The plays of D'Annunzio rely, as much as anything else, on sheer verbal virtuosity; and at first reading, they would seem totally anti-operatic. It is a measure of Tito's intelligence that he managed to reduce *Francesca* to serviceable length, as it is a measure of Zandonai's talent that he managed to make the still-verbose text into an opera that, whatever its final musical value may be, still possesses an undeniable dramatic tension and flow.

Other D'Annunzio texts were set by other composers. Mascagni—whom the poet had first attacked in a cruel article

entitled 'The Bandmaster'—essayed *Parisina* (1913), whose failure may have tempted him to try a rather Puccinian, sentimental subject for his next work, *Lodoletta*, in 1917 (based on a Ouida story which had, in fact, interested Puccini and had involved him and Casa Ricordi in extended, exhausting negotiations, before the composer's enthusiasm cooled). Franchetti also set D'Annunzio's most successful and most viable play, *La figlia di Jorio*, in 1906, which Ildebrando Pizzetti set again, much later, in 1954.

Pizzetti belonged to the generation that was still younger than the 'young school'; and with Gianfrancesco Malipiero and Alfredo Casella, he represented the anti-Puccini movement which, inevitably, had grown up in the wake—and in the face—of the composer's immense popularity.

Perhaps the unofficial spokesman of this group was a young musicologist, Fausto Torrefranca, born like Casella in 1883 (the other two composers were slightly older). In 1912 he published a little pamphlet, *Giacomo Puccini e l'opera internazionale*, which he had written a couple of years earlier. Torrefranca, referring to Puccini's 'cynical commercialism', predicted—through a very clouded crystal ball—that in ten years or so only the faint recol-

162. Cilea's *Adriana Lecouvreur*, Act IV. In the first decades of this century, in Italy, when an opera became popular, some photographer would rig up models in costume, pose them in scenes from the work (often with a bar or two of music and a few words of text), and sell the result, exploiting the piece's success. In this case, a photographer in Novara seems to have used actual singers, probably from a provincial production of Cilea's *Adriana Lecouvreur*, which had its première at the Teatro Lirico in Milan in 1902.

163. (*Right*) Feminism at La Scala. The first women's organizations in Italy arose in the factories and workshops in the last decades of the nineteenth century. In 1906 the Socialist Party formed The Socialist League for the Protection of Women's Interests. At the same time Anna Maria Mozzini (1837–1920) began agitating for women's political rights, including suffrage. Though the Italian movement never attracted the notoriety of similar movements in the United States and England, it was active, until—like all other progressive movements—it was suppressed by Mussolini.

lection of Puccini's music would remain, if that. But the burden of Torrefranca's attack was that the true Italian tradition in music was symphonic and instrumental, not operatic; the really great Italian musicians were not Verdi and Donizetti and Bellini, but Frescobaldi, Corelli, Veracini and Vivaldi (then names known only to specialists).

Although Malipiero, Pizzetti, and Casella all composed operas sooner or later, they were written in a firmly anti-traditional spirit. In Florence, when Puccini's *Trittico* was first performed there, Pizzetti—then music critic of *La Nazione*, the city's leading daily paper—ostentatiously stayed away and sent his assistant to review the première.

Pizzetti's *Fedra*, on a D'Annunzio text, was performed in 1914 (Puccini jokingly referred to it as 'la federa': the pillow-case). The year before, Malipiero, aged thirty-one, had set D'Annunzio's *Sogno d'un tramonto d'autunno* (An Autumn Sunset Dream), but it was not produced, and the composer's real operatic career began only after the Great War. Casella, the youngest of the trio, began writing operas much later.

Italy had joined the Triple Alliance in 1882, shortly after King Umberto and Queen Margherita had made a state visit to Vienna. In the ensuing years the pact was renewed several times, but in 1914, when Italy had to face the prospect of the First World War, there were sharply divided feelings about which side to join (or whether, indeed, to stay out of it altogether). In effect, the prime minister Salandra and his foreign minister Sonnino auctioned off Italy's allegiance: Britain and the Entente won, and by the Treaty of London—kept a secret from the Italian Parliament and the Italian people—the nation was pledged to enter the war on the side of the Allies.

The deepest division in the nation was between the interventionists and the neutrals. Among the most belligerent interventionists was D'Annunzio. Though he had fled Italy some time previously to escape his creditors, he returned from France in May of 1915, shortly before Italy's declaration of war. He made a ringing, aggressive speech at Quarto, the little coastal town from which Garibaldi and his Thousand had set sail in 1860 for Sicily.

The Socialists were non-interventionists. In fact, the party had been split over the question; and one faction, led by the pro-war Benito Mussolini, had broken off. This schism was the real beginning of the future dictator's career.

As usual, Puccini tried to ignore the political situation. Privately, he disliked the French and liked the Germans and the Austrians, who loved his music and even paid serious critical attention to it. Vienna was one of the few cities where he enjoyed himself, and it was hard for him to think of the Viennese as The Enemy.

So he was a non-interventionist, not only to protect his German-language royalties, but also because he was temperamentally pacific (although the frequent, not undeserved attacks of the jealous Elvira might have conditioned him otherwise). His aloof attitude, his coolness in the midst of the war fever, won him numerous enemies, his fellow-composers prominent among them. Leoncavallo, who had composed *Der Roland von Berlin* in 1904 at the express command of the Kaiser (it had been a failure all the same), dramatized his now anti-German sentiments by returning indignantly all his German decorations. Mascagni was more reserved, but Toscanini—a furious interventionist—almost stopped speaking to Puccini. And a whole array of French composers and artists publicly denounced him.

Leoncavallo was determined to become the bard of the 'holy war', in conscious imitation of Verdi, bard—as Leoncavallo insisted—of the Risorgimento. Thus the composer of *Pagliacci* wrote, hastily, *Goffredo Mameli*, performed at the Carlo Felice in Genoa on 27 April 1916. Given the date and the subject, the work—conducted by the composer—had an inevitable success.

Toscanini conducted concerts in the war zone. And during the spring of 1917, Boito, now well into his seventies, visited army headquarters near Monte Santo. While the mountain was being taken by the Italians, the composer was lunching with the general in command, who insisted that the old musician play something: 'Maestro, I have offered you the symphony of the mouths of fire,' the military man is reported to have said, in true D'Annunzian style, 'Now let us hear something more human, something of your own.' And Boito sat at the piano and played the notes of the Prologue of *Mefistofele*, his youthful work of fifty years earlier.

On his way back to Milan, he opened the train window to give some fresh air to a couple of convalescent young officers in his compartment; he caught a chill and, the moment he was home in Milan, had to go to his bed. He was in nagging poor health for months afterwards; the disaster of Caporetto, in the autumn, plunged him into deep depression. Finally, after long and patient suffering, Boito died on 10 June 1918. The next day Puccini wrote to Tito Ricordi: 'With Boito, the last of the host of our Sig. Giulio's comrades has gone!'

With Boito, too, the last of Verdi's companions—one of the few that Verdi accepted—had gone. He left behind the unfinished opera *Nerone*, the work that had tormented him for nearly six decades, the music that he had intended to be his monument, his masterpiece, and that instead had been the millstone of his mature life.

The 1916–17 season proceeded normally at La Scala, in spite of the war. On 20 November there was a 'Patriotic Evening Dedicated to the Allies', with speeches by several political figures, including Mussolini. The musical programme, conducted by Tullio Serafin, included 'Va, pensiero' and choruses from *I lombardi*, *Norma*, the Marseillaise, 'God Save the King', the Italian Royal March, the Inno di Garibaldi, and the Inno di Mameli. The following month—when the opera season was

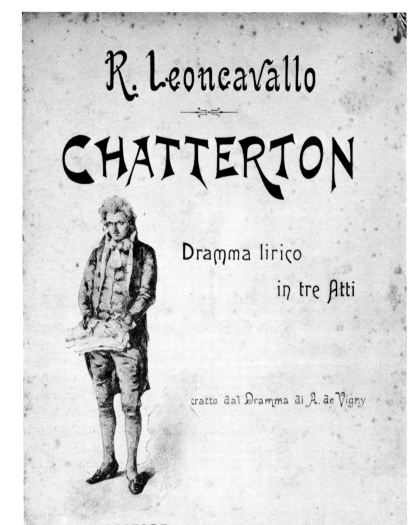

R. Leoncavallo

CHATTERTON

Dramma lirico

in tre Atti

tratto dal Dramma di A. de Vigny

EDITORE
ACHILLE TEDESCHI
BOLOGNA

164. Leoncavallo's *Chatterton*. Cover of libretto, 1896.
When Leoncavallo was twenty and a student of literature at the University of Bologna, he composed his first opera, *Chatterton*, to his own libretto based on the drama by Alfred de Vigny. A local impresario promised to mount the opera and, on the strength of this promise, extracted some money from the impecunious Leoncavallo. But then the impresario reneged, and the aspiring composer put his first effort away in a drawer for almost two decades. Later, after the success of *Pagliacci* in 1892 and what seemed the success of *I Medici* the following year, Leoncavallo remembered his early work. *Chatterton* was given its première at the Teatro Nazionale in Rome on 10 March 1896, but in spite of some sporadic revivals elsewhere, it did not win a place in the repertory.

over—there was another special programme, this time for the refugees from the Friuli region, overrun by the Austrians (for the occasion a *Canzone guerresca* by Giordano was performed). And on 3 March 1918 there was a Patriotic Band Concert, at which the Carabineri Band played the *William Tell* Overture, followed by the Band of the US 18th Infantry Regiment (*Stars and Stripes Forever*), the Band of the Garde Républicaine (*Benvenuto Cellini* Overture), and the Royal Guards Band (German: *Three Ancient Dances*; Douglas: *Tipperary*).

Before the war, the Scala had been managed—or governed—by a board, headed first by Duke Guido Visconti di Modrone, then by his son Uberto, who administered the funds contributed by the city and by the *palchettisti*, the owners of the boxes, who were, practically speaking, the owners of the theatre. It was an unsatisfactory system, and at the end of the war, when the theatre was closed, the Socialist mayor of Milan headed a movement to modernize and democratize the system. So the Ente Autonomo

165. Arturo Toscanini, caricature by Enrico Caruso.

Caruso sang many times with Toscanini; in fact, the tenor made his Scala debut, as Nemorino in *L'elisir d'amore*, under the baton of Toscanini, on 17 February 1901. In that same Scala season, Toscanini conducted Caruso in Boito's *Mefistofele*. But the real revelation of Caruso came, again under Toscanini, the following season, when on 11 March 1902 he created the role of Federico in Franchetti's *Germania*. The two men worked well together, with reciprocal respect, and they later collaborated during Toscanini's years at the Metropolitan (Toscanini conducted, among many other works, the world première of *La fanciulla del West*, with Caruso as Dick Johnson). In 1915, back in Italy, Toscanini organized an important, if brief, wartime season at the Teatro Dal Verme in Milan, where Caruso sang along with Rosina Storchio and Riccardo Stracciari.

was born; the Scala became independent of its box-holders, and was state-operated.

The modernization of the theatre was also physical: the proscenium apron—on which the singers, in earlier times, had stepped forward to perform their arias virtually in the midst of the public—was abolished. The orchestra pit, now sunk below stalls level, became a Wagnerian 'mystic gulf'. These reforms were the logical continuation of others that, against strong opposition, Toscanini had instituted during his tenure at the turn of the century. Then he had established the practice of lowering the house lights during the performance (another Wagnerian innovation), had abolished the traditional *bis*, the encores granted by popular singers, and had obliged ladies sitting in the stalls to remove their hats.

Toscanini had left Milan and La Scala to go to the Metropolitan in New York, but had quarrelled with Gatti Casazza there and had returned to Italy; he was now called once more to be the artistic director of the renovated and revitalized theatre. One of the first tasks that faced him was the preparation of Boito's *Nerone* for performance.

Toscanini had seen a score as far back as 1902 (one of the several occasions when Boito considered the work 'almost ready', then changed his mind). Since then, it had undergone more changes and cuts and additions. It was a problem to piece together a performing version from the chaos of pages and pages of music, sketches, annotations, and the various copies of the printed literary text, filled with marginal observations and modifications by the author. Toscanini was assisted first by the Triestan composer Antonio Smareglia and then, more importantly, by Vincenzo Tommasini. Finally, six years after Boito's death, *Nerone* was given at La Scala.

It was scheduled for 1 May 1924, May Day. The Fascists were

166. Mussolini at the Teatro San Carlo, Naples, 24 October 1922.
As it had witnessed the rise and fall of kings and governments, so the San Carlo witnessed the rise of Mussolini and the Fascist regime. In the last week of October 1922, the Fascist party held its first really important national congress in Naples. On 24 October, Mussolini fiercely attacked the cabinet of the Piedmontese lawyer Luigi Facta. Later, in the square outside the theatre, the Piazza San Ferdinando, Mussolini said even more vehemently: 'Either they give us the government, or we will take it, descending on Rome: now it is a matter of days, perhaps of hours.' It was a matter of days. On 28 October there was the so-called March on Rome, and by 31 October Mussolini was prime minister.

167. (Overleaf) Poster for Boito's Nerone at La Scala, with cancellation notice because of Puccini's death, 1924.
Boito's posthumous opera Nerone opened at La Scala, under Toscanini, on 1 May 1924, and was given nine more performances before the end of the season. Because of the exceptional interest the opera had aroused, it was revived again on 15 November of the same year for another thirteen performances. Puccini's almost-finished Turandot was also announced for that season. But on 29 November, during the run of Nerone, Puccini died. The news struck La Scala like a thunderbolt. The performance of Nerone, scheduled for that evening, was cancelled.

in power, but the Socialist Party still existed, and the possibility of demonstrations outside—or even inside—the theatre concerned the management. But Toscanini held firm, and the première took place on the day that had been set.

The seats had been sold out long in advance, and black-market prices for a stall went as high as three or four thousand lire, while the unofficial price of a box was ten thousand. People began to queue up outside the gallery entrance at seven in the morning, bringing folding chairs and picnic lunches. That evening, automobiles jammed the Via Manzoni and the Via Verdi (the street flanking the Scala), and the police had to fight off crowds that had come simply to see the crowd.

Toscanini had allowed only journalists into the dress rehearsal, and Puccini, who had appeared at the stage entrance, had been turned away. Swallowing his resentment, he returned for the opening night, surely remembering the important role that Boito had played in his life (even though in his final years Boito disapproved of Puccini's later works). Also present were Giordano and younger men like Franco Alfano, Italo Montemezzi, and Pizzetti. Critics came from all over Italy and from abroad; there were ambassadors, managers of foreign opera houses, representatives of the government.

Naturally, Nerone had a frenzied success. Toscanini and the singers (Rosa Raisa, Aureliano Pertile, Carlo Galeffi, Marcel Journet) received prolonged ovations, as did the designer, the lighting director and the others responsible for the impressive production. But the opera was born dead. It was promptly performed in other theatres; then it vanished from the repertory except for a very occasional, pious revival.

Puccini left Milan a day or so later and went back to Viareggio, dejected by his rebuff at La Scala and depressed also because of his health. For months he had been suffering from a chronic sore throat. He had consulted various doctors, who had recommended cures and insisted he stop smoking; eventually, after a biopsy, the truth was clear: Puccini had an inoperable tumour. The specialists recommended X-ray treatments, and it was decided that the composer would go to the Institut de la Couronne in Brussels.

Before leaving Italy, Puccini had a final meeting with Toscanini, at which all their differences were resolved and the old friendship was restored. Then, on 4 November, Puccini set out for Belgium.

During the first part of the treatment, he was able to leave the clinic. He even went to a performance of Butterfly at the Théâtre de la Monnaie. Clausetti, now the head of Casa Ricordi, visited him; so did Toscanini, and Puccini's devoted English friend Sybil Seligman. Elvira had to remain home in Viareggio with bronchitis; but her daughter Fosca was constantly at Puccini's side.

On 24 November Dr Ledoux, director of the clinic, operated, in order to apply radium directly to the tumour. The operation

168. Puccini's funeral in Brussels, 1924. After Puccini's death on 29 November the director of the Institut was so distraught that, on driving away from the clinic, he ran over a woman and killed her. With the Papal Nuncio Micara officiating, a Requiem Mass was sung for Puccini at the church of Sainte-Marie, on 1 December.

seemed a success. Although Puccini was unable to speak, he could take a few steps and read the newspapers. Then, on the 28th he collapsed, and the following morning he died.

The funeral was held in Brussels, then another solemn ceremony took place at the Duomo in Milan, with the orchestra and chorus of La Scala under Toscanini, who conducted the requiem scene from *Edgar*. The composer's remains were placed temporarily in the Toscanini family tomb in Milan, then moved two years later to a specially-built chapel in Puccini's house at Torre del Lago. Mascagni pronounced a commemorative oration.

But the public's farewell to Puccini took place on 25 April 1926, when his last opera, *Turandot*, was performed at La Scala. He had left it almost finished, and the final scenes had been tactfully filled in by Franco Alfano, a musician Puccini had known and liked. But on that opening night at La Scala, Alfano's careful patchwork was not heard. Before the glittering audience (only Mussolini was absent, because Toscanini had refused to conduct the Fascist anthem *Giovinezza* before the opera), as he reached the conclusion of Liù's death scene, Toscanini laid down his baton and said, in effect (he has been quoted variously): 'The opera ends here, because at this point the Maestro died. Death was stronger than art.'

The opera ends here. Toscanini might have been speaking not just of Puccini's last work but of Italian opera in general. Of course, other new Italian operas were composed and performed in the decades that followed, and some of them enjoyed a certain success, a certain theatrical life. But Puccini left no Crown Prince. With him, the glorious line, Rossini, Bellini, Donizetti, Verdi, came to a glorious conclusion.

ITALIAN OPERA IN CONTEXT: A BRIEF CHRONOLOGY

1792	29 February	Gioacchino Rossini born
1795		Saverio Mercadante born
1797		Gaetano Donizetti born
1800		Napoleon's victory at Marengo
1801		Vincenzo Bellini born
1805		Napoleon crowned king of Italy
	20 November	Beethoven's *Fidelio* (first version) first performed, Theater an der Wien, Vienna
1807	16 December	Spontini's *La Vestale*, Opéra, Paris
1810	3 November	Rossini's first opera, the one-act *La Cambiale di matrimonio*, Teatro San Moisé, Venice
1812	8 January	Rossini's *L'inganno felice*, Teatro San Moisé
	14 March	Rossini's *Ciro in Babilonia*, Teatro Municipale, Ferrara
	9 May	Rossini's *La scala di seta*, Teatro San Moisé
	26 September	Rossini's *La pietra del Paragone*, La Scala, Milan
1813	Late January	Rossini's *Il signor Bruschino*, San Moisé
	6 February	Rossini's *Tancredi*, La Fenice, Venice
	22 May	Rossini's *L'italiana in Algeri*, Teatro San Benedetto, Venice
1813	9 (or 10) October	Giuseppe Verdi born
		Richard Wagner born
1814	23 May	Beethoven's *Fidelio* (definitive version), Kärntnertortheater, Vienna
	14 August	Rossini's *Il turco in Italia*, La Scala
		Giovanni Ricordi opens his music-printing business in Milan
		Congress of Vienna (until 1815)
1815	18 June	Battle of Waterloo
1816	20 February	Rossini's *Il barbiere di Siviglia*, Teatro Argentina, Rome
	4 December	Rossini's *Otello*, Teatro del Fondo, Naples
1817	25 January	Rossini's *La cenerentola*, Teatro Valle, Rome
	31 May	Rossini's *La gazza ladra*, La Scala
1818	5 March	Rossini's *Mosè in Egitto*, Teatro San Carlo, Naples
1819	19 August	Mercadante's first opera, *L'apoteosi di Ercole*, Teatro San Carlo, Naples
	24 September	Rossini's *La donna del lago*, San Carlo
1820	14 June	Schubert's *singspiel* in one act, *Die Zwillingsbrüder*, Kärntnertortheater, Vienna
	19 August	Schubert's 3-act musical play, *Der Zauberharfe*, Theater an der Wien, Vienna
1821	18 June	Weber's *Der Freischutz*, Schauspielhaus, Berlin
1822	16 February	Rossini's *Zelmira*, San Carlo
1823	3 February	Rossini's *Semiramide*, La Fenice
	25 October	Weber's *Euryanthe*, Kärntnertortheater, Vienna
1824	4 February	Donizetti's *L'ajo nell'imbarazzo*, his first important success, Teatro Valle, Rome
1825	10 December	Boieldieu's *La Dame blanche*, Opéra-Comique, Paris
	12 December	Bellini's first opera, a student work, *Adelson e Salvini*, given at the Teatro del Conservatorio di San Sebastiano, Naples
1826	12 April	Weber's *Oberon*, Covent Garden
	30 May	Bellini's *Bianca e Gernando*, San Carlo
	9 October	Rossini's *Le Siège de Corinth*, his first work for Paris, at the Opéra
1827	12 June	Spontini's *Agnes von Hohenstaufen*, Berlin (first act only – first complete performance, 1829)
	27 October	Bellini's *Il pirata* at La Scala
1828	29 February	Auber's *La Muette de Portici* (or *Masaniello*), Opéra, Paris
	20 August	Rossini's *Le Comte Ory*, Opéra, Paris
1829	14 February	Bellini's *La straniera*, Scala
	16 May	Bellini's *Zaira*, Teatro ducale, Parma
	6 July	Donizetti's *Il castello di Kenilworth*, San Carlo
	3 August	Rossini's *Guillaume Tell*, Opéra, Paris
1830	11 March	Bellini's *I Capuleti ed i Montecchi*, La Fenice
	26 December	Donizetti's *Anna Bolena*, Teatro Carcano, Milan
1831		Giuseppe Mazzini founds *Giovine Italia* movement
	6 March	Bellini's *La sonnambula*, Carcano
	22 November	Meyerbeer's *Robert le Diable*, Opéra, Paris
	26 December	Bellini's *Norma*, La Scala

1832	12 May	Donizetti's *L'elisir d'amore*, Canobbiana, Milan
1833	2 January	Donizetti's *Il furioso all'isola di San Domingo*, Teatro Valle, Rome
	16 March	Bellini's *Beatrice di Tenda*, La Fenice
	17 March	Donizetti's *Parisina*, Teatro della Pergola, Florence
	9 September	Donizetti's *Torquato Tasso*, Valle
	26 December	Donizetti's *Lucrezia Borgia*, La Scala
1834		Amilcare Ponchielli born
1835	25 January	Bellini's *I puritani*, Théâtre-Italien, Paris
	23 February	Halévy's *La Juive*, Opéra, Paris
	12 March	Donizetti's *Marino Faliero*, Italien, Paris
	24 September	Bellini dies at Puteaux, near Paris
	26 September	Donizetti's *Lucia di Lammermoor*, San Carlo
	30 December	Donizetti's *Maria Stuarda* (uncensored version), La Scala
1836	4 February	Donizetti's *Belisario*, La Fenice
	29 February	Meyerbeer's *Les Huguenots*, Opéra, Paris
	22 March	Mercadante's *I briganti*, Italien, Paris
	29 March	Wagner's *Das Liebesverbot*, his first performed opera, given one disastrous performance at Stadttheater, Magdeburg
	1 June	Donizetti's *Il campanello*, Teatro Nuovo, Naples
	13 October	Adam's *Le Postillon de Longjumeau*, Opéra-Comique, Paris
	9 December	Glinka's *A Life for the Tsar*, Imperial Theatre, St Petersburg
1837	18 February	Donizetti's *Pia de' Tolomei*, Teatro Apollo, Venice
	10 March	Mercadante's *Il giuramento*, Scala
	29 October	Donizetti's *Roberto Devereux*, San Carlo
	22 December	Lorzing's *Zar und Zimmermann*, Stadttheater, Leipzig
1838	10 September	Berlioz's *Benvenuto Cellini*, Opéra, Paris
1839	9 March	Mercadante's *Il bravo*, La Scala
	17 November	Verdi's first opera, *Oberto*, Scala
1840–1842		Manzoni publishes *I promessi sposi*
1840	11 February	Donizetti's *La Fille du Régiment*, Opéra-Comique, Paris
	5 September	Verdi's *Un giorno di regno*, La Scala
	29 November	Pacini's *Saffo*, San Carlo
	2 December	Donizetti's *La Favorite*, Opéra, Paris
1842	9 March	Verdi's *Nabucco*, Scala
	19 May	Donizetti's *Linda di Chamounix*, Kärntnertortheater, Vienna
	20 October	Wagner's *Rienzi*, Hofoper, Dresden
	9 December	Glinka's *Ruslan and Lyudmila*, Imperial Theatre, St Petersburg
1842		Arrigo Boito born
1843	2 January	Wagner's *Flying Dutchman*, Hofoper, Dresden
	3 January	Donizetti's *Don Pasquale*, Italien, Paris
	11 February	Verdi's *I lombardi*, Scala
	5 June	Donizetti's *Maria di Rohan*, Kärntnertortheater, Vienna
	27 November	Balfe's *The Bohemian Girl*, Drury Lane, London
1844	9 March	Verdi's *Ernani*, La Fenice
	3 November	Verdi's *I due Foscari*, Argentina, Rome
	30 December	Flotow's *Stradella*, Stadttheater, Hamburg
1845	15 February	Verdi's *Giovanna d'Arco*, Scala
	12 August	Verdi's *Alzira*, San Carlo
	19 October	Wagner's *Tannhäuser*, Hofoper, Dresden
1846	17 March	Verdi's *Attila*, La Fenice
1847	14 March	Verdi's *Macbeth*, Pergola, Florence
	22 July	Verdi's *I masnadieri*, Her Majesty's Theatre, London
	25 November	Flotow's *Martha*, Kärntnertortheater, Vienna
	26 November	Verdi's *Jerusalem* (reworking of *I lombardi*), Opéra, Paris
1848	22–24 February	Insurrection in Paris; Louis-Philippe abdicates
	18–23 March	'Le cinque giornate': the Milanese expel the Austrians
	25 March	first Italian War of Independence
	25 October	Verdi's *Il corsaro*, Teatro Grande, Trieste
		Donizetti dies
	30 November	posthumous première of Donizetti's *Poliuto*, San Carlo
1849	27 January	Verdi's *La battaglia di Legnano*, Argentina, Rome
	5 February	Roman Republic proclaimed
	9 March	Nicolai's *Die lustigen Weiber von Windsor*, Hofoper, Berlin
	29 March	Victor Emanuel II becomes king of Piedmont
	14 July	Pope restored to power in Rome

1849	8 December	Verdi's *Luisa Miller*, San Carlo
1850	28 August	Wagner's *Lohengrin*, Hoftheater, Weimar
	16 November	Verdi's *Stiffelio*, Teatro Grande, Trieste
1851	11 March	Verdi's *Rigoletto*, La Fenice
	16 April	Gounod's *Sapho*, Opéra, Paris
		Louis-Napoléon becomes Napoleon III
1853	19 January	Verdi's *Il trovatore*, Apollo, Rome
		Giovanni Ricordi dies, and is succeeded by his son Tito
	6 March	Verdi's *La traviata*, La Fenice
1854	16 February	Meyerbeer, *L'Etoile du Nord*, Opéra-Comique, Paris
		Alfredo Catalani born
1855	13 June	Verdi's *Les Vêpres siciliennes*, Opéra, Paris
1856	16 May	Dargomozhsky's *Rusalka*, Imperial Theatre, St Petersburg
	30 August	Ponchielli's *I promessi sposi*, Teatro Concordia, Cremona
1857	12 March	Verdi's *Simon Boccanegra*, La Fenice
	16 August	Verdi's *Aroldo* (revised version of *Stiffelio*), Teatro Nuovo, Rimini
		Ruggiero Leoncavallo born
1858	21 October	Offenbach's *Orphée aux Enfers*, Bouffes-Parisiens, Paris
	15 December	Cornelius's *Der Barbier von Bagdad*, Hoftheater, Weimar
		Giacomo Puccini born
1859	17 February	Verdi's *Un ballo in maschera*, Apollo, Rome
	19 March	Gounod's *Faust*, Théâtre Lyrique, Paris
	4 April	Meyerbeer's *Dinorah*, Opéra-Comique, Paris
	29 April	second Italian War of Independence
1860	11 May	Garibaldi and the Thousand land in Sicily
	7 September	Garibaldi enters Naples: collapse of Bourbon reign
1861	14 February	first national Italian Parliament: Verdi is a deputy
		proclamation of the Unification of Italy
	6 June	death of Cavour
1862	9 August	Berlioz's *Béatrice et Bénédict*, Théâtre Bénazet, Weimar
	10 November	Verdi's *La forza del destino*, Imperial Theatre, St Petersburg
1863	30 September	Bizet's *Les Pêcheurs de perles*, Théâtre Lyrique, Paris
	4 November	Berlioz's *Les Troyens*, Théâtre Lyrique, Paris (only Part II performed)
		Pietro Mascagni born
1864	19 March	Gounod's *Mireille*, Théâtre Lyrique, Paris
	17 December	Offenbach's *La Belle Hélène*, Théâtre des Variétés, Paris
		Meyerbeer dies
1865	28 April	Meyerbeer's *L'Africaine* (posthumous), Opéra, Paris
	10 June	Wagner's *Tristan und Isolde*, Hoftheater, Munich
1866	30 May	Smetana's *The Bartered Bride*, Provisional Theatre, Prague
	17 November	Thomas's *Mignon*, Opéra-Comique, Paris
		Francesco Cilea born
1867		Arturo Toscanini born
	11 March	Verdi's *Don Carlos*, Opéra, Paris
	27 April	Gounod's *Roméo et Juliette*, Théâtre Lyrique, Paris
		Umberto Giordano born
1868	5 March	Boito's *Mefistofele*, Scala
	9 March	Thomas's *Hamlet*, Opéra, Paris
	16 May	Smetana's *Dalibor*, Municipal Theatre, Prague
	21 June	Wagner's *Die Meistersinger*, Hoftheater, Munich
	13 November	Rossini dies
1869	27 February	revised *Forza del destino* at La Scala
	22 September	Wagner's *Das Rheingold*, Hoftheater, Munich
1870	19 March	Gomes's *Il guarany*, Scala
	26 June	Wagner's *Die Walküre*, Hoftheater, Munich
	20 September	Italian troops enter Rome; end of Pope's temporal power
		death of Mercadante
1871	19 November	Wagner's *Lohengrin* in Bologna, first Wagner opera produced in Italy
	24 December	Verdi's *Aida*, Khedival Theatre, Cairo
1873	13 January	Rimsky-Korsakov's *The Fair Maid of Pskov* (or *Ivan the Terrible*), Maryinsky Theatre, St Petersburg
	22 May	Alessandro Manzoni dies in Milan
	24 May	Délibes's *Le Roi l'a dit*, Opéra-comique, Paris
1874		Giovanni Verga publishes *Nedda*, initiating the *verismo* movement in Italian literature

1874		Ponchielli's *I lituani*, Scala
	8 February	Mussorgsky's *Boris Godunov*, Maryinsky, St Petersburg
	5 April	Johann Strauss, *Die Fledermaus*, Theater an der Wien, Vienna
	22 May	Verdi's *Messa da Requiem*, in the church of San Marco, Milan
1875	25 January	Anton Rubinstein's *The Demon*, Imperial Theatre, St Petersburg
	3 March	Bizet's *Carmen*, Opéra-Comique, Paris
	10 March	Goldmark's *Die Königin von Saba*, Hoftheater, Vienna
1876	6 February	Tchaikovsky's *Vakula the Smith*, Maryinsky, St Petersburg
	8 April	Ponchielli's *La gioconda*, Scala (revised: 20 February 1880, Scala)
	16 August	Wagner's *Siegfried*, Festspielhaus, Bayreuth
	17 August	Wagner's *Götterdämmerung*, idem
	7 November	Smetana's *The Kiss*, Provisional Theatre, Prague
1877	27 April	Massenet's *Le Roi de Lahore*, Opéra, Paris
	2 December	Saint-Saens's *Samson et Dalila*, Hoftheater, Weimar
1878		Umberto I becomes king of Italy
1881	10 February	Offenbach's *Les Contes d'Hoffmann* (posthumous), Paris, Opéra-Comique
	24 March	Verdi's revised *Simon Boccanegra*, Scala
	23 April	Tchaikovsky's *Eugene Onegin*, Bolshoy, Moscow (a student performance took place on 28 March 1879 at the Imperial College of Music, Moscow)
	11 June	Smetana's *Libuse*, National Theatre, Prague
	19 December	Massenet's *Hérodiade*, Théâtre de la Monnaie, Brussels
1882	10 February	Rimsky-Korsakov's *The Snow Maiden*, Maryinsky, St Petersburg
	26 July	Wagner's *Parsifal*, Festspielhaus, Bayreuth
1883	14 April	Delibes's *Lakmé*, Opéra-Comique, Paris
1884	10 January	Revised version of Verdi's *Don Carlos* at La Scala
	19 January	Massenet's *Manon*, Opéra-Comique, Paris
	15 February	Tchaikovsky's *Mazeppa*, Bolshoy, Moscow
	31 May	Puccini's first opera, *Le Villi*, Teatro Dal Verme, Milan
1885	17 March	Ponchielli's *Marion Delorme*, Scala
	30 November	Massenet's *Le Cid*, Opéra, Paris
1886		Clarina Maffei dies
	21 February	Mussorgsky's *Khovanschina*, Kononov Theatre, St Petersburg
1887	5 February	Verdi's *Otello*, La Scala
	18 May	Chabrier's *Le Roi malgré lui*, Opéra-Comique, Paris
1888		Tito Ricordi dies; he is succeeded by his son Giulio
		Verga publishes *Novelle rusticane*; D'Annunzio publishes *Il piacere*
1888	7 May	Lalo's *Le Roi d'Ys*, Opéra-Comique, Paris
1889	12 February	Dvorak's *The Jacobin*, National Theatre, Prague
	21 April	Puccini's *Edgar*, La Scala
	14 May	Massenet's *Esclarmonde*, Opéra-Comique, Paris
1890	16 February	Catalani's *Loreley*, Teatro Regio, Turin
	17 May	Mascagni's *Cavalleria rusticana*, Costanzi, Rome
	4 November	Borodin's *Prince Igor* (posthumous), Maryinsky, St Petersburg
	19 December	Tchaikovsky's *Pique-dame*, Maryinsky
	31 October	Mascagni's *L'amico Fritz*, Costanzi, Rome
1891		death of Franco Faccio
1892	20 January	Catalani's *La Wally*, Scala
	16 February	Massenet's *Werther*, Hofoper, Vienna
	21 May	Leoncavallo's *Pagliacci*, Teatro Dal Verme, Milan
	6 October	Franchetti's *Cristoforo Colombo*, Teatro Carlo Felice, Genoa
1893	1 February	Puccini's *Manon Lescaut*, Teatro Regio, Turin
	9 February	Verdi's *Falstaff*, Scala
	23 December	Humperdinck's *Hansel und Gretel*, Hoftheater, Weimar
		Alfredo Catalani dies
1894	16 March	Massenet's *Thaïs*, Opéra, Paris
	10 May	Richard Strauss's first performed opera, *Guntram*, Hoftheater, Weimar
1895	16 February	Mascagni's *Guglielmo Ratcliffe*, Scala
1896	1 February	Puccini's *La Bohème*, Regio, Turin
	28 March	Giordano's *Andrea Chénier*, Scala
	7 June	Hugo Wolf's *Der Corregidor*, Nationaltheater, Mannheim
1897		death of Giuseppina Strepponi Verdi

1897	6 May	Leoncavallo's *La Bohème*, La Fenice
	27 November	Cilea's *L'arlesiana*, Teatro Lirico, Milan
1898	7 January	Rimsky-Korsakov's *Sadko*, Solodovnikov Theatre, Moscow
	17 November	Giordano's *Fedora*, Teatro Lirico, Milan
		Gramophone and Typewriter Co. (later HMV) established
1898	22 November	Mascagni's *Iris*, Costanzi, Rome
	7 December	Rimsky-Korsakov's *Mozart and Salieri*, Solodovnikov Theatre, Moscow
1899	24 May	Massenet's *Cendrillon*, Opéra-Comique, Paris
	3 November	Rimsky-Korsakov's *The Tsar's Bride*, Solodovnikov Theatre, Moscow
1900	2 February	Charpentier's *Louise*, Opéra-Comique, Paris
	12 July	Puccini's *Tosca*, Costanzi, Rome
		King Umberto I assassinated, succeeded by Vittorio Emanuele III
	10 November	Leoncavallo's *Zaza*, Teatro Lirico, Milan
1901	22 January	Queen Victoria dies
	27 January	Verdi dies
	31 March	Dvorak's *Rusalka*, National Theatre, Prague
	21 November	Richard Strauss's *Feuersnot*, Königliches Opernhaus, Dresden
1902	18 February	Massenet's *Le Jongleur de Notre-Dame*, Théâtre du Casino, Monte Carlo
	11 March	Franchetti's *Germania*, Scala
	30 April	Debussy's *Pelléas et Mélisande*, Opéra-Comique, Paris
	26 November	Cilea's *Adriana Lecouvreur*, Lirico, Milan
1903	15 November	d'Albert's *Tiefland*, Neues Deutsches Theater, Prague
1903	19 December	Giordano's *Siberia*, Scala
1904	21 January	Janacek's *Jenufa*, Deutsches Nationaltheater, Brno
	17 February	Puccini's *Madama Butterfly*, Scala (revised version 28 March 1904 in Brescia)
	30 March	Delius's *Koanga*, Stadttheater, Elberfeld
	30 November	Alfano's *Risurrezione*, Teatro Vittorio Emanuele II, Turin
1905	19 December	Strauss's *Salome*, Königliches Opernhaus, Dresden
1906	19 March	Wolf-Ferrari's *I quattro rusteghi*, Hoftheater, Munich
1907	20 February	Rimsky-Korsakov's *The Legend of the invisible city of Kitezh*, Maryinsky, St Petersburg
	21 February	Delius's *A village Romeo and Juliet*, Komische Oper, Berlin
	10 May	Dukas's *Ariane et Barbe-bleue*, Opéra-Comique, Paris
1909	25 January	Strauss's *Elektra*, Königliches Opernhaus, Dresden
	7 October	Rimsky-Korsakov's *The Golden Cockerel*, Solodovnikov Theatre, Moscow
	4 December	Wolf-Ferrari's *Il segreto di Susanna*, Hoftheater, Munich
1910	19 February	Massenet's *Don Quichotte*, Théâtre du Casino, Monte Carlo
	30 November	Ernest Bloch's *Macbeth*, Opéra-Comique, Paris
	10 December	Puccini's *La fanciulla del West*, Metropolitan, New York
1910	28 December	Humperdinck's *Die Königskinder*, Metropolitan, New York
1911		Italian war in Libya
	26 January	Strauss's *Der Rosenkavalier*, Königliches Opernhaus, Berlin
	19 May	Ravel's *L'Heure espagnole*, Opéra-Comique, Paris
	22 May	Debussy/D'Annunzio, *Le Martyre de Saint Sébastien*, Théâtre du Châtelet, Paris
	2 June	Mascagni's *Isabeau*, Teatro Coliseo, Buenos Aires
	14 October	Zandonai's *Conchita*, Teatro Dal Verme, Milan
	23 December	Wolf-Ferrari's *I gioielli della Madonna*, Kurfürstenoper, Berlin
1912		Giulio Ricordi dies
	13 April	Busoni's *Die Brautwahl*, Staatsoper, Hamburg
1913	1 April	Falla's *La vida breve*, Théâtre de l'Opéra, Nice
	10 April	Montemezzi's *L'amore dei tre re*, Scala
	4 June	Charpentier's *Julien*, Opéra-Comique, Paris
	15 December	Mascagni's *Parisina*, Scala
1914	19 February	Zandonai's *Francesca da Rimini*, Teatro Regio, Turin
	26 May	Stravinsky's *Le Rossignol*, Opéra, Paris
	28 July	World War I breaks out
1915	25 January	Giordano's *Madame Sans-Gêne*, Metropolitan, New York
	20 March	Pizzetti's *Fedra*, Scala
1916	28 January	Granados's *Goyescas*, Metropolitan, New York
	4 October	Strauss's *Ariadne auf Naxos* (final version; first version performed in Stuttgart, 1912)

1917	27 March	Puccini's *La rondine*, Théâtre du Casino, Monte Carlo
	30 April	Mascagni's *Lodoletta*, Costanzi, Rome
	11 May	Busoni's *Turadot and Arlecchino*, Stadttheater, Zürich
	12 June	Pfitzner's *Palestrina*, Residenz Theater, Munich
1918		Boito dies
		Leoncavallo dies
	24 May	Bartok's *Duke Bluebeard's Castle*, Kiralyi Operhaz, Budapest
	14 December	Puccini's *Il trittico*, Metropolitan, New York
1919	10 October	Strauss's *Die Frau ohne Schatten*, Staatsoper, Vienna
		Ruggiero Leoncavallo dies
1920		birth of the Fascist movement in Italy
	4 September	Francesco Balilla Pratella's *L'Aviatore Dro*, Teatro Comunale, Lugo (first 'futurist' opera)
	4 December	Korngold's *Die tote Stadt*, Stadttheater, Hamburg and Stadttheater, Cologne (simultaneously)
1921		Italian Communist Party founded
	2 May	Mascagni's *Il piccolo Marat*, Costanzi, Rome
	4 June	Hindemith/Kokoschka, *Mörder, Hoffnung der Frauen*, Landestheater, Stuttgart
		Hindemith's *Das Nusch-Nuschi* (on same bill as above)
	11 June	Honegger's *Le roi David*, Théâtre Jorat, Mézières
	23 November	Janacek's *Katya Kabanova*, Brno
	10 December	Alfano's *La leggenda di Sakuntula*, Teatro Comunale, Bologna
	30 December	Prokofiev's *The Love of Three Oranges*, Opera House, Chicago
1922	14 February	Zandonai's *Giulietta e Romeo*, Costanzi, Rome
	13 April	Respighi's *La bella addormentata nel bosco*, Teatro Odescalchi, Rome
	3 June	Stravinsky's *Renard* and *Mavra*, Opéra, Paris
	31 October	Mussolini becomes Prime Minister
	16 December	Pizzetti's *Debora e Jaele*, Scala
1923	26 April	Respighi's *Belfagor*, Scala
	25 June	Falla's *El Retablo de Maese Pedro*, Palais Polignac, Paris
1924	1 May	Boito's *Nerone*, Scala
		Murder of Matteotti
	6 June	Schönberg's *Erwartung*, Neues Deutsches Theater, Prague
	14 October	Schönberg's *Die Glückliche Hand*, Volksoper, Vienna
	4 November	Strauss's *Intermezzo*, Staatsoper, Dresden
	6 November	Janacek's *The Cunning Little Vixen*, Brno
	29 November	death of Puccini in Brussels
1925	7 March	Zandonai's *I Cavalieri di Ekebù*, Scala
	21 March	Ravel's *L'Enfant et les Sortilèges*, Théâtre du Casino, Monte Carlo
	22 April	Adriano Lualdi's *Il Diavolo nel Campanile*, Scala
	21 May	Busoni's *Doktor Faust*, Staatsoper, Dresden
	30 October	G. F. Malipiero's *L'Orfeide*, Stadttheater, Düsseldorf
	14 December	Berg's *Wozzeck*, Staatsoper, Berlin
1926	13 February	Honegger's *Judith*, Théâtre du Casino, Monte Carlo
	24 March	Malipiero's *Tre Commedie Goldoniane*, Hessisches Landestheater, Darmstadt
	25 April	Puccini's *Turandot*, Scala

LIST OF ILLUSTRATIONS

The author and John Calmann and Cooper Ltd. would like to thank those who kindly supplied photographs for reproduction in this book. Particular thanks are due to Giancarlo Costa, whose patient help was invaluable.

135. Teatro Costanzi, Rome. Gala evening, 1884. Racc. Bertarelli (Costa)
136. Mascagni's *Cavalleria rusticana*, finale. Lithograph, 1890. Milan, Biblioteca Sormani (Costa)
137. Socialist march, Rome, 1 May 1891. Photograph by Count Primoli (Rome, Fondazione Primoli)
138. Mascagni conducting. Photo engravings c.1900. Racc. Bertarelli (Costa)
139. Giuseppe Giacosa, Puccini, Luigi Illica, 1895. Scala (Costa)
140. Umberto Giordano, 1896. Scala (Costa)
141. Illica, Giordano, Alberto Franchetti, Cesare Galeotti. Milan, Biblioteca Sormani (Costa)
142. Leoncavallo playing *scopone* with friends, 1915. Photograph by Nunes Vais. Rome, Istituto Centrale per il Catalogo e la Documentazione
143. Francesco Cilea, c.1900. Taken from a magazine of the period. (Costa)
144. Giordano's *Andrea Chénier*, Act III. Engraving by Bonamore for Illustrazione italiana, 1896. Scala (Costa)
145. Verdi and the 'young school'. Milan, Museo del Risorgimento
146. Cesira Ferrani, 1893. Milan, Museo del Risorgimento (Costa)
147. Leoncavallo with the first interpreters of his *Zaza*, 1900. New York, John Ferrone Coll.
148. Puccini, caricature by Enrico Caruso (Photo courtesy of Cassell Ltd, London)
149. Autograph of the Schaunard-Colline mock duel in Puccini's *La Bohème*. 1895–6. Ricordi
150. Puccini in the garden at Torre del Lago, c. 1900. Photograph by Nunes Vais. Rome, Istituto Centrale

151. Haricléa Darclée, 1900. Racc. Bertarelli (Costa)
152. Verdi's Casa di Riposo in Milan. Ricordi
153. Giulio Ricordi, Verdi, Boito, and the contractor Noseda on the site of the Casa di Riposo. Ricordi
154. Crowds waiting to buy tickets for *Siegfried* at La Scala. Published in Illustrazione italiana. Milan, Civica Raccolta Stampe (Costa)
155. Verdi outside La Scala. Scala
156. Commemorative postcard of Verdi. William Weaver Coll.
157. Toscanini conducting at Verdi's burial, 1901. Milan, Conservatorio (Costa)
158. Caruso recording. Self-caricature (photo courtesy of Cassell Ltd)
159. Gabriele D'Annunzio at La Capponcina, 1906. Photograph by Nunes Vais. Rome, Istituto Centrale
160. Puccini's *Madama Butterfly*. Caricatures by Caruso, New York, 1907 (photo courtesy of Cassell Ltd)
161. Puccini's *La Fanciulla del West*. Photograph of Emmy Destinn and Pasquale Amato, with Enrico Caruso, 1910. William Weaver Coll.
162. Cilea's *Adriana Lecouvreur*, Act IV. Postcard
163. Femminismo alla Scala. William Weaver Coll.
164. Leoncavallo's *Chatterton*. Cover of Libretto, 1896. William Weaver Coll.
165. Arturo Toscanini. Caricature by Caruso (photo courtesy of Cassell Ltd)
166. Benito Mussolini at the San Carlo, Naples, 1922 (Costa)
167. Boito's *Nerone*: poster for performance cancelled because of Puccini's death, 1924. Scala (Costa)
168. Puccini's funeral in Brussels, 1924. William Weaver Coll.

A BIBLIOGRAPHICAL NOTE

A full bibliography of Italian opera for the period between 1800 and 1925 would be longer than this whole book. In fact, it would be an interesting book in itself, and I hope someone will compile it soon. Here, I can indicate only my main sources, with some suggestions for further reading.

For the lives of Rossini, Bellini, and Donizetti I have relied heavily on the biographies by my friend the late Herbert Weinstock; and, like him, I have also drawn extensively from the pioneering works of Radiciotti (on Rossini), Pastura (Bellini), and Zavadini (Donizetti). The writings of Stendhal, especially his *Vie de Rossini* and *Rome, Naples et Florence en 1817*, are essential for an understanding of the period, even if they must sometimes be taken with several grains of salt. For Rome in this early part of the century there are also the writings of Alberto Cametti, historian of the Teatro Apollo. The story of Lord Byron and Teresa Guiccioli is told in Iris Origo's *The Last Attachment*; Effie Ruskin's letters are in *Young Mrs. Ruskin in Venice* (ed. M. Lutyens).

One of the pleasures in writing this book was the opportunity it afforded to reread *The Bourbons of Naples* and *The Last Bourbons of Naples* by Sir Harold Acton. For life in Milan there is Emilia Branca's biography of her husband Felice Romani. The section on Paris, in addition to the sources already mentioned, was enriched by the reading of Théophile Gautier's *Histoire dramatique en France depuis vingt-cinq ans* and, to a lesser extent, by the confessions of Arsène Houssaye (translated and edited by Henry Knepler in *Man About Paris*).

For a Verdi bibliography I refer readers to Andrew Porter's chapter in *The Verdi Companion* (edited by William Weaver and Martin Chusid), which also contains chapters on Verdi's business dealings (by Bruno Cagli) and the political context of the time (by George Martin, whose biography of the composer is also strong in this area). I also consulted Piero Nardi's *Arrigo Boito* and Gaetano Mariani's *Storia della scapigliatura*. There are no proper biographies of Ponchielli or Leoncavallo, but there is much about them in Alfredo Colombani's valuable *L'Opera italiana nel secolo XIX*. A recent volume, *Antonio Carlos Gomes*, edited by Gaspare Nello Vetro, includes many interesting and little-known documents concerning the Brazilian composer and his Italian career. The Milanese publisher Sonzogno has issued copious anthologies devoted to Mascagni and Giordano.

For Rome at the end of the century I recommend wholeheartedly *Roman Century 1870–1970* by J. R. Glorney Bolton. For the story of Italian opera houses I have drawn frequently on *Great Opera Houses* by Spike Hughes. Most Italian opera houses have also published extensive chronologies, which I have used throughout (Alberto Basso's history of the Regio of Turin is especially rich in information), as I have taken extensively from the *Enciclopedia dello spettacolo*.

INDEX

Page numbers in *italic* refer to captions.